D0991717

CONSUMER GUIDE®

MUSCLE CARS

Contents

American Motors Corporation

Chrysler Corporation

Ford Motor Company

Louis Weber, President
Publications International, Ltd.
3841 West Oakton Street
Skokie, Illinois 60076

Library of Congress Catalog Card Number: 80-85362

ISBN: 0-89009-438-1

Principal Author: Phil Hall

Cover Design: Frank E. Peiler

Manufactured in the United States of America
1 2 3 4 5 6 7 8 9 10

Ford Motor Company *continued*

General Motors Corporation

Studebaker-Packard Corp.

Credits

Phil Hall, editor of Midwest Racing News, *is the principal author of* Muscle Cars. *He is a regular contributor to* Car Exchange *magazine, where his column on America's postwar high-performance automobiles, "Power," is a monthly feature. A great many of the photos for this volume were supplied from Mr. Hall's personal collection.*

We would also like to thank the following individuals and organizations for their kind assistance in providing color and black-and-white photographs: American Motors Corporation; Buick Motor Division; Cadillac Motor Division; Champion Spark Plug Company; Chevrolet Motor Division; Chrysler Corporation; Discovery Hall and Studebaker Museum, South Bend, Indiana; Ford Motor Company; David Gooley; Harrah's Automobile Collection, Reno, Nevada; Richard M. Langworth; Oldsmobile Motor Division; Neil Perry; Pontiac Motor Division; Nicky Wright.

Introduction

High performance at low cost—that's the essence of that uniquely American breed called Muscle Cars.

In the early '60s, automotive writers decided they needed a term for a new kind of American car growing more popular each year. Most of these cars had huge V-8 engines with astounding horsepower ratings. Many had stiffer suspensions for better handling, four-on-the-floor manual transmissions for maximum acceleration, and bold paint jobs, big tires, and rumbling exhausts for instant identification. They were youth-oriented cars, and sold for surprisingly little money. Most spent their time cruising the street or making a big impression at the drive-in. Some were owned by those ready to engage in a little impromptu speed test as soon as the traffic light turned green. Owners who wanted more go than the factory offered could find it as close as the nearest dealer. There, a mind-boggling array of special parts was available, some thinly disguised racing hardware, to turn your pride-and-joy into a race track terror.

At first, these high-performance models were dubbed "supercars." But when someone called them "muscle cars," the name stuck. It was an apt description for such potent machines. And as we remember them today, it's hard to believe cars were ever this powerful, or that there were so many of them.

The desire to go faster than everybody else has been a part of automotive history from the beginning. And in a sense, there have always been "muscle cars." People have always been fascinated with speed. When the horseless carriage came along, "how fast'll she go?" was a natural question. Soon, formal speed contests around closed tracks, like the Vanderbilt Cup and Indianapolis 500, were being held. In 1902, fledgling car builder Ransom Eli Olds challenged friend and fellow automaker Alexander Winton to a speed duel on the hard-packed sands of Ormond Beach, Florida. The race was judged a tie. Speed: 57 miles per hour.

Cars became much faster, of course, and competition was one of the main reasons. Racing gave engineers a chance to evaluate their designs under conditions far different than those at the company proving ground. The lessons learned usually ended up in the showroom. Racing also proved to be good business. In the early years of the century, just being able to finish an event like the Vanderbilt Cup or the Glidden Tour was quite an achievement. And because the public associated stamina in racing with reliability on the road, winning races became an important sales weapon. The phrase "race on Sunday, sell on Monday" was part of auto industry wisdom a good 40 years before the horsepower race of the '50s.

In the 1920s, higher performance usually went along with higher price. Makes like Stutz and Duesenberg were renowned for speed, but also offered style and exclusivity. Luxury makes like Cadillac, Lincoln, and Marmon brought out big multi-

cylinder engines, tremendously strong, amazingly smooth, and capable of providing surprisingly rapid performance. They were clothed in elegant coachwork sumptuously outfitted and carefully built mainly by hand. They were magnificent cars, but they were far too costly for most people.

Henry Ford changed all that. The man who put America on wheels put America behind V-8 engines in 1932. The flathead Ford V-8 offered much better performance than the anemic side-valve sixes and fours of its day, and became instantly popular. Now, you didn't have to be rich to go fast. Soon, performance became just as important as prestige in choosing a new car.

If performance sold cars before World War II, it literally changed the shape of the auto industry in the postwar years. General Motors created a sensation with the first high-compression overhead-valve V-8 in 1949, introduced initially in the Oldsmobile and Cadillac lines. Much lighter, more powerful, and more compact than the time-worn straight-eights of prewar days, it started an engineering revolution in Detroit. Soon, other carmakers were rushing to catch up. It wasn't long before these efficient, high-output powerplants found their way into lighter low-price models. The 1949 Olds 88 was the first. Others followed, and the horsepower race was on. By 1955, Chevrolet, Ford, and Plymouth—the traditional low-price three—all offered V-8 power.

Some makes didn't get into the race, and paid the price. Kaiser, the new arrival on the postwar scene, was popular in the seller's market of the late '40s. But the company suffered severe sales setbacks because of its old-fashioned six-cylinder engine (even though it was supercharged toward the end), and disappeared after 1955. Other independents fared little better. Hudson earned a performance reputation in the early '50s on the strength of its powerful six, which scored an incredible number of stock-car racing wins. But by the time Hudson got its own V-8, in 1955, it was too late. The public had turned elsewhere. Hudson (along with its new corporate partner, Nash) vanished after 1957. Packard also delayed, and slid into oblivion partly because of it.

Performance, of course, is a relative thing. An Olds 88 was considered a hot car in 1949, but it would have been blown off the road by a 1955 Chrysler 300. And that car wouldn't stand a chance against a 1966 Hemi-Belvedere. You can still find performance cars today, but they're a shadow of their late-'60s counterparts. However, in the context of today's situation—fuel economy standards, safety regulations, and the tightest-ever controls on exhaust emissions—cars like the '81 Chevrolet Camaro Z-28, Chevrolet Corvette, or Pontiac Firebird Turbo Trans-Am are pretty quick. Besides, does anyone really need 0–60 mph in 5 seconds off the showroom floor?

Muscle cars died out in the early '70s. Mostly it was a matter of economics. By that time, insurance rates on high-performance models had risen too high for most owners, particularly the younger buyers most attracted to them. And when gas prices started going up in 1974, sales went down. Eventually, the hot machines just faded away like ghosts. Today, interest in muscle cars rivals, even exceeds, that of the so-called "special-interest" models of the '40s and '50s. Muscle cars are part of an era we shall never see again, and for that reason alone have become prime collector's items.

So, return with us now to those thrilling days of yesteryear—to the time when you could but a screaming "boss" machine for about $3000; to the age of the "Beautiful Brutes," the "Lively Ones," the "Scat Pack," the "Wide-Track Cars," and all the rest; to the days of bucket seats, consoles, tachs, floorshifts, and Wide-Oval tires; to the era when "Little GTO" was both a hit song, and a hit car. *Muscle Cars* is for those who remember these flyers, and especially for those who have yet to discover them.

American Motors Corporation

Once known only for economy compacts, AMC got into the performance game with some of the most interesting muscle cars of the '60s—from the speedy AMX two-seater to the brash "Scrambler" and Rebel Machine—some rare, all rapid.

AMC AMX

Perhaps the boldest car ever to come from American Motors was the 1968-70 AMX. This two-passenger sporty coupe was not merely fancy trim and a hot engine applied to an existing package. Rather, it was a new approach for a performance product, one that neither copied from nor was imitated by other domestic automakers.

The AMX was derived from the four-passenger Javelin ponycar introduced for the 1968 model year. The "Jav's" body was new for AMC, as was its 109-inch-wheelbase chassis. The AMX was created by slicing a foot out of the Javelin aft of the front doors, resulting in a 97-inch wheelbase, an inch shorter than the Corvette's. There was no attempt at providing rear seats: the AMX was a two-seater, period.

To make it clear from the start that this was a muscle car, AMC announced the AMX with word that Craig Breedlove had set 106 speed records with the little bomb. The motoring press generally loved the car, but wasn't quite sure where it belonged in the scheme of things. Some writers compared it, unfairly perhaps, to the Corvette.

For 1969, the AMX was continued with only minor changes. For the spring selling season came a "Big Bad" option package, which featured loud paint, body-color bumpers front and rear, spoilers, and

Above: the 1968 AMX. Below: Craig Breedlove in the speed-record AMX. Above right: MoPar veteran Shirley Shahan dragged this AMX in 1970. Below right: the 1970 AMX featured slightly reworked sheetmetal.

other visual effects.

The last of the two-seat AMXs appeared for 1970, which would also be its last year as a separate model. There were slight sheetmetal changes and a few alterations in the power department. Replacing the 343 was a more potent 360 V8 rated at 290 horses. The 390's output also jumped by 10.

The AMX was a great image car, and in that sense was a success. In production numbers it wasn't: 6725 of the '68s were made, 8293 rolled off the assembly lines for 1969, and 4116 of the '70s were built. The three-year total came to a mere 19,134, way behind the Corvette total.

For 1971, the AMX became the top-line Javelin, and it remained a four-seater through the 1974 finale. The tag was revived for the 1978 model year on a fancy version of the compact Concord. Next, it was shuffled off to the subcompact Spirit for 1979, where it remained through 1980. None of these later AMXs are real performance cars, being identical to the regular models except for their flashier exteriors.

Early AMXs were, and still are, popular in sports-car racing and, to some extent, drag racing. They were too short to compete in most stock-car events. Today, an active and fiercely loyal club is devoted to these cars. Low production and high interest value make the two-seat AMX a highly sought-after collector's item. Despite its expedient production engineering, it was one of the more interesting cars of the late '60s.

AMX Performance

Year & Model	Engine (cid/bhp)	Curb Wt.[1]	lbs/ bhp[1]	0-60[2] (sec)	¼-mi.[2] (sec)	Base Price[3]
1968 AMX 2d cpe	390/315	3097	9.8	6.9	15.2	$3245

[1]Advertised; [2]Typical acceleration based on contemporary tests; [3]Advertised list price in contemporary dollars; n = Net advertised horsepower; cid = cubic inch displacement; bhp = brake horsepower; conv = convertible; cpe = coupe; fastbk = fastback; htp = hardtop; rdstr = roadster (2-seat); sdn = sedan; d = number of doors.

AMC Hornet

Replacing the Rambler in American Motors' 1970 lineup was the Hornet, a newly designed 108-inch-wheelbase compact. Its name, of course, harked back to the 1951-54 Hudson Hornet, a car with a great racing tradition. This new low-suds economy car was hardly in the same mold, but there was one brief attempt at a performance model, the 1970-71 SC/360.

For 1970, AMC offered its 304-cid V8 as the top power option in the Hornet line. The SC/360 was a special two-door utilizing a new 360-cid derivative of the firm's existing 343 V8. With two-barrel carb, this engine was rated at 245 horsepower. Next step up the short ladder was a four-barrel version with 285 advertised horses. Both engines ran on regular gas, a sign of the changing times. With the healthier version you got a hood scoop, and both models featured tape striping, a heavy-duty handling package, styled-steel wheels, and an optional four-speed manual transmission with Hurst linkage.

The SC/360 disappeared after 1971, as AMC had seen the writing on the wall, namely, Federal regulations which spelled the end of hot cars. The Hornet became just another compact. But while it was around, the SC/360 was a well-balanced, speedy package without being too outlandish. It also showed that at least a few people at AMC still liked to go fast—even in the early '70s.

Hornet SC/360 was offered only for 1970-71. Note big hood scoop.

Hornet Performance

Year & Model	Engine (cid/bhp)	Curb Wt.[1]	lbs/ bhp[1]	0-60[2] (sec)	¼-mi.[2] (sec)	Base Price[3]
1971 SC/360 2d sdn	360/285	3105	10.9	6.7	15.0	$2663

[1]Advertised; [2]Typical acceleration based on contemporary tests; [3]Advertised list price in contemporary dollars; n = Net advertised horsepower; cid = cubic inch displacement; bhp = brake horsepower; conv = convertible; cpe = coupe; fastbk = fastback; htp = hardtop; rdstr = roadster (2-seat); sdn = sedan; d = number of doors.

AMC Javelin

After Ford's runaway success with the Mustang in 1964, other carmakers went galloping to their drawing boards to bring out their own sporty compacts. American Motors was one of the last to enter what became known as the ponycar field. Its contender was the 1968 Javelin. Styled by Dick Teague, the two-door fastback hardtop sat on a 109-inch wheelbase, and was available in basic and fancier SST trim. Six-cylinder and V8 power were offered. The latter included 290 and 343 engines at the start of the model year. The top rating on the 343 was 280 horses.

With four-speed shift, the 343

Counterclockwise from top left: 1968 Javelin SST; 1969 SST with"Big-Bad" option; 1970 with race-car paint; 1973 Javelin SST; 1971 Penske Javelin; 1971 Javelin AMX.

Javelin tested out with a 0–60 mph time of around eight seconds, and ran the quarter mile in 15.4 seconds at 93 mph, according to a leading car magazine. This was average performance for a ponycar at the time.

Performance in the "buff books" was one thing, but it wasn't enough to ensure sales. For that, you had to win the Sports Car Club of America (SCCA) Trans-American Sedan Championship (Trans-Am), a road racing series created especially for ponycars. Rules here limited engines to stock displacement, no more than five liters (305 cid) for cars in the larger size class. Both Ford and Chevrolet had 302s for their Mustang and Camaro, but the only engine AMC could use was its 290. This meant the Javelin had to spot the competition a dozen cubes.

That didn't stop AMC from forming a team. For the third Trans-Am season in 1968, AMC hired ex-Corvette racer Jim Jeffords to head the Javelin campaign, along with Peter Revson and George Follmer, both first-class drivers. Javelin didn't win, but proved it could at least run with the pack. Mark Donohue's 10 victories in the Roger Penske Camaro iced the title for Chevrolet that year. AMC regrouped, and Ron Kaplan was tapped to captain the team in 1969. But the result was the same: the Penske Camaros won another crown.

What the Javelin needed to become a winner was more development. And AMC must have figured that if you can't beat 'em, have 'em join you. So, the company spirited away Penske and Donohue to give the Javelins their magic touch for the 1970 season. It almost worked. Donohue won several races, but Mustang reclaimed the title it had won in 1966 and 1967.

The 1971 season, however, be-

Javelin Performance

Year & Model		Engine (cid/bhp)	Curb Wt.[1]	lbs/ bhp[1]	0-60[2] (sec)	¼-mi.[2] (sec)	Base Price[3]
1968	STD 2d htp	343/280	3320	11.9	8.1	15.4	$2604
1970	SST 2d htp	390/325	3375	10.4	7.6	15.1	$2848
1972	AMX 2d htp	401/255n	3300	12.9	8.3	16.1	$3109
1973	AMX 2d htp	401/255n	3350	13.1	7.7	15.5	$3109

[1]Advertised; [2]Typical acceleration based on contemporary tests; [3]Advertised list price in contemporary dollars; n = Net advertised horsepower; cid = cubic inch displacement; bhp = brake horsepower; conv = convertible; cpe = coupe; fastbk = fastback; htp = hardtop; rdstr = roadster (2-seat); sdn = sedan; d = number of doors.

longed to Javelin, mostly by default. The factory-backed Ford and Chrysler teams didn't run that year, and there was no strong Chevy effort, so the only opposition came from privateers.

Back on the production scene, the 1969 Javelin was much the same as the '68 offering inside and out. A "Go" package with fake hood scoops was again listed, and a "Big Bad" option package became available for the top-line SST at mid-year. This featured bold paint colors, color-keyed urethane bumpers, a roof-mounted spoiler, stripes, and other trick appearance gear.

More functional changes came along for 1970. A new 304 V8 replaced the base 290, a 360 substituted for the 343, and the 390 was given 10 more advertised horses. Sheetmetal was also altered a bit. The 304 would have fit nicely into the Trans-Am formula, but a rule change for the 1970 season permitted larger engines to be de-stroked to get down to 305. Oh well. The Mark Donohue connection was visible in a special version of the SST, with a big ducktail spoiler mounted on the trunklid and bearing the popular road racer's signature. This model was known as the "Mark Donohue Special." Production totaled only 2501 units. AMC also offered a limited-edition street Javelin with the red-white-and-blue race-car paint treatment, plus front and rear spoilers. It was available from the start of the model year.

New sheetmetal made the 1971 Javelin longer, lower, wider, and slightly more aerodynamic, though inner body structure was unchanged. The most notable styling feature was a large bulge over each front wheel, something like the Corvette's, but less graceful. A big rear spoiler, similar to the one on the Donohue Special, was also available. After a three-year run on a two-passenger sporty car, the AMX nameplate was transferred to the Javelin line for the top model in the lineup. A two-barrel 360-cube V8 producing 245 horsepower was standard. Topping the option list was the new 401, which grew from the 390. It was AMC's largest-displacement engine ever. Rated at 330 horsepower, it was also the most powerful mill ever offered in a Javelin, and the last to require premium gas.

For 1972, the base model was deleted, and the 401 joined its cousins as a low-compression engine.

Javelin production ran through the 1974 model year. The 401 was available right to the end, unlike some other ponycars that lost their big-inch options. Styling continued the 1971 theme with minor changes.

AMC Rambler

The first automobiles produced by the Thomas B. Jeffery Company of Kenosha, Wisconsin bore the name Rambler. Production continued from 1902 through 1913, when the name was changed to Jeffery to honor the firm's founder. In 1916, Charles W. Nash resigned as president of General Motors and bought Jeffery. Starting with the 1918 models, he changed the name to honor himself.

The Rambler name was dormant until a handle was needed for a new line of 100-inch-wheelbase compacts that came out in 1950. The little Nash Rambler was hardly a performance car. Only a six-cylinder engine was used, and economy was the keynote. A longer 108-inch wheelbase appeared for 1954, but it wasn't until the all-new 1956 design that a Rambler had room for a V8 under its hood. Also on a 108-inch wheelbase, the '56s proved quite popular, and the shorter models were dropped.

Rambler finally got its V8 for 1957. This was an all-new 250 cubic-inch unit with a single two-barrel carb. It was the first V8 from the newly formed American Motors, and had been offered in the bigger Nash and Hudson lines from mid-'56. Later, a four-barrel version, rated at 203 horsepower, was made an option for the '57 Rambler. However, the 250 was not a hot performer—that didn't fit with Rambler's economy image. Meanwhile, the "horsepower race" had hit full stride throughout the industry.

Back in the '50s, an ideal way to get your name into print, both in the growing number of "car buff" magazines and in the daily newspapers, was to run on the hard sands of Daytona Beach during Speed Weeks each February. Speed Weeks was basically a manufacturers showdown, with heated tests for best acceleration and top speed. Many carmakers also held new-model previews there during or just before the performance trials. Despite its lack of a big budget for racing activities, American Motors decided to enter a hopped-up Rambler called the Rebel at the '57 trials.

Announced as a mid-year addition to the line, the Rebel was a four-door hardtop identified by a chrome spear along its flanks. This was filled with gold-anodized aluminum trim, a treatment not unlike that of the competing Plymouth Fury. Painted silver and wearing special script, the Rebel looked distinctive. Under the hood was the 327-cid V8 from the soon-to-be-extinct Nash and Hudson. Since it was basically a bored-out 250, it fit with no problem. The driveline was beefed up, as was the suspension, which garnered attention by having Gabriel heavy-duty adjustable shocks. But most of the interest in the Rebel was focused on its Bendix fuel injection unit, which reportedly produced 288 bhp. This differed from the mechanical setup on the '57 Chevrolet by being all-electric.

As presented at Daytona, the Rebel weighed just over 3300 pounds. The Speed Weeks cars ran without the injection, which was said to be coming later, using four-barrel carbs instead. Power output was the same as for Nash and Hudson at 255 bhp. The motoring scribes made 0–60 mph runs as low as 7.5 seconds, and predicted the in-

Rambler Performance

Year	& Model	Engine (cid/bhp)	Curb Wt.[1]	lbs/ bhp[1]	0-60[2] (sec)	¼-mi.[2] (sec)	Base Price[3]
1957	Rebel 4d htp	327/255	3353	13.1	7.5	17.9	$2786
1966	American Rogue 2d htp	290/200	3010	15.0	9.9	17.6	$2370
1969	SC/Rambler 2d htp	390/315	3150	10.0	6.3	14.2	$2998

[1]Advertised; [2]Typical acceleration based on contemporary tests; [3]Advertised list price in contemporary dollars; n = Net advertised horsepower; cid = cubic inch displacement; bhp = brake horsepower; conv = convertible; cpe = coupe; fastbk = fastback; htp = hardtop; rdstr = roadster (2-seat); sdn = sedan; d = number of doors.

Left: Fuel injection was promised for 1957 Rambler Rebel, but never appeared. Above: 1969 SC/Rambler was a surprising stormer. Note big hood scoop.

jection would put AMC's hottest machine in Corvette territory, around seven seconds. But the fuel injection never saw the assembly line. And after a mere 1500 Rebels had been built, AMC pulled the plug on performance.

It wasn't until 1966 that AMC showed interest again in the performance market. Replacing the trusty 327 was a new and lighter engine designed with room to grow. Surprisingly, it was first offered as a mid-year option for the little Rambler American, which previously had never had anything but a six. The American had been completely redesigned for 1964, with a cleanly styled body on a 106-inch wheelbase. It now had sufficient space between the front suspension towers for this wider 290-cid engine.

For 1967, the bigger AMC cars got a bored-out 290, the 343 V8. At midseason, this was extended to the American in its hottest form, which meant a rating of 280 bhp. To put icing on the cake, AMC dealers offered hop-up kits over the parts counter, which boosted output even more.

The American's role as a high-performance model was short-lived, however. The 1968 lineup starred the sporty all-new Javelin ponycar and its two-seat derivative, the AMX. The American was demoted back to its 1966 status, with the 290 being the most production cubes you could buy. At the start of the 1969 model chase, the American suffix was dropped. The line was now known as just plain Rambler.

Just before the end came, so did the fastest Rambler of all, the mid-year 1969 SC/Rambler. Hurst Performance Research combined with AMC on a machine designed to erase Rambler's reputation as a car for old fogeys. The "Scrambler" started as a two-door hardtop, the same pretty style that had been around for six years. A big, functional hood scoop was stuck on the hood, and styled-steel wheels were bolted on at all corners. The body was white, with a broad red splash along the sides and bold blue lettering on the hood. The interior was nearly stock, but the headrests were tri-colored. The brazen exterior might have caused a few "little-old-lady-in-a-Rambler" jokes, but it was backed up by the presence of a 390 V8 (a bored-and-stroked 343) rated at 315 bhp. This was hooked to a Borg-Warner four-speed manual trans rowed by a Hurst shifter. The whole thing was a light 3160 pounds, and sold for a remarkably low $2998.

In one car magazine test, the SC/Rambler clocked 0–60 mph in just over six seconds, and rushed through the quarter-mile in a hair over 14 seconds, hitting the traps at better than 100 mph. This rivaled many cars with fancier names, and beat most of them. But though demand was higher, only 1512 of the little beasties were made. Interestingly, that was a dozen more than the first high-performance Rambler, the Rebel. Needless to say, both are collector's items today.

Rambler ended as a make after 1969. The name continues on some AMC products built in foreign countries.

AMC Rebel/ Matador

Some American Motors cars have had more name changes than an undercover agent. Take, for example, the firm's 108-inch-wheelbase models. At their introduction in 1954, they were called Nash and Hudson Rambler, then just plain Rambler in 1957–60. The 1961–66 Rambler Classic (moved up to a 112-inch wheelbase in 1963) was renamed Rambler Rebel for '67, when a 114-inch chassis appeared. It was Rebel only for 1968–70, then Matador from 1971 through '78. Confusing, to say the least.

Whatever the name, all these cars were known for offering dependable transportation for the family man with a light foot. In the '50s, only the Rambler Rebel could be classed as a muscle car (see Rambler). Hot cars were conspicuous by their absence at AMC—until the 1967 Rambler Rebel.

Matador Performance

Year & Model	Engine (cid/bhp)	Curb Wt.[1]	lbs/ bhp[1]	0-60[2] (sec)	¼-mi.[2] (sec)	Base Price[3]
1974 Matador 2d htp	401/255n	4055	15.9	8.5	16.0	$3095

[1]Advertised; [2]Typical acceleration based on contemporary tests; [3]Advertised list price in contemporary dollars; n = Net advertised horsepower; cid = cubic inch displacement; bhp = brake horsepower; conv = convertible; cpe = coupe; fastbk = fastback; htp = hardtop; rdstr = roadster (2-seat); sdn = sedan; d = number of doors.

Completely new from stem to stern, the handsome Rebel offered a 280-horse 343 V8 as an option.

When the AMX came along part way through the 1968 model run, its optional 390-cid V8, rated at 315 horsepower, was added to the Rebel's arsenal. For some reason, the 390 was not a regular Rebel option for '69, but did return for 1970, now rated at 325 bhp. The 1970 model year was the last for the Rebel nameplate. But as with the last Rambler the year before, there was a special hot-dog model, the Rebel Machine, as a kind of "going-away" present.

Introduced in mid-October of 1969, the Machine was a standard two-door hardtop decked out with red and blue stripes on its white body (other body colors were offered later). It got the obligatory hood scoop, more sedate than the one on the SC/Rambler, but had a built-in tachometer. Beneath the scoop sat a 390 with the highest horsepower rating ever for an AMC production engine: 340 bhp at 5100 rpm.

For 1971, the Rebel turned into a Matador (a name last seen in 1960 on a full-size Dodge). The 390 V8 grew for the last time to 401 cid as the big-inch offering. The top version was rated at 330 bhp.

There was never a muscle-car counterpart to the Machine in the Matador line, but a factory-backed car was entered in 1972 NASCAR Grand National championship races. Roger Penske, who brought AMC its first Trans-Am sedan racing title the year before, prepped the Matadors, but they did not do well in their inaugural running. The 1973 season opened with a win by driver Mark Donohue at Riverside, but the boxy Matador didn't have the right aerodynamics to be competitive on the super-speedways.

Above: 1970 Rebel Machine looked ready for the drags but was too heavy.
Below: The slippery 1975 Matador X fastback.

That problem was solved by the arrival of a sleek two-door fastback coupe for 1974. It showed obvious signs of having been styled in the wind tunnel, and some writers suggested the all-new body had been introduced just to make AMC more competitive in NASCAR. Whatever its background, it worked: Matadors started winning. But the first energy crunch came along just as the '74s premiered. Sales took a beating, despite Matador's better showing on the tracks.

You could still get the 401 in a Matador right on through 1974, but aside from the "X" trim package, there was no separate performance-oriented model in AMC's intermediate line. Production continued through 1978, after which the Matador was quietly dropped.

Engine Charts

American Motors

Type	Bore × Stroke (in.)	CID	BHP @ rpm*	Torque @ rpm*	Fuel# System	Avail. (years)
ohv V8	4.00 × 3.25	327	255@ 2600	345@ 2600	4 bbl.	1957
ohv V8	4.08 × 3.28	343	280@ 4800	365@ 3000	4 bbl.	1967-69
ohv V8	4.17 × 3.57	390	315@ 4600	425@ 3200	4 bbl.	1968-69
ohv V8	4.17 × 3.57	390	325@ 5000	420@ 3200	4 bbl.	1970
ohv V8	4.17 × 3.57	390	340@ 5100	430@ 3600	4 bbl.	1970
ohv V8	4.17 × 3.68	401	330@ 5000	430@ 3400	4 bbl.	1971
ohv V8	4.17 × 3.68	401	255@ 4600n	345@ 3300n	4 bbl.	1972-73
ohv V8	4.17 × 3.68	401	235@ 4600n	335@ 3200n	4 bbl.	1974

*SAE gross ratings except where noted; † hemispherical heads; # carburetion: no. carbs × bbls.; e = estimated; FI = fuel injection; n = net advertised figures; SC = supercharged; TC = turbocharged.

Chrysler Corporation

With its astounding hemispherical-head V8, Highland Park created a high-performance legend in the '50s and '60s. Chrysler cars rewrote the record books on the drag strips and in stock-car racing. From nimble compacts to luxury models, Chrysler was ready with go!

Chrysler

In June 1924, noted race driver Ralph DePalma broke the record for climbing Mt. Wilson in California, then went on to set a mark of 1000 miles in 1007 minutes at a board track in Fresno. His car was a 1924 Chrysler, then in its first year on the market. It was an auspicious beginning.

Over the years, Chrysler earned an enviable reputation for reliability and engineering. Styling was another matter. It took the firm years to recover from the disastrous Airflow design of the '30s. Management became so conservative about styling that, by 1940, Chrysler had evolved into a bulky, stodgy-looking car powered by plodding six- and eight-cylinder flathead engines.

All that changed in 1951. The big straight-eight lump was replaced by a much lighter and more efficient V8 with significant engineering features. Called FirePower, it displaced 331.1 cubic inches, exactly the same displacement (and bore and stroke dimensions) as Cadillac's overhead-valve unit of 1949. But that's where the similarity ended. Chrysler's engine had hemispherical combustion chambers and twin rocker-arm shafts for each head. The result was a combustion chamber shape that allowed room for the big valves needed for deep breathing and maximum power from each piston stroke. Initially, the FirePower belted out 180 horsepower compared to Cadillac's 160, making it the industry's most powerful engine that year. It quickly became known as the "hemi," and was destined to become a performance legend.

The FirePower was first offered only in the top-line New Yorker and Imperial models. The New Yorker sat on a massive 131.5-inch wheelbase, and in its lightest club coupe form, tipped the scales at a hefty 4145 pounds. At mid-year, the hemi found its way into the lower-priced Saratoga, which would handily outrun the New Yorker. The reasons were that it was six inches shorter and lighter by an average of 200 pounds.

1951 hemi V8 was first offered on New Yorker series.

Pioneer auto writer Tom McCahill of *Mechanix Illustrated* magazine entered a stock New Yorker at the Daytona Beach Speed Weeks in February 1951, and won his class, averaging 100.13 mph in the flying mile. His was the only U.S. car to top the century mark that year in stock form. Tommy Thompson drove a New Yorker to victory in a NASCAR event in Detroit, where the stands were full of Motor City executives. This win was significant because it showed the hemi's staying power while other cars literally fell apart in front of the fans. Also in 1951, a Saratoga two-door was entered in the Carrera Panamericana (the famed Mexican Road Race). Bill Sterling won the stock-car class, and placed third overall. Outboard-motor honcho Carl Kiekhaefer was the sponsor, and would later campaign Chryslers in many events.

In stock form, the FirePower had only a single two-barrel Carter carburetor, so it was understressed and underfed. Hop-up artists inside and outside the company recognized early on that the hemi had great power potential. All it needed was higher compression, extra carburetion, and changes to cam and timing. It was several years before that potential would be realized.

Not much changed for the 1952 Chryslers, but there was a modest facelift for '53. The hemi still churned out 180 bhp that year, though Cadillac had reached 190 the year before, and was now up to 210.

A few extra horses were found for '54 with the addition of a four-barrel carb. Oldsmobile, Buick, and Cadillac had all offered four-barrels as early as 1952. The hemi's compression ratio remained at 7.5:1, but advertised output was now 235 bhp, again tops in the industry, and five up on Cadillac. This engine was standard on New Yorker Deluxe and the Imperial. The newfound horses helped Chrysler in racing. Brewster Shaw set a new flying-mile record at Daytona with an average speed of 117.065 mph, and Lee Petty was right behind at 116.90, both in New Yorkers. Petty went on to win the 160-mile NASCAR event held on the beach shortly after the speed runs. To top it off, Petty went on to take the NASCAR Grand National driving championship that year, driving Chryslers on the longer tracks and Dodges on the shorter circuits.

Chryslers for 1955 had all-new styling, touted as the "$100 Million Dollar Look." They also lost their six-cylinder engines and the Imperial, which became a separate make. New Yorker models again had the hemi, still at 331.1 cubes. A compression boost to 8.5:1 brought advertised output to 250 bhp, but it wasn't as much as Cadillac and Packard offered.

Early in 1955, Chrysler returned to the top of the horsepower heap in spectacular fashion with the 300, one of the most famous postwar performance cars of all time. The designation signified advertised horsepower, obtained by the same means familiar to any hot-rodding teenager. Displacement was still 331.1, but breathing was improved with a pair of four-barrel carbs, and output got help from a hot cam and solid lifters. Suspension was heavy-duty. The 300 was available only with automatic transmission. Body styles were limited to a single two-door hardtop on the standard 126-inch Chrysler wheelbase, and carried the distinctive front-end design from the Imperial.

In 1955, a big car could still do well in speed trials and stock-car racing—if it had enough horsepower. The 300 certainly did. At Daytona, it was the talk of Speed Weeks. W. J. Koechling shattered the year-old flying-mile mark by better than 10 mph with a run of 127.580 mph. The holder of the former 117.065-mph record drove another 300 at 126.452 mph. Tim Flock, in a 300 entered by Carl Kiekhaefer, took the 160-mile stock-car oval event. The only speed laurel not in Chrysler's crown that year was the standing-start-mile beach run, which was won by, of all things, a Cadillac.

The Kiekhaefer operation, which was independent of the factory, entered the big white cars in NASCAR events throughout the '55 season. When it was over, Flock was the second straight Chrysler driver to take the title, and the make won 27 of the 45 events on the schedule. Up north on the AAA (American Automobile Association) stock-car circuit, the "Kiekhaefer Krew" took 10 of 13 races. It was clear that Chrysler's future in racing and in the performance field would be carried by the 300s. For a while they lived up to expectations—and then some.

The 1956 version of the 300 was a late introduction. There was updated rear styling with higher fins, and the hemi got its first displacement increase, a larger bore bringing 354 cubic inches. As installed in the 300, with twin four-barrels, the bottom line was 340 bhp. Would it be the Chrysler 340? Nope, the tag for 1956 was 300B.

Speed Weeks was still fun time for the 300s. Brewster Shaw was back on top in the flying mile, shattering his 1955 mark with a run of 139.373 mph. At $75 over the price of the automatic, the 300B was offered

Chrysler Performance

Year & Model		Engine (cid/bhp)	Curb Wt.[1]	lbs/ bhp[1]	0-60[2] (sec)	¼-mi.[2] (sec)	Base Price[3]
1951	New Yorker 4d sdn	331/180	4260	23.7	14.4	19.3	$3378
1952	Saratoga 4d sdn	331/180	4010	22.3	14.8	19.5	$3215
1954	New Yorker 4d sdn	331/235	4065	17.3	12.3	19.1	$3433
1955	300 2d htp	331/300	4005	13.4	9.8	17.4	$4110
1956	300B 2d htp	354/340	4145	12.2	9.0	17.0	$4419
1957	300C 2d htp	392/375	4235	11.3	7.7	16.6	$4929
1958	300D 2d conv	392/380	4475	11.8	9.1	17.1	$5603
1960	300F 2d conv	413/375	4310	11.5	7.1	16.0	$5841
1961	300G 2d htp	413/375	4260	11.4	8.3	16.2	$5411
1962	300 2d htp	413/340	3750	11.0	8.7	16.7	$3323
1962	300H 2d htp	413/380	4010	10.6	7.7	16.0	$5090
1963	300J 2d htp	413/390	4000	10.3	7.9	16.5	$5184
1965	300L 2d htp	413/360	4245	11.8	8.8	17.3	$4153
1970	300-H 2d htp	440/375	4440	11.8	7.1	15.3	$4234

[1]Advertised; [2]Typical acceleration based on contemporary tests; [3]Advertised list price in contemporary dollars; n = Net advertised horsepower; cid = cubic inch displacement; bhp = brake horsepower; conv = convertible; cpe = coupe; fastbk = fastback; htp = hardtop; rdstr = roadster (2-seat); sdn = sedan; d = number of doors.

The 1955 300 on the banks of Chrysler's Chelsea, Michigan proving grounds.

with a heavy-duty three-speed manual transmission. Shaw's car had the device, but he apparently hadn't entirely mastered it. A missed shift in the flying-mile run left him edged out by a Dodge D-500—by a mere .024 mph. Tim Flock repeated his 1955 triumph in the 160-mile oval track event. In all, there were 56 Grand National races on the NASCAR schedule, and the Kiekhaefer Chryslers took 22, more than any other make. Buck Baker won the driving title for Kiekhaefer. But with the onslaught of factory-backed Fords, Mercurys, and Chevrolets, plus the Chrysler's greater weight, it was clear that the glory days of the big white machines would soon be over. At the end of the season, Kiekhaefer announced he would not be back in '57. Except for a brief NASCAR effort by Buck Baker and his son Buddy in the early '60s, Chrysler would no longer be a major factor in stock-car racing.

In the heady atmosphere of the mid-1950s, there was no way a carmaker could keep an engine at the same displacement for five years, as Chrysler had with the hemi, and expect it to keep selling. So, the 354 of 1956 turned out to be a one-year size. For 1957, bore and stroke stretches brought displacement to 392, the largest in these years. In the New Yorker, the hemi churned out 325 horses. The 300 was again a late starter, and everyone wondered how high its horsepower would be. The mystery was solved when the 300C was announced with 375 bhp, achieved by the usual methods. And for the first time there was an engine option, a 390-bhp monster with a hotter cam.

To go along with the new engine size and output was the package it came in. While wheelbase remained at 126 inches, styling was all-new, with the high fins, low roof, and big windows of Virgil Exner's "Forward Look." As with past 300s, the body was stock Chrysler from the firewall back, but up front was a distinct grille treatment no longer shared with Imperial. The huge gaping mouth was trapezoidal in shape, and not unlike the Studebaker Hawk or earlier Ferraris in appearance. Also new was torsion-bar front suspension, with balljoints instead of kingpins.

Contemporary road tests put the 300C's 0–60 time at about eight seconds, and top speed at around 150 mph. Daytona's Speed Weeks didn't shed any light on the latter. Beach conditions were less than ideal, and the winning car of Red Byron went through the flying-mile traps at an average of "only" 134.138 mph. But, Brewster Shaw didn't miss a shift this time, and took the standing-start mile at an average of 86.873 mph, edging a Mercury.

The 300C offered the familiar two-door hardtop and a new convertible. That formula was repeated for the 1958 300D, which was given only minor trim changes. The hemi returned for what would be its final year, still with 392 cubes of muscle. Standard rating with twin four-barrels was now 380. Another 390-bhp job was optional, but this

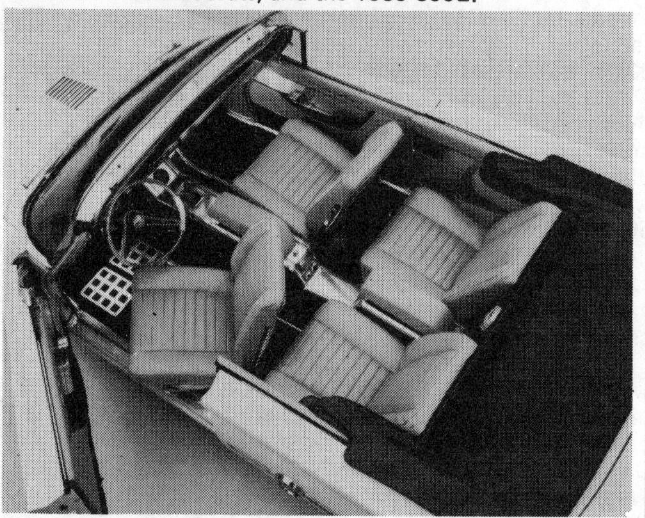

A quartet of "Beautiful Brutes," counterclockwise from top left: 1957 300C, 1958 300D, the 1960 300F interior with swivel bucket seats, and the 1959 300E.

Above: 300G of 1961 set letter-series cars' final speed marks. Below: "Family" 300 was launched for '62. Upper right: The 1964 non-letter 300. Lower right: 1970 300-H was a standard hardtop modified by Hurst. Special paint and trunklid spoiler were featured.

one had Bendix electric fuel injection instead of carburetors to feed the big cylinders. The 300D ran into an Indian uprising at Daytona, where a tribe of hot Pontiacs was trying to take over. Only Shaw's standing-start mile of 87.485 mph stopped a sweep by the half-dozen Pontiacs right behind him. Pontiac took the flying mile that year, but didn't break the 300B's 1956 mark of 139-plus.

Wedgehead engines replaced the hemi for model year 1959, mainly because it was too costly to build. That year's 300E got the largest version (along with the New Yorker and Imperial), 413 cid. Output remained the same as the last hemi despite the additional 21 cubes. Chrysler was shut out at Daytona, leading some to say the 300 had had it. But there was more to come.

New for 1960 was the 300F, now with less distinctive frontal styling that was merely a variation of that on the regular Chryslers. Its interior *was* different, however, sporting four individual seats and a full-length center console. Occupants were cradled by a new unit body that was a shade lighter than the old body-and-frame cars. Torsion-bar front suspension was retained. Two new performance items debuted this year. One was ram induction, which gave the 413 375 advertised horsepower with long tubes, and 400 with the optional short-tube setup. Also optional, at around $400 a crack, was a Pont-á-Mousson four-speed manual transmission as used in the French-made Facel-Vega.

Flying-mile competition was again a 300 show. The F models took the top six positions, led by Gregg Ziegler's average of 144.927 mph, which finally erased the 1956 mark. Standing-start tests didn't turn out so well because of a last-minute change in tire pressures that brought less speed instead of more.

The last page in the 300's performance saga was written by the 300G. Convertible and hardtop models were still listed on the same 126-inch New Yorker wheelbase as previously. Only one engine was cataloged, the long-ram, 375-horse version of the 413. Gone was the four-speed trans, and in its place a heavy-duty three-speed unit.

The speed trials on the Daytona sands were discontinued after 1961. By then, most activities had been transferred over to the new Daytona International Speedway, as critics said speeds were getting too high for the unpredictable beach. But there was one last blaze of glory for the 300. Ziegler repeated flying-mile honors at a near-record 143.027 mph, and Harry Faubel flew to a standing-start-mile win at 90.661 mph.

Though the 300 gave Chrysler a fantastic image, it didn't do much for sales. The most popular of the early letter-series was the 300C, of which 2302 were built. Production dropped to as low as 690 for the E, and just 1617 of the 300Gs were made.

For 1962, Chrysler decided to capitalize on the 300's reputation with a lower-priced volume version in its regular lineup. The new non-letter series appeared with two- and four-door hardtops and a convertible. Built on a 122-inch wheelbase shared by the bottom-line Newport, this "family" 300 was priced between it and the New Yorker. Standard was a 305-horse, 383-cid wedgehead V8. The real letter-series was still around, but that year's 300H was demoted to the 122-inch chassis, and you had to look closely at its insignia to tell it apart from the non-letter models. Its interior, though, still had four buckets, and the suspension got the heavy-duty treatment. The same engines were available on all 300s, which left little reason to buy the H. Not surprisingly, production of the letter car fell to an all-time low of 558.

To avoid confusion with the number 1, there was no 300 "I." Instead, the 1963 model became the 300J, and only a two-door hardtop was available. Standard for the first time was a single carburetor, a four-barrel, which brought the 413 down to 340 bhp or 390 with optional ram induction. Production sank again to another all-time low, only 400.

Prices and equipment were cut for the 1964 model run. The 300K hardtop's sticker was better than $1000 lighter. The convertible was reinstated, however, and production rose to 3647, an all-time record. Standard for both models was the 340-bhp engine, with a 360 four-barrel 413 optional, along with the 390-bhp ram setup. But by now, the significance of the letter series was only historical, if not sentimental.

Predictably, then, the last of the letter-series came along for 1965. The 300L two-door hardtop and convertible were completely revamped along with other Chryslers that year. Only the 360-horse 413 was fitted; optional engines were nil. Only 2845 were produced. The regular 300 series continued through 1971, however.

A last attempt at recapturing past glories came in 1970 with the 300-H. This was not a revival of the letter series. Here, the H stood for Hurst Performance Research. These were mostly standard 300 two-door hardtops sold through Chrysler dealers. All had special road wheels, wider-section white-letter tires, a 440-cid V8, heavy-duty suspension, and, of course, a Hurst shifter for the TorqueFlite automatic. There was also a gold-and-white paint job, rear deck spoiler, and custom interior. Production totalled only 400.

DeSoto

Chrysler Corporation's entry in the medium-priced field never received the recognition, or sales, it deserved. Yet, some of the fastest production cars of the '50s bore the name DeSoto.

DeSoto Performance

Year & Model		Engine (cid/bhp)	Curb Wt.[1]	lbs/ bhp[1]	0-60[2] (sec)	¼-mi.[2] (sec)	Base Price[3]
1952	FireDome 4d sdn	276/160	3760	23.5	15.7	20.4	$2740
1955	Fireflite 4d sdn	291/200	3940	19.7	12.8	19.2	$2727
1957	Adventurer 2d htp	345/345	4040	11.7	8.2	16.7	$3997
1960	Adventurer 2d htp	383/330	3945	12.0	8.8	16.8	$3663

[1]Advertised; [2]Typical acceleration based on contemporary tests; [3]Advertised list price in contemporary dollars; n = Net advertised horsepower; cid = cubic inch displacement; bhp = brake horsepower; conv = convertible; cpe = coupe; fastbk = fastback; htp = hardtop; rdstr = roadster (2-seat); sdn = sedan; d = number of doors.

DeSoto had been introduced in 1928 to fill the price gap between the brand-new Plymouth and the mid-price Dodge. Straight-eight engines were offered in the early years, but for most of its existence DeSoto had only L-head sixes of moderate power. It also was repositioned on the dollar ladder to sell for more than a Dodge and a little less than a Chrysler.

DeSoto's first change of fortune came at the dawn of the horsepower race, when a new V8 arrived for 1952. It was based on the 331.1-cube Chrysler FirePower hemi-head mill introduced the year before, but displaced 276.1 cubic inches. Power output was 160 compared to 180 for the Chrysler. Christened the "Fire-Dome V8," it went into a new top-line series bearing that name. *Motor Trend* magazine tested one with automatic, and made it to 60 mph in 15.72 seconds, topping out at just over 98 mph. Tom McCahill, of *Mechanix Illustrated*, always the leadfoot, did better, doing 0–60 mph in 12.2 seconds, with a top end of 97.

DeSoto got a reskinned body for 1953, but the FireDome V8 was left alone. The first power increase came for 1954, where a boost in compression ratio from 7.1 to 7.5:1 brought the total to 170.

For the all-new 1955 models, displacement was kicked up to 291 cubes, via a stretch in bore, and six-cylinder engines were canned. Firedome (with a different spelling) was now the lesser of two series, and carried a twin-barrel carb good for 185 bhp. The new top-dollar Fireflite got a Carter four-barrel and an even 200 bhp. Dual exhaust appeared as a mid-year option for the Fireflite. No horsepower rating was given, but the package was probably good for an extra 10 horses.

One of DeSoto's rare appearances in the world of high-performance came at Daytona Beach in 1955. At the annual Speed Weeks, a power pack-equipped Fireflite sedan was clocked at 112.295 mph in the flying mile to win its class in record time.

For the 1956 model year displacement went up again. This time it was done by a nearly half-inch increase in stroke, bringing the count to 330.4 cid. This left the powerplant undersquare, with a 3.72-inch bore and 3.80-inch stroke. Fireflites were now rated at 255 horses, nothing to get excited about, but nothing to be ashamed of either. DeSoto broke away from being "average" this year with its first high-performance model, the Adventurer two-door hardtop. Powered by a new 341.4-cube hemi producing 320 bhp, the Adventurer had the second most powerful engine in the industry that year (trailing Chrysler's 340-bhp 300B). A 0.06-inch bore enlargement brought up displacement, and a compression boost from 8.5 to 9.25:1 brought up power. A Carter four-barrel carb rested atop the Adventurer engine. DeSoto was chosen to pace the Indianapolis 500 that year. The pace car was a Fireflite convertible decked out with gold-anodized aluminum side trim similar to the Adventurer's.

Both these cars helped create some performance publicity for DeSoto, though the Adventurer was strictly a limited-production item. The first year, only 996 were made.

For 1957, DeSoto got Virgil Exner's all-new "Forward Look" styling along with other Chrysler products. There were now three series: Fireflite, Firedome, and a new low-priced Firesweep, the latter based on the shorter '57 Dodge platform. The Adventurer returned to the top of the line, again after the start of the model year. As with Chrysler's 300C, the two-door hardtop was later augmented by a new convertible. Some 1950 were produced, which would be the high-water mark for the model.

Above: DeSoto's first Adventurer appeared for '56, was one of Chrysler's hot quartet that year. Below: The 1957 edition with "Forward Look" styling. Upper right: 1958 Adventurer. Lower right: 1959 Adventurer.

For power, the Adventurer's bore was squared up with stroke at 3.80 inches, and displacement went to 345 cubes. An extra four-barrel was added, and horsepower was advertised the same as engine size. That one-horsepower-per-cubic-inch trick was quite an achievement for 1957, but DeSoto got little recognition for it.

Only minor trim changes on the outside marked the 1958 models. Alterations of a more major nature were made on the inside: DeSoto's hemi was sent down memory lane. In its place came a series of wedge-head V8s, less powerful but much less expensive to build. DeSoto drew 350- and 361-cubic-inch versions. That year's Adventurer had a pair of four-barrels and the same horsepower rating as the smaller '57 hemi, 345 bhp. A very few were fitted with Bendix electric fuel injection, good for 355 bhp. One of these cars would be a rare find today. Sales for the industry in general, and Chrysler Corporation in particular, took a nosedive that recession year, so only 432 Adventurers were called for.

Despite that, the model continued for 1959. Hardtop and convertible versions were retained, and production picked up a bit to 687. For the first time, the Adventurer's performance spread to the rest of the line. The 361 wedge was bored out 0.12 inch to 4.25 for 383 cubes. A pair of four-barrels was standard, and output went up to 350 bhp. This setup was optional for Fireflite, Firedome, and even Firesweep models.

DeSoto and other Chrysler cars (except Imperial) switched to unit-body construction for 1960. The Adventurer name survived, but its meaning didn't. It was now simply the upper series, offering not only a two-door hardtop, but a four-door one as well, not to mention a four-door sedan. Fireflite remained as a cheaper alternative. Other models were axed in the face of disappointing 1959 sales. However, there was still a hot engine option for Adventurers, the "Power Charge." This was a 383 with ram-induction, and was rated at 330 bhp. In model year production, DeSoto sank to 25,581 units. Just three years earlier, 117,514 had been built.

For 1961, only two models were announced, a two- and four-door hardtop. Series names were gone: the cars were just called "DeSoto." The only engine available was a 265-horse 361 able to burn regular gas. A soft medium-price market, which had killed Edsel, kept DeSoto from seeing New Year's Day 1961. Production had ended by Christmas, with just 3034 of the '61s built.

Dodge

From its beginnings in 1914, Dodge had been known mainly for dependability. As the first step up from Plymouth in Chrysler Corporation's hierarchy, Dodge had been very successful through the early '50s. But its cars were rather dull.

That all started to change in 1953. Wheelbase was cut from 123.5 inches to 119 on some models, and from 115 to 114 on others. Styling was still high and boxy, though generally more eye-appealing than in 1949-52. The most important innovation that year was the Red Ram V8, a pocket-size version of Chrysler's FirePower hemi. Displacing 241.1 cubic inches, this powerplant was actually a smaller version of the 1952 DeSoto hemi. Output was listed at 140 horsepower, and the V8 was initially confined to the top-line Coronet series. Tom McCahill wrung one out for *Mechanix Illustrated* magazine. He recorded 0-60 mph in 15.11 seconds, and wound the needle past the 100-mph mark. He also predicted great things for the 1953 Dodge in stock-car racing.

Dodge Performance

Year & Model		Engine (cid/bhp)	Curb Wt.[1]	lbs/ bhp[1]	0-60[2] (sec)	¼-mi.[2] (sec)	Base Price[3]
1953	Coronet 4d sdn	241/140	3385	24.2	16.1	19.3	$2220
1954	Royal 4d sdn	241/150	3425	22.8	16.2	20.3	$2373
1956	Custom Royal 2d htp	315/260	3505	13.5	8.8	16.9	$2693
1957	Custom Royal 4d sdn	325/285	3690	11.4	9.4	17.2	$2881
1958	Custom Royal 4d htp	361/320	3720	11.6	9.3	17.3	$3142
1960	Dart Phoenix 4d sdn	383/340	3610	10.6	8.5	16.3	$2715
1962	Dart 330 2d htp	413/385	3540	9.2	7.4	15.1	$2570
1962	Dart 2d sdn	413/410	3440	8.4	5.8	14.4	NA
1963	Dart Ramcharger 2d sdn	426/425	3218	7.6	4.2	12.5	NA
1964	Polara 2d htp	426/365	3740	10.2	7.7	15.9	$2745

[1]Advertised; [2]Typical acceleration based on contemporary tests; [3]Advertised list price in contemporary dollars; n = Net advertised horsepower; cid = cubic inch displacement; bhp = brake horsepower; conv = convertible; cpe = coupe; fastbk = fastback; htp = hardtop; rdstr = roadster (2-seat); sdn = sedan; d = number of doors.

To help that prediction come true, the factory "authorized" under-the-table sale of special performance parts designed for the sport, similar to the way Hudson unofficially backed those who campaigned Hornets. Dodge didn't exactly set NASCAR on fire, but did notch a half-dozen victories against some pretty stiff competition.

For 1954, cars with automatic transmission got 10 extra horses thanks to a compression increase from 7.1 to 7.5:1. McCahill found the change brought the 0–60 time down to 14.2 seconds.

Dodge's traditional conservative look was blown away for good by all-new sheetmetal for 1955. Wheelbase rose to 120 inches across the board. A bore expansion gave the Red Ram a new 270.1-cid displacement. A four-barrel carb made its debut as an option later in the model year, resulting in 193 bhp.

Tailfins grew for 1956, and so did the Dodge V8. It was now up to 315 cubes, thanks to a stroke increase of better than a half-inch, making the stroke bigger than the bore. Initially, 230 bhp was the most you could get. But early in the calendar year, the D-500 option blasted on to the scene. Chrysler was into specific high-performance models now, with cars like the Plymouth Fury, DeSoto Adventurer, and Chrysler 300B. There was no such offering at Dodge, however. Instead, D-500 power could be had on *any* model in the line, right down to the lightest and cheapest Coronet two-door sedan.

For the drastically new 1957 models, the Red Ram hemi got 10 more cubes for a total of 325. In D-500 trim, with single four-barrel carb, it put out 285 bhp. There was also a dual-quad engine called the Super D-500, and super it was with a 310-bhp rating. A very few 1957s had the 354-cid, 340-horse engine from the Chrysler 300B, and carried the label D-501.

Trim was shuffled for 1958, but the hemi was shuffled off the engine list. Like other Chrysler divisions, Dodge substituted the firm's new wedgehead V8.

While several makes cut their performance options for 1959, Dodge didn't. Engine sizes and power outputs went up, so civilians might have been able to give those police cars a run for it. The D-500 and Super D-500 were now based on the wedgehead 383, and delivered 320 and 345 bhp, respectively. Racing appearances by the 1958–59 models were sparse as Dodge took a back seat to Pontiac.

Starting with the 1960 models, Dodge changed its product philosophy. The line was subdivided with a lower-priced, 118-inch-wheelbase series, similar to Plymouth, and dubbed Dart. The big Dodge continued on its own 122-inch wheelbase (shared by Dart wagons), and was listed with the hotter engines for awhile. But clearly the hottest performers were now the Darts, which were lighter and smaller. The Dart's engine options ran virtually parallel with Plymouth's. (For details of Dart muscle options, see the Plymouth section.) Ram-Induction was picked up for both 361 and 383 V8s. With twin four-barrel carbs and 30-inch long intake tubes, it wore the D-500 label.

Reverse-swept fins, which thankfully never caught on, were unique to the 1961 Dodge and Dart. To start the model year, performance options settled around the 383, which came in 325-bhp (four-barrel), 330-horse (long ram tube), and 340-horse (short ram tube) versions. Later that season, Chrysler's 413 became available, with power outputs from 350 to 375.

Left: Dodges were more compact for 1953, offered new Red-Ram hemi V8. Above: All-new '57s were dubbed "Swept-Wing" by ad men.

Upper left: 1960 Dodge Dart. Above: Downsized 1962 models (440 4-door hardtop shown) became hot dragstrip contenders (left) when equipped with Ram Charger package and 413 wedge. Lower left: Styling was cleaned up for '63 (Polara convertible shown). Below: Smoother roof arrived on '64 Polara hardtops.

Like Plymouth, the 305-bhp 361 was supposed to have enough power for the trimmer '62s, but racers at the strip had a hard time believing it after the 413. To keep the troops happy, the 413 returned at mid-year, and was offered in a lightened package (like the Plymouth Super/Stock) designed mainly for dragging. Dodge called its version the Ram Charger. Short-ramming brought a potent 410 bhp.

If you've kept up with model changes so far, see if you can follow this one. The compact Lancer of 1961–62 was completely revised (along with Plymouth's Valiant) and took the Dart name for 1963. Wheelbase was stretched on the mid-size line (now called 330, 440, and Polara) from 116 to 119 inches (except for wagons. The performance engine was now a 426 wedge with a single four-barrel for the stock-car boys and 400 bhp. An optional setup with 11:1 compression and short ram tubes produced 415 bhp, and 425 was available from a 13.5:1 version. Like Plymouth, the 426 came along in time for late-season events.

For 1964, the production models got a smoother, more aerodynamic front end and two-door hardtops a sleeker roof. The early performance engine was the wedgehead 426 III, not unlike the previous year's II. But it was the return of the fabled hemi that made the big news. The Dodge name-callers tagged it, and the muscle models it powered, Hemi-Charger. Racers grabbed this non-production option as fast as they could. The hemi's paper ratings came out at 415 bhp with a single four-barrel, and 425 bhp with short-ram induction. (These figures were no doubt grossly conservative, though most hemis didn't stay in stock tune very long, anyway.) In NASCAR, the hemi proved to be the answer (along with a number of additional factory-supported cars) and Dodge took 14 wins, two more than Plymouth. That was still short of Ford's 30, however.

Dodge jumped on the model merry-go-round again for 1965. It still had the full-size cars on a 121-inch wheelbase (now named Polara, Custom 880, and Monaco), but these were too big and heavy for maximum go. The intermediate Coronet, however, was just right. This was essentially facelifted from the mid-size '64 line, with wheelbase upped slightly to 117 inches. From here on, Coronet would do Dodge's muscle flexing, later joined by the Charger.

Dodge Challenger

Dodge was the last of the domestic manufacturers to field a ponycar. Appropriately enough, it was called the Challenger, and debuted as a 1970 model. It was quite similar in appearance to the second-generation Plymouth Barracuda, offering the same body styles on a two-inch longer wheelbase. Initially there were six versions in two series, standard and R/T. Each offered a two-door hardtop with standard or formal-roof rear window (the latter was dubbed Special Edition) and convertible.

Dodge Challenger Performance

Year & Model	Engine (cid/bhp)	Curb Wt.[1]	lbs/ bhp[1]	0-60[2] (sec)	¼-mi.[2] (sec)	Base Price[3]
1970 Challenger R/T 2d conv	440/390	390	10.0	7.1	14.6	$3535

[1]Advertised; [2]Typical acceleration based on contemporary tests; [3]Advertised list price in contemporary dollars; n = Net advertised horsepower; cid = cubic inch displacement; bhp = brake horsepower; conv = convertible; cpe = coupe; fastbk = fastback; htp = hardtop; rdstr = roadster (2-seat); sdn = sedan; d = number of doors.

Later a low-priced coupe, the Deputy, was added at the bottom end.

There was enough room under the Challenger's hood for any of 11 Dodge engines at the time. The selection ran from the mild-mannered 198 cubic-inch slant six to the "Superman" hemi and 440 V8s.

Challengers and Barracudas became the darlings of MoPar lovers on the dragstrips. But Dodge's big competition push with its ponycar came in the hard-fought SCCA Trans-American series. The division backed a small team headed by veteran driver Sam Posey. The cars were constructed by Autodynamics. As a spin-off of this effort, customers were offered a new race-inspired Challenger, the T/A. (Of course, Dodge couldn't call it the Trans-Am—Pontiac had already taken that handle.) This mid-year package included such goodies as a fiberglass hood with a mean-looking scoop, front and rear spoilers, heavy-duty suspension, and side exhaust pipes connected to a Six-Pack version of the small-block 340 V8.

Horsepower wasn't advertised. Neither was the T/A's race record. The new team was simply no match for the experienced Ford Mustangs or Roger Penske's Javelins, which dominated the series that year.

Dodge scrapped its Trans-Am effort for 1971, and the Challenger T/A went with it. Most other models and engines returned. Sales dropped, however, and at the end of the model year, the big engines and convertibles joined the T/A in that big garage in the sky.

For 1972, the most power you could buy came from the 340. The R/T was replaced by a nondescript Rallye model that had only a tame 318 V8 standard. For 1973, the Rallye became an option. Curiously, six-cylinder mills were dropped just in time for the fuel crisis. A 360 replaced the 340 as the top V8 for 1974, but the model year was cut short in spring, when it was announced that the Challenger would be dropped.

Left from top: 1970 Dodge Challenger R/T; Challenger T/A prototype; Sam Posey in the Trans-Am racer. Above from top: R/T continued for 1971; Rallye was the hot '72; Challenger's last appearance was in 1974.

Dodge Charger

Most Dodge models, options, and engines in the 1960s had Plymouth counterparts. The divisions shared components to keep costs down and to give both dealer networks the widest possible variety of products. Not everything was duplicated, however. For example, Plymouth got the go-ahead to produce a fastback version of its compact Valiant, which debuted as the Barracuda in mid-1964. Dodge came up with nothing. But turnabout is fair play, so at the beginning of the 1966 calendar year, Dodge got to show off a fastback version of its mid-size Coronet, the Charger.

The Charger shared front and side styling with the 1966 Coronet, but had a long sloping roof which flowed down into the trunk area. It was similar to the fiesty fish in having a fold-down rear seatback (a pair actually, as there were twin buckets in back).

One of Charger's missions was to win stock-car races. Dodge had captured only two events in NASCAR Grand National competition in the rules-plagued year of 1965. What could be better than this sleek fastback to put the make in the winner's circle? Well, it turned out that the Charger had aerodynamic troubles. On the supertracks, like Daytona, the car's rear wheels tended to lift noticeably—not very desirable for handling stability at speeds approaching 200 mph. Not until a small rear spoiler was added were the Chargers really able to charge.

The factory-backed Fords sat on the sidelines for '66 because the hemis were allowed to run and Ford's overhead-cam engine wasn't. So, Chrysler products ruled NASCAR. Dodge took the most wins of any single make, 18. David Pearson won the driving championship, becoming the first exclusive Dodge pilot ever to do so.

Charger carried on almost unchanged for 1967. An exception was the addition of the new 440 Magnum V8, rated 375 bhp, to the engine roster. Richard Petty dominated NASCAR with his Plymouth in '67, and only five events went to Dodge.

"Scat Pack" is what the ad types

Above: First-edition Dodge Charger was designed for the stock-car tracks but also did well at the drags. This is Bob Thomson's 1967 "Dodge Rebellion" dragster. Right: Second generation got sensational new styling with curvaceous contours. Engines ran from the 318 V8 to the awesome 426 hemi. "Flying-buttress" rear roof pillars were unique to Charger this year, but "tunnelback" design was later modified for high-speed stock-car racing.

called Dodge's hot models for '68, and the sleekly restyled Charger was the best-looking of the bunch. Though still based on Coronet underpinnings, the Charger's new "Coke bottle" shape brought rave reviews and record sales. A total of 96,108 were built. R/T was now the hot ticket, with its standard 440. The hemi was still optional.

At Daytona, the Dodge squad was elated as the new Charger lapped the track at around 184 mph, considerably faster than the previous model. But smiles turned to frowns when the newly styled Ford Torino and Mercury Cyclone fastbacks came in five miles an hour faster. So, the 1968 NASCAR season turned out to be another long one for Dodge drivers. Again, they could muster only five wins.

For the '69 models there was only a minor facelift, and no body changes with an eye to better aerodynamics on the long tracks. But shortly after the regular line bowed, Dodge announced a slipperier car designed expressly for the superspeedways. Dubbed Charger 500 (no doubt to honor 500-mile events), it had a flush-mounted grille (instead of a recessed opening as on other models), a full fastback roof with flush backlight (instead of the tunnelback configuration), and smoother windshield mouldings. The 500 came with the hemi stan-

Dodge Charger Performance

Year & Model		Engine (cid/bhp)	Curb Wt.[1]	lbs/ bhp[1]	0-60[2] (sec)	¼-mi.[2] (sec)	Base Price[3]
1967	Charger 2d htp	440/375	3750	10.0	8.0	15.5	$3128
1967	Charger 2d htp	426/425	3950	9.3	6.4	14.2	$3128
1968	Charger R/T 2d htp	440/375	3775	10.1	6.5	14.9	$3379
1969	Charger 500 2d htp	426/425	3950	9.3	5.7	13.7	$3860
1970	Charger R/T 2d htp	440/375	3900	10.4	7.2	14.7	$3711
1971	Charger Super Bee 2d htp	440/385	3985	10.4	6.9	14.7	$3245
1971	Charger Super Bee 2d htp	426/425	4083	9.6	5.7	13.7	$3245
1973	Charger SE 2d htp	440/275n	4160	15.1	7.4	15.2	$3267

[1]Advertised; [2]Typical acceleration based on contemporary tests; [3]Advertised list price in contemporary dollars; n = Net advertised horsepower; cid = cubic inch displacement; bhp = brake horsepower; conv = convertible; cpe = coupe; fastbk = fastback; htp = hardtop; rdstr = roadster (2-seat); sdn = sedan; d = number of doors.

From top: Buddy Baker at '68 World 600; 1969 Charger 500; the incomparable '69 Daytona; 1970 Charger R/T.

From top: 1971 Charger R/T; 1972 Charger Special Edition; 1974 Charger Rallye; 1978 Magnum XE, Charger's successor.

dard and the 440 as an option. Dodge built just enough of these cars to make them legal under NASCAR rules, 500. It might have done the job against Ford's 1968 racers, but the target moved. Dearborn replied with slicked-up models of its own, the Ford Torino Talladega and Mercury Cyclone Spoiler II.

On April 13, 1969 Dodge's ultimate answer to supertrack aerodynamics arrived, the Charger Daytona. Based on the basic 500 shell, it featured a sloped, pointed nose to help break up air flow in front, and a full-width rear wing mounted on towering vertical struts. The air foil was supposed to keep the rear end glued down. Unlike the original Charger, the Daytona came off the assembly line virtually race-ready. NASCAR told Dodge to build 500 of the winged things. It did, and, after the mandatory waiting period, got to race it. For street use, the 440 was standard, the hemi optional.

Of more interest was the racing version, which made its first appearance at the new Alabama International Motor Speedway in Talladega. (It was only fair the Daytona be introduced there, as the Ford Talladega had first raced at Daytona.) The car was victorious in its rookie run, as Richard Brickhouse took the checkered flag in the Ray Fox entry. But the win wasn't as sweet as it might have been: a drivers' strike kept the big-name MoPar and Ford drivers away. In all, Dodge captured 22 Grand National races in 1969, its best total ever. But it wasn't enough to beat Ford's.

Things had calmed down by introduction time for the 1970 Charger. The Daytona was gone, and the 500 became a mere production item with only plusher trim to set it apart from the standard offering and no special bodywork. The Six-Pack option for the 440 V8 had appeared on the 1969 Coronet Super Bee, and was extended to the Charger this year.

Even though the Daytona was out of production, it was still legal for NASCAR, and continued to carry the Dodge banner on the superspeedways. Bobby Isaac drove a Daytona to the NASCAR title in 1970, the second Dodge pilot to do so. In all, the make accounted for 17 checkered flags that season.

Charger underwent its second body change and first wheelbase alteration, from 117 to 115 inches, for the 1971 model year. That season, all intermediate coupes became Chargers, while Coronet was restricted to sedans and wagons. The roof was now a semi-fastback, and the hood was slightly sloped. A big kickup in the rear fenders was blended into the roof. The '71 design looked very smooth, and seemed well-suited for things like superspeedway touring. The R/T nameplate was retained, and the former Coronet Super Bee now got Charger emblems. Compression ratios were cut, and power ratings took a dip on most engines.

By now, muscle cars were losing popularity with the buying public, largely due to soaring insurance rates. Reflecting the downturn were the Charger offerings for 1972. Now minus the R/T and Super Bee, the line had only one vestige of the old days, a meek Rallye option. A luxury-oriented Special Edition model sat at the top of the price ladder, with slightly sleeker roof styling helping air flow a bit. Power options were thinned out. The street hemi disappeared, leaving the 440, the last engine to require premium fuel, in four- and six-barrel versions. Richard Petty no longer had full factory backing, and switched from Plymouth to Dodge in mid-1972, because of the Charger's better aerodynamics. He went on to take the NASCAR crown, and helped account for Dodge's five wins.

Rear quarter windows were enlarged on the 1973-74 Chargers (except for the SE, which had gimmicky louvers). The smooth overall shape continued, as did the 440, which now succumbed to a low-compression diet. Petty stayed with Dodge, and ran a 1973-74 Charger through the 1977 racing season. In 1973 he won six events, including the Daytona 500. The next year he took Daytona again, scored all of Dodge's 10 victories, and nailed down the NASCAR title to boot. There was revised styling for 1975, but Petty stuck with his earlier model. He knew what he was doing: he took 13 of Dodge's 14 first-place flags, and his sixth Grand National title. In 1976, the old Charger was still charging, and won six more events, half going to Petty. A rules extension for the 1977 campaign allowed the 1974 Charger to stay around for one more year. Dodge scored its final seven wins, five of which belonged to "King Richard."

Despite its racing prowess, the production Charger was bumped into the personal-luxury market for 1975. The restyled Special Edition now shared a squared-line bodyshell with the new Chrysler Cordoba.

Charger lasted through 1978, but few examples made any noise in competition. Dodge brought out a companion model, the Magnum XE for 1978, complete with glass-covered headlights and a sloped-back nose. Although it looked slick enough to race, the Magnum bombed on the tracks. And adding injury to insult, Richard Petty switched to Chevrolet.

Dodge Coronet

The 1965 Coronet was tapped to carry the Dodge delta insignia in the world of high-performance. As a new troop, it got all the high-speed ammunition in the Dodge arsenal to fight battles on dragstrip or superspeedway. It was based on the 1964 330/440/Polara series, but sat on a 117-inch wheelbase, an inch longer than before. Sheetmetal was new from the beltline down. All this made Coronet the division's first official entry in the intermediate field.

Initially, the big hemi V8 was not a Coronet production option, so NASCAR said it wasn't race-legal. If you wanted to race a hemi in 1965, you had to drive a big Polara (though the hemi wasn't a production item for that line, either). Later, NASCAR partially relented. For the street folks, the 426 wedge was civilized by means of a single four-barrel carb and a "mild" 10.3:1 compression ratio. The result was 365 advertised horsepower. Besides the hemi, the Coronet's limited-production sheet showed the Ram Charger drag package. With this you now got fenders and hood made of steel instead of aluminum, mostly because of the NHRA's new rules for the Super/Stock class, which mandated

Above: Coronet was Dodge's mid-size 1965 entry. Right: "Mr. Norm's" Blown Hemi funny car; note rearranged wheelbase. Below: Coronet was rebodied for 1966. 500 (shown) was top-of-the-line this year.

Dodge Coronet Performance

Year	& Model	Engine (cid/bhp)	Curb Wt.[1]	lbs/ bhp[1]	0-60[2] (sec)	¼-mi.[2] (sec)	Base Price[3]
1965	Coronet 500 2d htp	426/365	3740	10.2	7.7	15.7	$2674
1966	Coronet 440 2d conv	426/425	3900	9.2	6.1	14.5	$2766
1967	Coronet R/T 2d htp	440/375	3800	10.1	7.2	15.4	$3379
1969	Coronet Super Bee 2d htp	383/335	3555	10.6	6.6	14.7	$3138
1969	Coronet Super Bee 2d htp	440/390	3900	10.0	7.1	14.6	$3138

[1]Advertised; [2]Typical acceleration based on contemporary tests; [3]Advertised list price in contemporary dollars; n = Net advertised horsepower; cid = cubic inch displacement; bhp = brake horsepower; conv = convertible; cpe = coupe; fastbk = fastback; htp = hardtop; rdstr = roadster (2-seat); sdn = sedan; d = number of doors.

heavier race weight. Many Super/Stock victories were claimed by Dodge in 1965. One was at the NHRA Nationals, where Bob Harrop took the trophy in SS/A aboard his 1965 Coronet.

Specially equipped performance models were hot items in the mid-'60s. Coronet's entry came with the 1967 R/T. This offered a standard 375-horse rendition of the biggest engine in the stable, the 440 V8, basically an enlarged 426 wedge.

Coronet got a new suit of clothes for 1968, but Charger was given even fancier duds. Initially, the engine lineup read the same as 1967, and the R/T was still the hot number. Over at Plymouth, the bargain-basement muscle car, the Road Runner, had younger buyers bustin' down the showroom doors. Not wanting to be left out, the Dodge folks went to the parts bin and came up with the Coronet Super Bee. This was one of the hot models that made up the "Scat Pack," which had a big bee as its symbol. To provide instant identification for the Pack, Dodge wrapped racing stripes around their hind quarters, and these became known as "bumble-bee stripes." Like the Road Runner, the Super Bee was a basic two-door coupe powered by a 335-bhp 383 V8, though that was just for openers. The package also included a four-speed tranny and heavy-duty suspension. Unlike the Road Runner, it was a bit fancier inside, having a Charger instrument panel and the mid-line Coronet 440 interior trim. To go with the stripes was a new logo, but the Super Bee didn't get a horn that buzzed.

A hardtop joined the Super Bee coupe for 1969. Both got added muscle at mid-year when the 440 Six-Pack became available. Six-Pack referred to a trio of two-throat carbs, good for 390 rated horses. Dodge had used all sorts of performance tricks over the years, but this was its first tri-carb setup. The option also featured a fiberglass hood, complete with a big scoop.

The Scat Pack found a home in "Scat City," according to the 1970 sales literature. To tell the fans all about it, Dodge formed the Scat Pack Club. You invested $3.00 to get a decal, patch, newsletter, and other goodies. Coronet was invested with a minor facelift. Engines stayed mostly the same, and the hot Super Bee and R/T models were continued. A few Coronets appeared on the stock-car circuits, and Dick Landy ran them on the strips, where they still did well. But at the end of the model year, it would all be over.

Coronet performance models were wiped out for 1971, and only mundane four-door sedans and wagons were listed. Coronet coupes became Chargers, and convertibles vanished. The Super Bee survived as a Charger, but only for this year.

Dodge Dart

Lancer was Dodge's first compact, basically a reworked Plymouth Valiant. It had a short life, starting as a 1961 model and ending after '62. It was hardly a hot performer as it was offered only with six-cylinder engines. However, some of these had the interesting Hyper-Pak option that drew 196 horsepower from 225 cubes (see Plymouth Valiant).

After a two-year trial, the Lancer name was shelved, and Dart script was affixed to Dodge's elongated 1963 compacts. Wagons remained on the previous 106.5-inch wheelbase, but other models now had 111 inches between front and rear wheels. At first, Dart followed Lancer in having only six-in-a-row engines. But a few months into the 1964 model year a V8 was added. This was a 273 cubic-inch debored

Above: 1968 Coronet Super Bee, part of the "Scat Pack."
Right: 1969 Coronet R/T.

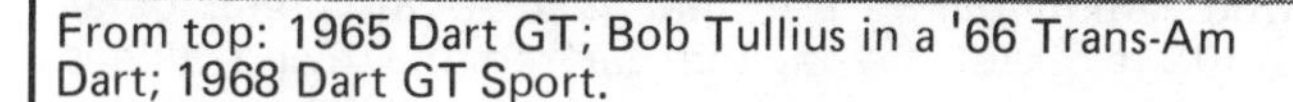
From top: 1965 Dart GT; Bob Tullius in a '66 Trans-Am Dart; 1968 Dart GT Sport.

Swinger 340 (top) was hottest Dart for 1970. Fastback Demon (above) arrived for 1971 to take over.

variation of the 318, and produced an advertised 180 bhp.

Dart was redone for 1967. Wheelbase remained at 111, but there was now enough underhood space for a big-block V8 if needed. Dodge soon took advantage of this, and squeezed in a 383, rated at 280 horses.

The hot Dodges for 1968 were called the "Scat Pack." Dart's member in the bumble-bee-striped fraternity was the GT Sport, usually referred to as the GTS. There were two-door hardtop and convertible versions powered by a new standard engine, a 340-cube extension of the 318. The 383 was still optionally available, now at an even 300 horses. But even that wasn't enough to run with the hottest stocks at the drags. So, the implausible Hemi-Dart was concocted along the lines of the earlier Ram Charger intermediates. For a little over $4000 you got a stripped hemi-powered two-door, with beefed-up drivetrain and suspension, and fiberglass body parts including a scooped hood. The car also had lightweight window glass and side panes that had to be pulled up by a strap because the window-winding mechanisms were left out. So were sound-deadening material and sealers, all to keep weight down. The Hemi-Dart was approved for the Super/Stock B class by NHRA. Some had the 440 Magnum V8 and also ran in that class. Production (very limited) with both engines continued in 1969.

The standard '69 lineup continued the GTS duo, but now featured a low-priced pseudo-muscle car, the Swinger 340. This was a two-door hardtop with the 275-horse version of the 340.

After the Challenger ponycar came out for 1970, Dart's performance status diminished. The GTS, 383 V8, Hemi-Dart, and convertibles were all killed, leaving the Swinger 340 as the only performance-oriented model. Meanwhile, the Duster derivative of the Valiant was making a big splash for Plymouth. Dodge got its own version of the 108-inch-wheelbase coupe for 1971. Called the Demon, it was available with the 340 V8, and replaced Swinger as the division's most muscular compact. The Demon name never caught on, though (some fanatics objected to its link with the Devil), so after the 1972 model run, the car was renamed Dart Sport and offered with the 340 V8, which was supplanted the next year by a 360 version. Although the 360 Sport was technically dropped after 1975, you could still buy this car for one more year (if you didn't live in California) with four-barrel carb and 200 bhp net.

Dart died after 1976 in favor of the Aspen. In its last two years, Dart saw limited action in stock-car competition as an outgrowth of Chrysler's Kit Car program.

Dodge Lancer/Dart Performance

Year & Model		Engine (cid/bhp)	Curb Wt.[1]	lbs/ bhp[1]	0-60[2] (sec)	¼-mi.[2] (sec)	Base Price[3]
1961	Lancer 770 2d htp	225/196	2670	13.6	8.6	16.4	$2164
1965	Dart GT 2d htp	273/235	2850	12.1	9.3	16.4	$2628
1968	Dart GTS 2d htp	340/275	3120	11.3	6.0	15.2	$3189
1971	Dart Demon 2d sdn	340/275	3360	12.2	6.5	14.5	$2721

[1]Advertised; [2]Typical acceleration based on contemporary tests; [3]Advertised list price in contemporary dollars; n = Net advertised horsepower; cid = cubic inch displacement; bhp = brake horsepower; conv = convertible; cpe = coupe; fastbk = fastback; htp = hardtop; rdstr = roadster (2-seat); sdn = sedan; d = number of doors.

Plymouth

If there ever was a slow starter in the muscle car field it was Plymouth. Introduced in the late 1920s as Chrysler Corporation's low-priced make, it was a sales success right from the start. Plymouth's only powerplant from the early '30s right on through 1954 was a low-power flathead six, which became known for sturdiness and longevity. But you couldn't buy a Plymouth with 100 horsepower until 1953.

Plymouth finally got its first high-output engine in the all-new "Young at Heart" 1955 models. Displacement of this "Hy-Fire" V8 was 241 and 260 cubic inches. Top output came from the latter, 177 bhp with a four-barrel carb bolted on. That left Plymouth a number of ponies shy of Ford's and Chevrolet's hottest options for the year.

Taller tailfins and bigger engines (270 and 277 cubes) arrived for the facelifted 1956 line. The top power rating was now an even 200, but even more was needed to keep from being outpaced in the horsepower race. More turned up just in time in the first really hot Plymouth, the 1956 Fury, introduced at mid-year. Fury was a two-door hardtop trimmed and priced to sit at the top of the model line. You could get any color you wanted as long as it was white. A bodyside spear filled with textured gold-anodized aluminum trim provided visual interest. Needless to say, Fury also packed the most powerful engine ever offered for the make. This was a 303-cube V8 rated at 240 bhp, breathing through a Carter four-throater.

To prove Plymouth knew how to play the speed game, a Fury made the obligatory speed runs on the sands at Daytona Beach on January 10th that year. As the press looked on, the car ran the flying mile at

Plymouth Performance

Year & Model		Engine (cid/bhp)	Curb Wt.[1]	lbs/ bhp[1]	0-60[2] (sec)	¼-mi.[2] (sec)	Base Price[3]
1956	Fury 2d htp	303/240	3650	15.2	9.6	17.0	$2866
1957	Fury 2d htp	318/290	3595	12.4	8.6	16.5	$2925
1958	Fury 2d htp	350/305	3510	11.5	7.7	16.1	$3067
1959	Fury 2d htp	361/305	3605	11.8	8.5	16.4	$2771
1960	Sport Fury 2d htp	361/310	3520	11.4	7.5	15.6	$2720
1961	Fury 2d htp	383/330	3540	10.7	7.4	15.1	$2718
1963	Sport Fury 2d htp	383/330	3235	9.8	7.2	15.9	$2851
1964	Sport Fury 2d htp	426/365	3470	9.5	6.8	15.2	$2864

[1]Advertised; [2]Typical acceleration based on contemporary tests; [3]Advertised list price in contemporary dollars; n = Net advertised horsepower; cid = cubic inch displacement; bhp = brake horsepower; conv = convertible; cpe = coupe; fastbk = fastback; htp = hardtop; rdstr = roadster (2-seat); sdn = sedan; d = number of doors.

From top: Fury was Plymouth's hottest setup in 1956, continued for '57 and '58. Right from top: Sport Fury arrived for '59; fins were big for 1960; '61s had none.

Fury was downsized for '62 (top), became better-looking for '63 (above). 1964 Sport Fury (upper right) was favored by Richard Petty (lower right) who won big with it during the 1964 NASCAR season.

124.01 mph, which got the typewriters into high gear.

"Suddenly It's 1960" was the catch phrase for the all-new '57 line. Like the rest of Chrysler Corporation, Plymouth's dramatically styled new models were lower, longer, and wider than their '56 predecessors, and had soaring tailfins. The chassis was redesigned, too. Wheelbase was bumped from 115 to 118 inches on all but wagons, now at 122. The front suspension went from conventional coils to longitudinal torsion bars. To move this bigger package was a larger powerplant, the now-familiar 318-cid V8. Called the Fury V-800, it carried a pair of Carter four-barrels, and claimed 290 horsepower. It could be had in any model right down to the lowly Plaza two-door sedan.

Returning for 1958 was the third-edition Fury, still a limited-production item, and again listed with the 318-cube V-800 as standard. But now there was something hotter. Big-block wedgehead V8s were dealt to all but the Chrysler and Imperial lines that year, and Plymouth's number was a 350 tagged "Golden Commando."

With the general de-emphasis on performance in the late '50s, Plymouth watered down the Fury name for 1959. It was now a separate series, second from the top in price, and expanded to include four-door models. The previous Fury was replaced at the top of the heap by the new Sport Fury two-door hardtop and convertible. These did not have a heavy-hitter engine as standard, though, just a 260-horse 318.

Suddenly it *was* 1960, and the 1957 design was dropped. All Chrysler products except Imperial adopted uni-body construction that year, though the torsion-bar front suspension, now a MoPar trademark, was retained. Fins made their last and gaudiest appearance on a Plymouth, and the Sport Fury vanished. Plymouth buyers weren't shortchanged in the muscle department, however. The most potent engine option so far was now available. A larger brother to the 361, it had a 0.13-inch healthier bore for a 383-cube displacement. And there was a new system to improve breathing, ram-induction (or as Plymouth's writers called it, "SonoRamic").

Basically, ram-induction consisted of a pair of four-barrel carbs mounted on intake manifolds some 30 inches long. This meant the carb feeding the left cylinder bank was far to the right of the engine compartment, and vice-versa. As the fuel/air mixture neared the intake valve, it picked up speed through the long induction tubes, causing a "ram" effect, which boosted power.

Plymouth lost its fins for 1961, along with the SonoRamic 361. The 383 was now listed in single four-barrel form at 325 horses, as the long-tube version with 330, and in short-tube trim at 340 bhp. The 383 may have been competitive in 1960, but not in '61. Ford moved up to 390 cubes and Chevrolet to 409, both well ahead in displacement. Plymouth responded at mid-year with the 413, a larger version of the 383, which up to now had been slotted only into big Chryslers and Imperials.

A lot changed at Plymouth for '62. The radically styled new models were downsized, dropping in wheelbase from 118 to 116 inches. Other dimensions also shrank, including weight by an average of 350 pounds.

But while the reduction in bulk was not popular with buyers, racers and performance fans loved it. At first, the 383 and 413 engines were deleted, because the 305-horse 361 was deemed sufficient for the lighter '62. It might have been okay for the average motorist, but not for dyed-in-the-wool speed freaks. To remain competitive in drag racing, Plymouth ran off a batch of lightweight specials, called Super/Stocks, powered by the 413-cube short-ram engine. The name referred to their class in drag racing (with classes based on pounds per advertised horsepower). The S/S had a nominal 410 horses, though that was surely a very conservative figure. Something closer to 500 would be more like it.

The gloves came off for 1963. NASCAR, NHRA, and other sanctioning bodies had imposed seven-liter (427 cubic-inch) limits on engine sizes. To get closer to this, Chrysler chewed an extra 0.06 inch out of each cylinder on the 413, and ended up with the 426 wedge. This became the top power option for Plymouth's much better-looking 1963 models.

With single four-barrel carb, the 426 produced 400 advertised horses. The short-ram setup and 11:1 compression was good for 415, and with short ram and a 13.5:1 squeeze, 425 galloped out. The 426 was available to special order only, as was a new version of the Super/Stock package for drag racing. This included aluminum front fenders and hood, complete with scoop, plus removal of most trim and unneeded hardware. The S/S thus came to within a few pounds of the 3200-pound weight minimum for the Super/Stock class.

If all that wasn't enough, a mid-year change brought more goodies. The 426 II "Superstock" combo arrived, with improved head design; a new cam, carbs, intake manifold, and exhaust manifold for NASCAR use, and other modifications.

Winning was becoming a way of life with Plymouth. In 1963 it captured 19 NASCAR Grand National first-place finishes (14 taken by Richard Petty), second only to Ford's 23.

A smoother nose and a rounded roof slope on two-door hardtops made the 1964 Plymouths the most aerodynamic yet. New that year was the 426 III, not unlike the 426 II except that, strangely, there was no four-barrel carb listed. Also new was a 426 street engine with a single four-barrel and 365 bhp. Even the dimmest Plymouth salesman knew about that one. The Super/Stock package was again available for quarter-mile service. Initially it came with the 426 III, but that was only for openers. Plymouth and Dodge had been doing well in stock-car racing, especially compared to the '50s, but were still unable to win on NASCAR ovals of a mile or longer. To solve that problem (and blow the remaining drag competitors into the weeds) Chrysler brought back the hemi.

Based on the 426 wedge block (though not exactly the same), this new hemi had a head design similar to that of the original 1951-58 Chrysler FirePower V8. But this time, the competition heads were made of aluminum.

Though the sanctioning bodies were let in on it, the revived hemi wasn't announced to the public until February 9, 1964, shortly before the Daytona 500. Plymouth dubbed its version the "Super Commando" (the division loved that name). Although reports from the engineering labs told tales of dyno needles breaking at 600 horsepower, the advertised ratings turned out the same as those for the 426 wedge: 400, 415, and 425 bhp. So much for truth in advertising. The Super Commando was marketed in accordance with Chrysler policy, and was not available in regular production. You were supposed to be able to get one over the parts counter for around $1800, or you could get one from the factory under the hood of a Super/Stock.

The leading NASCAR teams had no problems getting their hemis, however. While other makes couldn't get over 170 mph on the 2.5-mile Daytona tri-oval, the hemi-powered cars were romping around at around 175 mph. Paul Goldsmith won the pole for the 500 at 174.910 mph, leading MoPars into the first five spots. Critics said they wouldn't go the distance, but were proved wrong by Richard Petty's convincing win. Following in second and third were Jimmy Pardue and Goldsmith, for a 1-2-3 Plymouth sweep. Petty went on to win the 1964 Grand National title, the first ever for a Plymouth driver.

Model year 1964 was the last for a fairly simple Plymouth lineup. For 1965, the cars that had been downsized in '62 became a separate series called Belvedere, and were Plymouth's intermediate contenders. The Fury name was applied to a true full-size model on a 119-inch wheelbase (wagons rode a 121-inch span). To add to the confusion, both lines had sub-series like Fury I, II, and III, and Belvedere I and II. Sport Fury was the bucket-seat top-of-the-line big car; Satellite was its counterpart in the mid-size range. While the model hierarchy may have been fuzzy, it was clear that Belvedere would carry Plymouth's muscle-car colors from here on.

Plymouth Barracuda

Ford is generally credited with starting the "ponycar" craze with the Mustang. But it's instructive to recall that Plymouth introduced its Barracuda only a month later. The Barracuda offered buyers most of the features found in the small Ford, and a few that weren't.

While Mustang was based on fairly well-disguised Falcon components, the Barracuda was quite open about its relationship to the Valiant. (In fact, it even wore Valiant script in its first season and Valiant emblems for the first two.) Basically, it was a fastback version of Plymouth's compact, with a different superstructure embodying a huge wraparound rear window. Its grille was only slightly different, and its front fenders previewed those of the '65 Valiant. The Barracuda's fold-down rear seat opened up the trunk, so that long, narrow items like skis could be carried inside. Ford offered something similar in its 1965 Mustang 2+2 fastback. There was no convertible to counter the Mustang ragtop, though one came along later. The most powerful engine available was the 273-cube V8, producing 180 horsepower in mild tune. Though nowhere near as popular as Mustang, Barracuda scored 23,443 units in its first model

Plymouth Barracuda Performance

Year & Model		Engine (cid/bhp)	Curb Wt.[1]	lbs/ bhp[1]	0-60[2] (sec)	¼-mi.[2] (sec)	Base Price[3]
1965	2d fastbk	273/235	2950	12.6	8.0	16.1	$2627
1967	2d fastbk	273/235	3100	13.4	8.8	16.6	$2720
1967	2d fastbk	383/280	3150	11.3	7.4	15.9	$2720
1968	2d htp	340/275	3125	11.4	8.1	15.2	$2711
1969	'Cuda 440 2d fastbk	440/375	3405	9.1	5.6	14.0	$2813
1970	AAR 'Cuda 2d htp	340/290	3350	11.6	7.2	15.5	NA
1972	'Cuda 2d htp	340/240n	3625	15.1	8.5	16.3	$2953

[1]Advertised; [2]Typical acceleration based on contemporary tests; [3]Advertised list price in contemporary dollars; n = Net advertised horsepower; cid = cubic inch displacement; bhp = brake horsepower; conv = convertible; cpe = coupe; fastbk = fastback; htp = hardtop; rdstr = roadster (2-seat); sdn = sedan; d = number of doors.

From top: 1965 Barracuda; '66 models had front-end facelift; 1967 Barracuda was all-new; 'Cuda option bowed for '69 with 340, 383, or 440 V8s.

From top: 1970 'Cuda 383; 1970 AAR 'Cuda, Plymouth's Trans-Am special; unique paint for '72 'Cuda; the last Barracuda, the '74.

year (abbreviated, as the car wasn't announced until May 15, 1964).

For 1965, Barracuda gained its first performance package, the Formula S. This featured the 273-cid four-barrel "Commando V8" with 235 bhp, along with heavy-duty suspension, fatter wheels and tires, and special trim. Barracudas were entered in a few sports-car rallies, some with factory backing. Production went up to 64,596 for the model year, making it the most popular single model in the Plymouth line.

For 1966, there was a front-end facelift of the original design. Production declined to 38,029 units. Some Barracudas made the drag-racing scene that year, and not with 273s under the hood. Enterprising car builders stuffed them with hemis to compete with the overhead-cam 427 Mustangs from Ford Country.

Barracuda and Valiant were both all-new for 1967, and still closely related. Wheelbase went up from 106.5 to 108 inches. To compete with Mustang, as well as the Chevrolet Camaro, Pontiac Firebird, and Mercury Cougar (all newcomers that season), Plymouth expanded its school of Barracudas. A convertible and a uniquely styled notchback hardtop joined the revamped fastback, all with rather pleasing new contours. To help sales, hardtops and convertibles were axed from the Valiant line. The redesign brought more underhood room for a big-block engine, and Plymouth wasted little time in making a 280-horse version of the 383 a Barracuda option. This could be combined with the Formula S package, which was still on the books. In all, it was a pretty good year, with near-record production of 62,543 units.

For the mildly changed 1968 edition, the 273 was replaced as the base V8 by the 318. A small-block 340 V8, which had a 0.13-inch larger bore than its 318 parent, was a new option. This was good for 275 bhp by means of a four-barrel carb and 10.5:1 compression. The 383 was back, now at 300 horses. It was neat for the street, but a drag at the strips where more of everything was needed. In reply, Plymouth issued a very limited number of hemi-powered Barracudas for quarter-mile action, mostly for the factory-blessed team of Ronnie Sox and Buddy Martin. Like the Super/Stocks of the early- to mid-'60s, the Hemi-Cudas were lightweight specials with only the barest of necessities to be street-legal.

The third and final year for the '67 body style, 1969, saw a new performance option appropriately called the 'Cuda. At first, this meant either the 275-horse 340 or an upgraded 383 with 330 bhp. Later came a 440, rated at 375 bhp. Information on '69 hemi-engined Barracudas is sketchy, with conflicting information on how many, if any, were built.

The second-generation Barracuda appeared for 1970. The fastback was gone, but the convertible and two-door notchback hardtop remained. Width bulged from 69.6 to 74.9 inches, so there was now enough room for a hemi and the whole pit crew between the fender walls. 'Cuda became a full-fledged series, with a standard 335-horse 383. The 275-pony 340 was optional, followed by four-barrel and three-times-two-barrel versions of the 440, and finally the hemi. And that wasn't all: Plymouth went Trans-Am racing in 1970, signing up Dan Gurney to prepare a car for driver Swede Savage. To celebrate the relationship, the AAR 'Cuda was announced as a mid-year production model. AAR stood for Gurney's All-American Racers operation. The package gave you the 340 with triple two-barrel carbs, front and rear spoilers, and the usual ID striping. The big-engined models were the choice of Sox and Martin and other drag racers, and did very well.

With all this hoopla, the Barracuda contingent of the "Rapid Transit System" accounted for 54,799 units in 1970. That was well up on 1969's total of 31,987, but not close to projections, nor the record.

Due to lack of success, the Trans-Am program was folded after the 1970 season, but Plymouth continued to support drag competition. The same lineup of models and engines, more or less, returned for 1971, minus the AAR 'Cuda. Production slipped badly to 18,690 units.

The 1972 Barracuda lost a lot of its performance teeth. Gone were the convertibles and all the big-block engines, including the 383, hemi, and 440. This left the base Barracuda and 'Cuda hardtops, and the hottest power option was now the 240-bhp (net) 340. Apparently the public didn't mind, and ordered 18,450, only a few less than the full line generated the year before.

Production actually climbed for 1973. The six-cylinder engine was dropped, the 318 became standard, and the 340 was still available. The following season, a 360 displaced the 340. By now, the energy crisis was hurting sales of eight-cylinder cars, and, with no six available, Barracuda went deep-six in sales. Production was halted in the spring of 1974.

Plymouth Belvedere

The 1965 Belvedere picked up where the "standard" '64 Plymouths left off. Previously used for the middle-priced series, the name now applied to an entire line of intermediate models distinct from the new full-size Fury, also introduced that year. The Belvedere was dimensionally similar to the '64 Plymouth, but had different sheetmetal below the beltline. Because the muscle-car action was in the mid-size arena, the new line got most of Plymouth's performance goodies.

One of these was the 426 hemi, replacing the wedgehead 426 III as the racer's choice. Two versions were available.

After taking heat during the 1964 season because the hemi was not a true production option, NASCAR disallowed it in the Belvedere for 1965. (It was allowed in the bigger Fury.) Chrysler withdrew in protest, and took its cars elsewhere. A late-season change of heart brought them back, but Plymouth tallied only four NASCAR wins.

Things weren't all roses in Drag City, either. The NHRA ruled that Plymouth's Super/Stock models had to be heavier, which made their trick front-end sheetmetal superfluous. So, the '65 S/S cars reverted to steel for hood and fenders, though some were built with fiberglass parts as factory experimentals for events sponsored by other sanctioning bodies. F/X racing was becoming popular, and started to overshadow the Super/Stock class. Fords ran mostly F/X, notably the big-engine Mustangs, but the MoPars stayed in S/S, so there were few head-to-head confrontations.

New sheetmetal graced the '66 Belvedere, but that was of minor importance to muscle fans because the hemi was finally offered for the street. Buyers who checked the right box on the order form (and plunked down $1105) got a somewhat tamer version of the racing engine. This meant twin Carter AFB four-barrel carbs mounted inline, rather than in a ram setup, and cast-iron heads with a milder 10.25:1 compression ratio. Cam and timing were also cooled down to suit runs to the grocery store. Despite all this, the horsepower rating continued to be—you guessed it—425. Experts said that was still about 125 bhp shy of reality.

Racing folk and interested parties were still able to purchase competi-

Plymouth Intermediate Performance

Year & Model		Engine (cid/bhp)	Curb Wt.[1]	lbs/ bhp[1]	0-60[2] (sec)	¼-mi.[2] (sec)	Base Price[3]
1966	Belvedere Satellite 2d htp	426/425	3940	9.3	7.4	14.5	$2695
1967	Belvedere GTX 2d htp	440/375	3830	10.2	7.0	15.4	$3178
1968	Road Runner 2d sdn	383/335	3650	10.9	7.3	15.4	$2896
1968	GTX 2d conv	426/425	3950	9.3	6.3	14.0	$3590
1969	GTX 2d htp	440/375	3860	10.3	5.8	13.7	$3433
1970	Road Runner 2d htp	440/390	3675	9.4	6.6	14.1	$3034
1971	Road Runner 2d htp	383/300	3950	13.2	6.7	14.8	$3120
1971	Road Runner 2d htp	440/385	4050	10.5	6.7	15.0	$3120

[1]Advertised; [2]Typical acceleration based on contemporary tests; [3]Advertised list price in contemporary dollars; n = Net advertised horsepower; cid = cubic inch displacement; bhp = brake horsepower; conv = convertible; cpe = coupe; fastbk = fastback; htp = hardtop; rdstr = roadster (2-seat); sdn = sedan; d = number of doors.

From top: 1965 Belvedere Satellite; GTX was the hot 1967 setup; Road Runner hardtop from mid-'68; ragtop followed for '69.

From top: 1969 GTX; 1970 Road Runner had power bulge with 440-6bbl. engine; 1970 GTX; Superbird was the ultimate '70 Runner.

tion hemis through the usual channels, so they were reinstated for all Grand National events. Ford was not happy, and withdrew for most of the season. Richard Petty won his second Daytona 500 in '66, and Plymouths accounted for 16 wins (half by Petty), second to Dodge's 18. On the quarter-mile courses, MoPars continued their domination in the top stock classes.

In late summer 1966, a few factory-backed racing Belvederes carried the letters GTX in stock-car competition. The meaning wasn't clear until the "win-you-over" '67 models were announced a few weeks later: GTX was the label for a new high-performance hardtop and convertible.

Standard GTX power came from a new Belvedere engine, the Super Commando. This name meant 440 cubes, achieved via increasing the bore of the 426 wedge by 0.07 inch. The 440 was first seen in the '66 Plymouth Fury and other full-size Chrysler products, but didn't become a performance engine until the 1967 model run. Even so, it was not highly stressed.

Plymouth's race wins in '67 are too numerous to list here, but Richard Petty's NASCAR performance is worth mentioning. He scored a record 27 triumphs (out of Plymouth's season total of 31), including 10 straight, on his way to a second Grand National driving championship. Both the 27 and 10 figures were records, which have never been broken to this day.

Another new skin was wrapped around the Belvedere line for 1968, and the GTX was back with the same engine offerings. However, the spotlight shifted downrange to a downright cheap relative, the Road Runner. Named after the popular Warner Brothers cartoon character, this was a taxicab-basic Belvedere two-door coupe powered by a most untaxi-like engine. Included in the $2896 price was a 335-horse version of the 383, plus four-speed tranny, heavy-duty suspension, and a funny horn that went "beep-beep" like the cartoon animal. The interior was stark, and only Road Runner decals graced the unadorned exterior tin.

Above: 1971 Road Runner shared all-new bodyshell with Sebring/Sebring Plus coupes. Note big loop grille. Upper right: Rear-quarter "strobe stripes" identify the 1972 Road Runner. Lower right: Road Runner reverted to being an option for 1974.

The motoring press loved the Road Runner, as did budget-conscious performance buyers. A total of 44,799 of the '68 models found homes, compared to 18,940 for the GTX. Helping the Road Runner's total was the mid-year addition of a two-door hardtop.

Ford dominated the NASCAR tracks in 1968, especially the superspeedways, with its fastback Torinos. Fords accounted for 20 Grand National wins, while Plymouth was forced to take second with 16.

A ragtop Road Runner was added for 1969, along with a slightly less cut-rate interior. Other than that, things began pretty much the way they had ended the previous year for the mid-size Plymouths. The Super Commando got 15 more advertised horses with the mid-year option of three two-barrel carbs (a first for Plymouth) stuck to an Edelbrock intake manifold. Called the 440-6bbl., it came with a fiberglass hood which had a built-in scoop. Road Runner again won the sales race, this time topping 84,000 units, but it was a different story at the race track. Star driver Richard Petty didn't celebrate his 10th anniversary with Plymouth, switching to Ford instead for the '69 campaign. Plymouth's inferior aerodynamics, plus needed development work on the hemi were the prime reasons.

To get Petty back (and improve on its dismal '69 season—just two Grand National wins) Plymouth hatched the ultimate Road Runner for 1970, the Superbird. A near twin to the 1969 Dodge Charger Daytona, the 'Bird had the same sloped, pointy nose and a big strut-mounted rear airfoil. The body was basic Belvedere, the rear window mounted flush. Standard power came from the 375-horse 440, and the hemi was optional, of course. NASCAR rules that year said that to qualify a car, you had to make one for each dealer. Plymouth dutifully bolted together 1920 of its winged warriors, compared to just over 500 Daytonas.

The Superbird (plus some cash) was enough to bring Richard back to the fold. A team car was also fielded for rookie Pete Hamilton, who promptly went out and won the Daytona 500. Plymouth also signed Dan Gurney away from Ford to run some stock-car events and the Trans-Am. In all, Plymouth notched 21 NASCAR wins in 1970.

The Superbird wasn't the only attraction among Plymouth's power hitters, now called the "Rapid Transit System." The three other Road Runners were back, as was the GTX hardtop, though the convertible wasn't. The performance market went soft as Road Runner sales dropped better than 50 percent and GTX production skidded to 7748.

Plymouth reacted by dropping some of its muscle stuff from the all-new 1971 intermediates, now called Satellite if sedan or wagon and Sebring or Sebring Plus if coupe. The latter's wheelbase shrank an inch to 115, convertibles became history, and there was no such thing as a Superbird. Four-door models grew a bit, and were mounted on a 118-inch wheelbase. Road Runner and GTX were still around, but only in hardtop form. Compression ratios and the need for premium fuel were altered on many engines throughout the industry that year, and Plymouth was no exception. Standard for the Road Runner was a regular-gas 383 with 300 bhp. Optional were the hemi and six-barrel 440, both of which couldn't give up the high-test brew. Ratings were 425 and 385 horses, respectively. The GTX started with a four-barrel 440 at 370 bhp, and offered the Road Runner options. A mid-year arrival took the Road Runner into the small-block world for the first time, a 275-bhp 340 V8. Demand for the performance pair continued to dwindle. Just 14,218 Road Runners were asked for and a mere 2942 GTXs. Plymouth again had a very good year in NASCAR. Richard Petty took 21 of its 22 wins and a third national championship. Included in that total was his third Daytona 500.

Only minor cosmetic changes marked the 1972 Satellite/Sebring, but there was even less performance material. The GTX departed, and the hemi returned to its status as an over-the-counter commodity.

When the 1973 models came out, the muscle-car action had shifted to the compact end of the spectrum.

continued on page 41

Muscle Cars Color Gallery One

1. 1949 Oldsmobile Rocket 88 Holiday
2. 1951 Hudson Hornet Hollywood
3. 1954 Lincoln (Mexican Road Race car)

1

2

3

4

5

1. 1954 Buick Skylark
2. 1955 Chrysler 300
3. 1955 Chrysler 300
4. 1955 Buick Century
5. 1957 Studebaker Golden Hawk
6. 1957 Mercury Turnpike Cruiser
7. 1957 Chevrolet Bel Air

6

7

1. 1958 Chrysler 300D
2. 1958 Chrysler 300D
3. 1958 Chrysler 300D 392-cid FirePower V8
4. 1958 Chrysler 300D control panel
5. 1958 Pontiac Bonneville
6. 1958 Plymouth Fury
7. 1959 Cadillac Eldorado Biarritz

5
BONNEVILLE

6

7

1. 1958 Ford Thunderbird
2. 1961 Chevrolet Corvette
3. 1961 Oldsmobile Starfire
4. 1963 Studebaker Lark Daytona
5. 1963 Ford Galaxie 500/XL

4
516 HJ

5
1963

1. 1963 Studebaker Avanti
2. 1963 Studebaker Avanti
3. 1963 Studebaker Avanti

Plymouth Fury

Plymouth and Dodge pioneered high-performance intermediates with their downsized 1962 models. This may have made them good goers, but it didn't make for good sales. There was still a solid big-car market in the early- to mid-'60's. Starting with the 1965 lineup, Plymouth set out to recapture a chunk of it with its new 119-inch-wheelbase Fury. Fury was not intended to have a muscle-car image (although a mixup in the NASCAR rules resulted in a few showing up on the race tracks). The demand for potent plushmobiles was relatively small, so Plymouth reserved its hottest engines for the intermediate Belvedere.

A break in this philosophy came in 1970, when Plymouth offered high-performance versions of everything as part of its "Rapid Transit System." In the full-size line, the hot ticket was the Sport Fury GT, a two-door hardtop decked out with Plymouth's biggest engine, the 440 cubic-inch V8, with a single four-barrel carb and 350 horsepower. A 390-horse edition was optional, featuring a trio of two-barrels. Heavy-duty suspension was standard in both years. For 1971, a 370-bhp 440 was standard, also with single-quad carb.

The Sport Fury GT was not an answer to a market trend, nor did it start one. Only 375 of the '71s were built, and probably not a great many more of the '70s (figures unavailable). At least it ranks as a rare machine if nothing else.

Plymouth Valiant

Detroit's Big Three introduced their first compacts in 1960 to meet consumer demand for more economical transportation. Ford flourished with its conventional Falcon, and Chevy had the radical rear-engine Corvair. Chrysler's Valiant was somewhere in between.

It wasn't long before somebody thought of hopping up and racing the compacts. Chevrolet offered a mid-season, factory-installed performance package for its 1960 Corvair, and Ford went the dealer-installed route for its Falcon. But Valiant blew them all off the track with the "Hyper-Pak" option for its 170 cubic-inch slant six. Utilizing the ram-induction principle from the big Plymouth V8s, this featured an extended intake manifold (several lengths were tried) capped by a four-barrel carb. The exhaust manifold was split to form dual exhausts, and the head was flattened for a 10:1 compression ratio, up from the stock pressure of 8.5:1. The result was an advertised output of 148 horsepower at 5200 rpm, well up from the regular engine's 101 bhp.

Hyper-Pak continued as a dealer option through 1961, and was applied at mid-year to the larger, long-stroke 225-cube six. This setup was rated at 196 bhp, and was supposedly reserved for the Dodge Lancer. No doubt a few went into Valiants as well.

Valiants competed with minor

Top left: Sport Fury GT was Plymouth's muscular biggie, but only lasted for 1970–71. Few were made. Above: 1961 Valiant hardtop. Top right: 1970 Duster 340, the "whirlwind compact." Middle right: 1971 Duster 340. Lower right: 1975 Duster drag car fires up.

Plymouth Valiant Performance

Year & Model		Engine (cid/bhp)	Curb Wt.[1]	lbs/ bhp[1]	0-60[2] (sec)	¼-mi.[2] (sec)	Base Price[3]
1970	Duster 340 2d cpe	340/275	3105	11.3	6.2	14.7	$2547
1974	Duster 360 2d cpe	360/245n	3250	13.3	8.2	15.8	$3107

[1]Advertised; [2]Typical acceleration based on contemporary tests; [3]Advertised list price in contemporary dollars; n = Net advertised horsepower; cid = cubic inch displacement; bhp = brake horsepower; conv = convertible; cpe = coupe; fastbk = fastback; htp = hardtop; rdstr = roadster (2-seat); sdn = sedan; d = number of doors.

success in sports-car, drag, and rally events. But they were primarily designed and marketed as economy cars. The line got its first V8 as a mid-year option for 1964. Not long afterwards, the Barracuda appeared, and hogged most of the performance goodies.

The 1970 Duster 340 was the first Valiant that can be considered a "performance" car. This attractively styled two-door fastback coupe came with a 275-bhp version of the 340 small-block as standard equipment, along with racy appearance touches to set it apart from the cheaper Dusters. While it didn't have the big inches of the supercars, the Duster 340 proved to be an efficient little screamer. *Car Life* magazine tested the automatic version, which ran 0–60 mph in a very respectable 6.2 seconds. The quarter was accomplished in 14.72 seconds at a terminal speed of 94.24 mph. With a base factory sticker reading $2547, the Duster 340 attracted nearly 25,000 customers, which no doubt hurt sales of the all-new Barracuda that year.

The Duster 340 lasted through 1973. It then became the Duster 360 for '74 by an increase in displacement, and stayed on through 1976, (though it was an option in its final year, not a separate model).

Engine Charts

Chrysler

Type	Bore × Stroke (in.)	CID	BHP @ rpm*	Torque @ rpm*	Fuel# System	Avail. (years)
ohv V8†	3.81 × 3.63	331	180@ 4000	312@ 2000	2 bbl.	1951-53
ohv V8†	3.81 × 3.63	331	235@ 4400	330@ 2600	4 bbl.	1954
ohv V8†	3.81 × 3.63	331	300@ 5200	345@ 3200	2 × 4 bbl.	1955
ohv V8†	3.94 × 3.63	354	340@ 5200	385@ 3200	2 × 4 bbl.	1956
ohv V8†	4.00 × 3.91	392	375@ 5200	420@ 4000	2 × 4 bbl.	1957
ohv V8†	4.00 × 3.91	392	390@ 5600	430@ 4000	2 × 4 bbl.	1957
ohv V8†	4.00 × 3.91	392	380@ 5200	435@ 3600	2 × 4 bbl.	1958
ohv V8†	4.00 × 3.91	392	390@ 5200	435@ 3600	FI	1958
ohv V8	4.19 × 3.75	413	380@ 5000	450@ 3600	2 × 4 bbl.	1959
ohv V8	4.19 × 3.75	413	375@ 5000	495@ 2800	2 × 4 bbl.	1960-61
ohv V8	4.19 × 3.75	413	400@ 5200	465@ 3600	2 × 4 bbl.	1960
ohv V8	4.19 × 3.75	413	380@ 5200	450@ 2800	2 × 4 bbl.	1962
ohv V8	4.19 × 3.75	413	390@ 4800	485@ 3600	2 × 4 bbl.	1963-64
ohv V8	4.19 × 3.75	413	360@ 4800	470@ 3200	4 bbl.	1965

DeSoto

Type	Bore × Stroke (in.)	CID	BHP @ rpm*	Torque @ rpm*	Fuel# System	Avail. (years)
ohv V8†	3.63 × 3.34	276	160@ 4400	250@ 2000	2 bbl.	1952-53
ohv V8†	3.63 × 3.34	276	170@ 4400	255@ 2400	2 bbl.	1954
ohv V8†	3.72 × 3.34	291	200@ 4400	274@ 2800	4 bbl.	1955
ohv V8†	3.78 × 3.80	341	320@ 5200	356@ 4000	4 bbl.	1956
ohv V8†	3.80 × 3.80	345	345@ 5200	355@ 3600	2 × 4 bbl.	1957
ohv V8	4.13 × 3.38	361	345@ 5000	400@ 3600	2 × 4 bbl.	1958
ohv V8	4.13 × 3.38	361	355@ 5000	400@ 3600e	FI	1958
ohv V8	4.25 × 3.38	383	350@ 5000	425@ 3600	2 × 4 bbl.	1959
ohv V8	4.25 × 3.38	383	330@ 4800	460@ 2800	2 × 4 bbl.	1960

Dodge

Type	Bore × Stroke (in.)	CID	BHP @ rpm*	Torque @ rpm*	Fuel# System	Avail. (years)
ohv V8†	3.44 × 3.25	241	140@ 4400	220@ 2200	2 bbl.	1953-54
ohv V8†	3.44 × 3.25	241	150@ 4400	222@ 2400	2 bbl.	1954
ohv V8†	3.63 × 3.25	270	193@ 4400	245@ 2800	4 bbl.	1955
ohv V8†	3.63 × 3.80	315	260@ 4800	330@ 3000	4 bbl.	1956
ohv V8†	3.63 × 3.80	315	295@ 4800	335@ 3200e	2 × 4 bbl.	1956
ohv V8†	3.69 × 3.80	325	285@ 4800	345@ 2800	4 bbl.	1957
ohv V8†	3.69 × 3.80	325	310@ 4800	350@ 3200	2 × 4 bbl.	1957
ohv V8	4.13 × 3.38	361	320@ 4800	400@ 2800	2 × 4 bbl.	1958
ohv V8	4.13 × 3.38	361	333@ 4800	400@ 2800	FI	1958
ohv V8	4.25 × 3.38	383	345@ 5000	420@ 3600	2 × 4 bbl.	1959
ohv V8	4.25 × 3.38	383	330@ 4800	460@ 2800	2 × 4 bbl.	1960-61
ohv V8	4.25 × 3.38	383	340@ 5000	440@ 2800	2 × 4 bbl.	1960-61
ohv I6	3.40 × 4.13	225	196@ 5200	212@ 4200	4 bbl.	1961
ohv V8	4.19 × 3.75	413	350@ 4600	470@ 2800	4 bbl.	1961
ohv V8	4.19 × 3.75	413	375@ 5000	465@ 2800	2 × 4 bbl.	1961
ohv V8	4.19 × 3.75	413	410@ 5400	460@ 3600e	2 × 4 bbl.	1962
ohv V8	4.25 × 3.75	426	415@ 5600	470@ 4400	2 × 4 bbl.	1963-64
ohv V8	4.25 × 3.75	426	425@ 5600	480@ 4400	2 × 4 bbl.	1963-64

*SAE gross ratings except where noted; † hemispherical heads; # carburetion: no. carbs × bbls.; e = estimated; FI = fuel injection; n = net advertised figures; SC = supercharged; TC = turbocharged.

Type	Bore × Stroke (in.)	CID	BHP @ rpm*	Torque @ rpm*	Fuel# System	Avail. (years)
ohv V8†	4.25 × 3.75	426	400@ 5600	465@ 3800	4 bbl.	1964
ohv V8†	4.25 × 3.75	426	415@ 6000	470@ 4600	2 × 4 bbl.	1964
ohv V8†	4.25 × 3.75	426	425@ 6000	480@ 4600	2 × 4 bbl.	1964-65
ohv V8†	4.25 × 3.75	426	415@ 5600	470@ 4400	4 bbl.	1965
ohv V8	4.25 × 3.75	426	365@ 4800	470@ 3200	4 bbl.	1964-65
ohv V8†	4.25 × 3.75	426	425@ 5000	490@ 5000	2 × 4 bbl.	1966-71
ohv V8	4.25 × 3.38	383	280@ 4200	400@ 2400	4 bbl.	1967
ohv V8	4.32 × 3.75	440	375@ 4600	480@ 3200	4 bbl.	1967-70
ohv V8	4.04 × 3.31	340	275@ 5000	340@ 3200	4 bbl.	1968-71
ohv V8	4.25 × 3.38	383	335@ 5200	425@ 3400	4 bbl.	1968-70
ohv V8	4.25 × 3.75	440	390@ 4700	490@ 3600	3 × 2 bbl.	1969-70
ohv V8	4.04 × 3.31	340	290@ 5200	345@ 3400	3 × 2 bbl.	1970
ohv V8	4.32 × 3.75	440	370@ 4600	480@ 3200	4 bbl.	1971
ohv V8	4.32 × 3.75	440	385@ 4700	490@ 3200	3 × 2 bbl.	1971
ohv V8	4.04 × 3.31	340	240@ 4800n	290@ 3600n	4 bbl.	1972-73
ohv V8	4.32 × 3.75	440	280@ 4800n	375@ 3200n	4 bbl.	1972
ohv V8	4.32 × 3.75	440	330@ 4800n	410@ 3600n	3 × 2 bbl.	1972
ohv V8	4.34 × 3.38	400	260@ 4800n	335@ 3600n	4 bbl.	1973
ohv V8	4.32 × 3.75	440	280@ 4800n	380@ 3200n	4 bbl.	1973
ohv V8	4.00 × 3.58	360	245@ 4800n	320@ 3600n	4 bbl.	1974
ohv V8	4.32 × 3.75	440	275@ 4400n	375@ 3200n	4 bbl.	1974
ohv V8	4.00 × 3.58	360	230@ 4000n	300@ 3200n	4 bbl.	1975
ohv V8	4.32 × 3.75	440	260@ 4400n	355@ 3200n	4 bbl.	1975
ohv V8	4.00 × 3.58	360	200@ 4000n	280@ 3200n	4 bbl.	1976
ohv V8	4.34 × 3.38	400	240@ 3200n	325@ 3200n	4 bbl.	1976
ohv V8	4.00 × 3.58	360	175@ 4000n	275@ 2000n	4 bbl.	1977-78
ohv V8	4.00 × 3.58	360	195@ 4000n	280@ 2400n	4 bbl.	1979

Plymouth

Type	Bore × Stroke (in.)	CID	BHP @ rpm*	Torque @ rpm*	Fuel# System	Avail. (years)
ohv V8	3.81 × 3.32	303	240@ 4800	310@ 2800	4 bbl.	1956
ohv V8	3.91 × 3.31	318	290@ 5400	325@ 4000	2 × 4 bbl.	1957-58
ohv V8	4.06 × 3.38	350	305@ 5000	370@ 3600	2 × 4 bbl.	1958
ohv V8	4.06 × 3.38	350	315@ 5000	370@ 3600	FI	1958
ohv V8	4.12 × 3.38	361	305@ 4600	395@ 3000	4 bbl.	1959-62
ohv V8	4.25 × 3.38	383	330@ 4800	460@ 2800	2 × 4 bbl.	1960-61
ohv V8	4.25 × 3.38	383	340@ 5000	440@ 2800	2 × 4 bbl.	1960-61
ohv I6	3.40 × 3.13	170	148@ 5200	153@ 4200	4 bbl.	1960-61
ohv V8	4.19 × 3.75	413	350@ 4600	470@ 2800	4 bbl.	1961
ohv V8	4.19 × 3.75	413	375@ 5000	465@ 2800	2 × 4 bbl.	1961
ohv V8	4.19 × 3.75	413	410@ 5400	460@ 3600e	2 × 4 bbl.	1962
ohv V8	4.25 × 3.75	426	415@ 5600	470@ 4400	2 × 4 bbl.	1963-64
ohv V8	4.25 × 3.75	426	425@ 5600	480@ 4400	2 × 4 bbl.	1963-64
ohv V8	4.25 × 3.75	426	365@ 4800	475@ 3200	4 bbl.	1964-65
ohv V8†	4.25 × 3.75	426	400@ 5600	465@ 3800	4 bbl.	1964
ohv V8†	4.25 × 3.75	426	415@ 6000	470@ 4600	2 × 4 bbl.	1964
ohv V8†	4.25 × 3.75	426	425@ 6000	480@ 4600	2 × 4 bbl.	1964-65
ohv V8	3.63 × 3.31	273	235@ 5000	280@ 4000	4 bbl.	1965-67
ohv V8†	4.25 × 3.75	426	415@ 5600	470@ 4400	4 bbl.	1965
ohv V8†	4.25 × 3.75	426	425@ 5000	490@ 4000	2 × 4 bbl.	1966-71
ohv V8	4.25 × 3.38	383	280@ 4200	400@ 2400	4 bbl.	1967
ohv V8	4.32 × 3.75	440	375@ 4600	480@ 3200	4 bbl.	1967-70
ohv V8	4.25 × 3.38	383	300@ 4400	400@ 2400	4 bbl.	1968
ohv V8	4.25 × 3.38	383	335@ 5200	425@ 3400	4 bbl.	1968-70
ohv V8	4.32 × 3.75	440	390@ 4700	490@ 3600	3 × 2 bbl.	1969-70
ohv V8	4.04 × 3.31	340	275@ 5000	340@ 3200	4 bbl.	1969-71
ohv V8	4.04 × 3.31	340	290@ 5200	345@ 3400	3 × 2 bbl.	1970
ohv V8	4.32 × 3.75	440	370@ 4600	480@ 3200	4 bbl.	1971
ohv V8	4.32 × 3.75	440	385@ 4700	490@ 3200	3 × 2 bbl.	1971
ohv V8	4.04 × 3.31	340	240@ 4800n	290@ 3600n	4 bbl.	1972-73
ohv V8	4.32 × 3.75	440	280@ 4800n	375@ 3200n	4 bbl.	1972-73
ohv V8	4.32 × 3.75	440	330@ 4800n	410@ 3600n	3 × 2 bbl.	1972
ohv V8	4.34 × 3.38	400	255@ 4800n	340@ 3200n	4 bbl.	1972-73
ohv V8	4.00 × 3.58	360	245@ 4800n	320@ 3600n	4 bbl.	1974
ohv V8	4.32 × 3.75	440	275@ 4400n	375@ 3200n	4 bbl.	1974
ohv V8	4.00 × 3.58	360	230@ 4000n	300@ 3200n	4 bbl.	1975
ohv V8	4.34 × 3.38	400	235@ 4000n	320@ 3200n	4 bbl.	1975
ohv V8	4.00 × 3.58	360	200@ 4000n	280@ 3200n	4 bbl.	1976
ohv V8	4.34 × 3.38	400	240@ 4400n	325@ 3200n	4 bbl.	1976
ohv V8	4.00 × 3.58	360	175@ 4000n	275@ 2000n	4 bbl.	1977-78
ohv V8	4.00 × 3.58	360	195@ 4000n	280@ 2400n	4 bbl.	1979

*SAE gross ratings except where noted; † hemispherical heads; # carburetion: no. carbs × bbls.; e = estimated; FI = fuel injection; n = net advertised figures; SC = supercharged; TC = turbocharged.

Ford Motor Company

Dearborn's honor roll of hot cars is a long one. From the fabled Mexican Road Race Lincolns and speedy two-seat Thunderbirds of the '50s to the hot Mustangs, Cobras, Torinos, and Cyclones of the '60s, Total Performance has always been a way of life in Ford Country.

Edsel

Edsel will always be remembered as the auto industry's biggest flop. It was Ford's attempt to broaden its base in the medium-price field, and proved to be the wrong car at the wrong time. So it may come as a surprise that the 1958 Edsel, at least, could be a pretty rapid mover.

Conceived at the height of the "horsepower race," the first-year Edsel offered good performance throughout its model line, from the bottom to the top. Positioned to straddle Ford and Mercury in price, the line consisted of four series. The cheaper Ranger and Pacer shared basic bodies with Ford, and rode the same 118-inch wheelbase. The top-line Corsair and Citation rode a 124-inch stretch, and shared the Mercury bodyshell. Wagons used the Ford structure and 116-inch wheelbase. The two lower lines were powered by a slightly bored-out version of Ford's new 352 V8. This packed 361 cubes, and was called the "Express V8." Output came to 303 horsepower, a scant three more than Ford's best. The big jobs pulled 345-bhp from a smaller version of the Mercury/Lincoln 430 dubbed the "Super Express," and sized at 410 cubes. Both Edsel engines carried four-barrel Holley carbs and, with a 10.5:1 compression ratio, demanded premium fuel.

Mechanix Illustrated magazine tested a loaded Corsair four-door hardtop that tipped the scales at 4381 pounds. This car managed a respectable 0–60 mph time of 8.7 seconds, and the report estimated top speed at 120 mph. Of all the '58 cars tested by writer Tom McCahill, only Pontiac had better acceleration.

The 1959 Edsel reflected the public's new concern with economy—and dismal first-year sales for the new make. All models were related to that year's Ford, and rode a 120-inch wheelbase. The lineup contracted, smaller Ford 292-and 332-cid engines were substituted, and even a six was now available. Topping the power list was the 303-horse 361 as an option for all models. *Motor Life* magazine confirmed the '59s were down on performance, as its 303-bhp Corsair couldn't do 0–60 mph in less than 10 seconds.

Edsel's final model year, 1960, was a short one. Styling was completely revised on an all-new bodyshell shared with Ford. A regular-gas 352 V8 with 300 bhp was now the top power option. The sales

1958 Edsel Ranger (left) and Pacer shared bodyshell and engines with Ford. Above: Last Edsel was 1960 model. Ragtop is rare.

Edsel Performance

Year & Model		Engine (cid/bhp)	Curb Wt.[1]	lbs/ bhp[1]	0-60[2] (sec)	¼-mi.[2] (sec)	Base Price[3]
1958	Corsair 4d htp	410/345	4235	12.3	8.7	16.9	$3425
1959	Corsair 4d sdn	361/303	3696	12.2	10.2	17.6	$2812

[1]Advertised; [2]Typical acceleration based on contemporary tests; [3]Advertised list price in contemporary dollars; n = Net advertised horsepower; cid = cubic inch displacement; bhp = brake horsepower; conv = convertible; cpe = coupe; fastbk = fastback; htp = hardtop; rdstr = roadster (2-seat); sdn = sedan; d = number of doors.

pace was still snail-like, and only 3000 of the 1960 models were built. Production closed in November 1959.

Despite its lack of popularity, the Edsel wasn't really a bad car in most respects, just a very average one. It did offer performance that was competitive with other medium-price cars of the day, although no Edsel can truly be thought of as a muscle car. In the years since this $250-million fiasco disappeared, Edsel has achieved almost a cult status in a certain segment of the old-car hobby. Perhaps because of their performance (not to mention their greater numbers), the '58s have proven most popular. The 1960 models are the rarest and, because of that, command the highest prices on the collector market.

Ford

On a cold January morning in 1904, Henry Ford set a world's speed record in his "999" racer, with a run of 91.370 mph. Since then, Ford cars and feats of performance have been closely connected. Even in the early years of the marque, Fords were entered in many durability and speed contests. Because they were low-priced cars and sold in huge numbers, a great many individuals and companies started to design special speed parts for them. Soon, there was a booming business in making Model As and Model Ts quicker. Ford's early performance history, in fact, was written largely by these modifieds.

For 1932, the company got in on the action itself. The result was the first low-priced car to offer a V8 engine. It was a relatively simple design, with a displacement of 221 cubic inches and 65 horsepower. An even smaller version at only 135.9 cubic inches was offered for 1937–40, and was known as the V8-60 because of its 60-bhp output. Neither of these was exactly a powerhouse, but they became very popular for midget auto racing. They were also somewhat smoother than the side-valve fours and sixes of other cars, which gave Ford an important sales tool. The flatheads became the favorite of home mechanics, and appealed to every teen-ager interested in a new-fangled type of home-made modified called a "hot rod." Again, aftermarket suppliers rushed out a plethora of parts to give the little flathead V8 more muscle. Stock-car racing garnered growing interest in the 1930s, and cut-down Fords were in the thick of it. Through the 1940s and into the early '50s, Ford was still without V8 competition in its price class. Though some medium-priced cars had V8s and could handily outrun the flatheads, Ford's performance heritage kept a steady stream of power-seeking customers flocking to the showrooms. The original 221 V8 remained in the Ford line through 1942. After the war, there was a 239.4-cid version, which had been introduced for the companion Mercury in 1939. This offered 100 bhp, 10 more than the 221.

Ford's first all-new postwar models arrived for 1949, with much smoother styling that proved very popular. The suspension was also updated, with coil springs in front and leaf springs in the rear replacing the transverse-leaf-spring front and torque-tube drive that had been Ford hallmarks (some said drawbacks) for many years. The V8 remained at 100 bhp until the next major body change in 1952. That year, Ford debuted its modern overhead-valve six rated at 101 bhp. To keep pace, the V8 got a compression boost from 6.8 to 7.2:1 for 110 bhp. *Motor Trend* magazine tested both engines, and found the '52 six could do 0–60 mph in 19.45 seconds compared to 20.47 for the V8. The in-line job was also faster through the quarter-mile.

The modern overhead-valve V8 finally arrived for Ford's 1954 models. Displacement was still 239.4 cubes, but the new powerplant was of short-stroke (bore bigger than stroke) configuration, and much more efficient than the old

Left: 1940 is still a hot-rodder's favorite. Above: 1951 Ford was still without V8 competition in the low-price field.

Above: 1956 Ford Fairlane could be had with 292-cid V8 new that season. Right: "Fireball" Roberts hurtles a '57 Custom Tudor around the dirt-beach track at Daytona in 160-mile race.

flathead. Advertised output came to 130 bhp.

The next year, Ford's traditional rivals in the low-price field had V8s too, plus all-new styling. Chevrolet's powerful 265-cid engine, in particular, looked like big trouble. Ford was ready, or so it thought, with a pair of larger V8s. First came a bored-and-stroked version of the 239 giving 272 cubes, and rated at 162 bhp with a single two-throat Holley carb. For more horses, a four-barrel and dual exhausts were offered to deliver 182 bhp. Later, Ford went to its parts bin for the 292 V8 previously reserved for Mercury and the dashing new '55 Thunderbird. This unit fit the standard Ford since it was just a bigger-bore 272. Available power went up to 198 bhp.

It didn't take long for word to get around that Chevy's 265 had tremendous performance potential. Compared to the Ford engines, it was lighter, and had a free-revving valve train that allowed it to wind up faster and higher. Speed merchants set about extracting more power from it, much as they had done in earlier times with the flathead Ford. Stock-car racers eyed the Chevy because it could be quickly converted to race trim fairly cheaply, yet still run with the best of the medium-priced cars like the Olds 88, which still dominated NASCAR in those years. Chevrolet helped by offering power packs that upped horses. Fords were still raced more than any other make at the time, but the factory did little itself. Now that its performance leadership in the low-price field was being seriously challenged for the first time in more than two decades, Ford knew it had to get involved.

NASCAR was the choice. The start would be the 1955 Southern 500, held on Labor Day at Darlington International Raceway, a 1⅜-mile banked, paved oval, and the South's first high-speed track. Indianapolis 500 great Pete DePaolo was hired to set up a team, and he quickly signed Curtis Turner and Joe Weatherly to do the driving. The factory helped out by announcing a special "Interceptor" version of the 292 (ostensibly for police use) with 205 bhp. While they ran, the Fords stole the show. But they needed more development, especially the suspensions, which gave way and gave the Southern 500 to Herb Thomas in a Smokey Yunick 1955 Chevrolet. At the end of the season, Ford went back to its drawing board.

The 272 and 292 V8s continued for 1956. The Y-block design was treated to a bore-and-stroke increase for 312 cid. The top setup offered 225 bhp with single four-barrel carb, and was supposedly offered only with automatic transmission. Dual four-barrel carbs came up at mid-year for both Mercury and Thunderbird. This option wasn't listed for the standard Ford, but it's possible some cars got it. Fords couldn't match the mighty Chrysler 300s in NASCAR during 1956, but did manage 14 wins (including the Southern 500).

For 1957 there were two sizes of standard Fords. The lower-priced Custom and Custom 300 series used a 116-inch wheelbase. The fancier Fairlane and Fairlane 500 rode a 118-inch chassis. Styling was the same for all models except for trim details. The 312 was retained, now at 245 bhp for the standard setup or 270 with dual quads. Chevrolet moved up to 283 cid that year—and up to 283 bhp with its new fuel injection system. Ford replied with two hotter 312s after the start of the model year. A twin four-barrel setup produced 285 horses, and there was a McCulloch supercharged mill claimed to produce 300 bhp.

Meanwhile, NASCAR banned superchargers, fuel injection, and

Ford Performance

Year	Model	Engine (cid/bhp)	Curb Wt.[1]	lbs/ bhp[1]	0-60[2] (sec)	¼-mi.[2] (sec)	Base Price[3]
1951	STD 2d sdn	239/100	3043	30.4	17.8	21.2	$1417
1954	Customline 4d sdn	239/130	3216	24.7	17.2	20.4	$1793
1956	Fairlane 4d sdn	292/202	3400	16.8	11.6	18.6	$2093
1957	Fairlane 500 4d sdn	312/245	3525	14.4	11.1	18.2	$2286
1958	Fairlane 500 2d htp	352/300	3550	11.8	10.2	17.7	$2435
1960	Starliner 2d htp	352/360	3617	10.0	7.1	15.4	$2610
1962	Galaxie 500 2d htp	406/405	3880	9.6	7.0	15.3	$2674
1963	Galaxie NASCAR Stock Car 2d htp	427/410	3715	9.1	6.3	14.2	NA
1965	Galaxie 500/XL 2d htp	427/425	4096	9.6	4.8	14.9	$3233
1966	7-Litre 2d htp	428/345	4118	11.9	8.0	16.4	$3621

[1]Advertised; [2]Typical acceleration based on contemporary tests; [3]Advertised list price in contemporary dollars; n = Net advertised horsepower; cid = cubic inch displacement; bhp = brake horsepower; conv = convertible; cpe = coupe; fastbk = fastback; htp = hardtop; rdstr = roadster (2-seat); sdn = sedan; d = number of doors.

multiple carburetion in April. In June, the Automobile Manufacturers Association (AMA) issued a decree that effectively banned factory-backed race teams and the use of performance in advertising. But though the teams were disbanded, racing parts were still available to them under the table. One such organization, Holman & Moody of Charlotte, North Carolina, got a warehouse full of Ford goodies. Partner Ralph Moody took one of the supercharged cars to USAC, where they were still legal, and won four races (including all three Milwaukee events). He also earned enough money to help finance an independent Ford racing parts operation through H&M. Even without superchargers, Fords still did well in NASCAR, taking 27 Grand Nationals in '57. It was a record for the make, and tied the all-time high mark held jointly by Hudson and Chrysler. Ford was also a winner in the sales race. Its restyled '57 line topped the facelifted Chevrolets, making Ford number one for the first time since 1935.

A new big-block V8 was the engineering highlight for the warmed-over 1958 Fords. There were two sizes, 332 and 352 cubes, the latter offered with up to 300 horses. The 292 was the only surviving small-block. Ford took the AMA ban seriously, so there was no high-output 352. Nevertheless, the big engine was fairly popular in stock-car racing where the 116-inch wheelbase two-door sedans were entered as in '57. Fords won 16 NASCAR Grand National races, but Chevrolet copped 23 running its '57 cars. Newcomer Fred Lorenzen won the USAC title for Ford that year.

For 1959, all full-size Fords rode the 118-inch wheelbase, and adopted squared-off conservative lines. There was no change in the 352's power rating. The make won 10 Grand National races that season, and another six were scored by Thunderbird for a total of 16 against Chevrolet's 14.

The dawn of the '60s brought a renewed interest in performance at Ford, thanks partly to a new division general manager, Lee A. Iacocca. The 1960 standard Fords were the biggest and widest ever. Wheelbase went up to 119 inches, but the increase in sheetmetal acreage wasn't too great. A new Starliner two-door hardtop appeared with very smooth lines that made it look like a natural superspeedway competitor.

Not so competitive was the 300-horse 352, the largest in the stable. Thunderbird had switched to the 350-bhp Lincoln 430-cid V8, but that was too heavy for stock-car racing. To motivate the new Starliner, and bring back buyers who had strayed to other makes, Ford introduced its first performance engine in three years, the Interceptor 360. With a single four-barrel carb and 10.6:1 compression, the 352 was persuaded to kick out 360 bhp. Initially the 360 only came with a three-speed manual transmission.

Ford sent a letter to the AMA, indicating its intent to build high-performance cars again because it could no longer support the ban. As proof of that, a Starliner with the 360 averaged 142 mph at Daytona for 40 laps. Ford was heading back for the fast lane.

It had been a while since Ford had done much in drag racing. The new 360s turned out in decent numbers at the strips, setting records in the standard-shift class. More ammunition came in June 1960 with the announcement of a triple two-barrel setup as a dealer-installed option. No horsepower rating was given, but the hardware was announced in time to be legal at the NHRA Labor Day Nationals. Ford topped the Grand National stock car winners' list that year, taking 15 events.

Trimmer and more powerful Fords were issued for 1961. An increase in bore and stroke brought the 352 up to 390 cid, putting Ford in the big-inch league with Pontiac's 389. Three versions were initially listed, a "common" 300-horse job, a police-oriented 330-bhp unit, and the high-performance 375-bhp Thunderbird Super V8. Don't let the Thunderbird title fool you: every Ford V8 that year bore the name, whether it was available in the T-Bird or not. Though squared-off rooflines got space in the ads, the Starliner carried on and would see superspeedway duty. A 375-bhp model tested out at over 153 mph at Daytona. The original 390's single four-barrel carb was joined at mid-year by triple two-barrels and a compression ratio boost yielding 401 bhp. This option was also deemed legal for drag racing. There were other modifications later in the season, but no power increases were claimed. Also late in the year, the big Ford got its first four-speed manual transmission, a Borg-Warner unit.

Despite all the hot stuff, the competition was hotter, so Ford turned up a lot of "almosts." The make notched only seven NASCAR wins in '61, its lowest total since 1955, but one victory was satisfying as Nelson Stacy took the Southern 500 at Darlington.

The 390's reign as Ford's top performance offering was short-lived. After the 1962 model year was underway, the 406 appeared, with a 0.08-inch larger bore. In standard four-barrel form it delivered a claimed 385 horses. The tri-carb combo and compression increase took the number up to 405 bhp. The Starliner disappeared, leaving the less slippery square-cut models to battle on the long tracks. Ford teams tried to get a Starliner-type roof approved for use on convertibles, and the factory even announced a removable "Starlift" roof option, but NASCAR said no. Only six Grand National events were won

1962 Ford Sunliner could be equipped with new 406 V8.

by Ford pilots. The drag racing effort also needed help. Special lightweight Plymouth, Dodge, and Pontiac dragsters were out in force, and the big Ford was too heavy to keep up. Aluminum bumpers and fiberglass body panels were fabricated for the option list, but not in sufficient quantities to qualify as "production." Cars with the lightweight pieces had to run in the factory-experimental class.

As was becoming standard Ford practice, the 1963 full-size models bowed with the most powerful engines from the previous year. In June 1962, Ford had declared it would no longer follow the AMA edict, and the first evidence of that arrived for 1963½: two-door hardtops with a slanted rear roofline for the Galaxie 500 and 500/XL series. Though called a "fastback," it wasn't as smooth as the Starliner, but it was a step in the right direction for stock-car racing. The major sanctioning bodies had imposed a maximum engine limit of 427 cubic inches starting with the 1963 model year. That's the number Ford came up with, thanks to another bore increase on the big-block. Ratings came up to 410 bhp with single four-barrel carb and to 425 with two. Drag racers weren't left out, either. An S/S kit with fiberglass body panels was now available, and took 164 pounds off the front end. Some complete cars fitted with the kit and stripped interiors came off the assembly line. Though lighter, these big Fords still couldn't catch the Plymouths and Dodges in Super/Stock action. Things were better in NASCAR where 23 events went to Ford drivers.

Major facelifts were ordained for the 1964 big cars, but for once there were no major changes in engine displacement or output. A mid-year option was a High-Riser manifold for the 427, but like the competition, Ford shyed away from claiming increased horsepower. The division's drag-racing campaign was shifted to the intermediate Fairlane. A limited number of 427-engine models, called Thunderbolt, were assembled for factory-experimental competition. The big Ford had had it.

There were size problems in NASCAR as well. Starting in 1962, the standard Dodges and Plymouths were smaller than the standard Ford, but it made little difference, as they were down on power. After Chrysler brought back its hemi for the '64 season, the MoPar stockers ran away from the big Fords on the superspeedways. Ford protested, and tried to legalize an overhead-cam 427. NASCAR said no, so the High-Riser option and a "high-rev" package were certified instead. While the Chrysler forces won some big ones, Ford won more races, scoring a record 30 victories for the season.

All-new top to bottom described the 1965 full-sized Ford. But despite its recent race triumphs, most of the hoopla surrounded the top-line LTD, billed as being "Quieter than a Rolls Royce." The mid-size '65 Fairlane still couldn't carry a big-block off the assembly line, so the big Fords again had to carry the ball in stock-car racing, while most of the competition used intermediates. A rules dispute with NASCAR kept the Plymouth and Dodge teams out for much of the 1965 season, so Ford rolled to the greatest number of Grand National wins ever, 48 out of 55 starts. In quarter-mile events, the sporty Mustang now began to appear with trick engines for the factory-experimental class, while the big cars had a terrible time in the production classes.

By 1966, demand for burly big cars had slackened considerably. The intermediates and sporty compacts were now the tire-burner's favorites. Ford's Fairlane was all-new this year, and could now accommodate big-blocks. A few 427s started sneaking in almost at once.

Above: Ford called its 1963s "Super Torque." Shown is Galaxie 500/XL. Lower left: 427 muscle helped big Fords at the drags. Upper right: 1964 Galaxie 500/XL. Below: 1966 7-Litre with 428 V8.

The stock-car runners started off the season with the big cars, sat out most of it, then returned for the finale in Fairlanes.

Ford had been running the cubic-inch race for years before it fielded a full-size model with a standard big-inch powerplant. This was the 1966 Galaxie 500 7-Litre, offered in two-door hardtop and convertible styles, and equipped with a low-output big-block sized at 428 cid. It had a smaller bore and a longer stroke than the 427, and was designed for smoothness rather than brute power. In standard tune it delivered 345 bhp, and 360 was optional, both with four-barrel carbs. The 7-Litre was not popular, however, and just over 11,000 were made. It moved to option status for 1967, then into oblivion.

The hairy 427 hardly fit the posh image Ford wanted for its big cars, but stayed in the lineup through the 1967 model year. Both four-barrel and twin-four forms were offered. To meet the new Federal emission standards for 1968, the 427 was tamed by a single four-barrel carb, bringing power down to 390 bhp. Just to confuse customers, a hot version of the 428 came out at mid-year to replace the 427, which had served well for five years.

The standard Fords were now big, heavy cars, and had long since given up any pretense of real performance. Mustang and Fairlane were doing the job as the division's muscle cars—and a very good one at that.

Mid-size Fairlane was heated up for '63 with 271-bhp 289.

Ford Fairlane/ Torino

Cars got longer, lower, and wider in the late '50s. Detroit's new compacts came along in 1960 to help balance things out. But this left a size gap that seemed too obvious for carmakers to ignore. Ford was one of the first to capitalize on the market for what came to be known as intermediates with its 1962 Ford Fairlane and Mercury Meteor. Wheelbase for this pair was 115.5 inches and overall length 197.6. Weight was just under 3000 pounds. Two- and four-door sedans were initially offered under each nameplate. The unitized body/chassis structure was similar to that of the compact Falcon, and standard power was supplied by the Falcon six.

Significantly, there was also a new 221 cubic-inch V8, the same size as Ford's first V8 in 1932. This design was all-new and quite modern, with a thin-wall block that had room to grow. Rated horsepower was a modest 145. At mid-year, a 0.3-inch stroke increase brought 260 cubes and 164 bhp. Later, another bore increase, from 3.80 to 4.00 inches, brought displacement to 289 cubes. A high-performance 271-bhp version, complete with four-barrel carb and 11.0:1 compression, became a mid-1963 Fairlane option. It was the first performance engine to be offered in an intermediate.

The 271 was fine until Pontiac ran away from the hot-car field by dropping its 389 V8 into the mid-sized Tempest and calling it GTO. Chrysler products were also running around the dragstrips with ram-inducted 426s, leaving Fairlane in the minor leagues. Ford had a big-league engine, the 427, but the Fairlane didn't have enough room between its suspension towers to give it a home.

Finally, for 1964, Ford found a way to stuff the 427 into a Fairlane. It called for reworking the front end, something that couldn't be done on a mass-production assembly line, but was feasible on a limited number of cars. Accordingly, there was a short run of two-door sedans equipped with fiberglass body panels and bumpers and plexiglass windows. Thus was born the Thunderbolt. Though it resembled the stock Fairlane, the Thunderbolt was different in almost every other way. With the 427 aboard, it weighed within a sneeze of the NHRA's 3205-pound minimum. The Thunderbolt did well against the MoPars in the Super/Stock class.

The first production Fairlanes able to carry a big-block were the totally redesigned 1966 models. The new bodyshell didn't change overall dimensions much, but its extra underhood room enabled Ford to come up with an answer to the GTO and other muscle machines. This turned up as the Fairlane GT (GTA with automatic). A two-door hardtop and convertible were offered with a 315-bhp 390 V8 as standard, or 335 optional. That would have given a 1964 GTO a good run, but Pontiac upped the ante to 360 bhp that year, which again left the Fairlane in the shade. Later in the model year Ford

Ford Fairlane/Torino Performance

Year & Model		Engine (cid/bhp)	Curb Wt.[1]	lbs/ bhp[1]	0-60[2] (sec)	¼-mi.[2] (sec)	Base Price[3]
1966	Fairlane GTA 2d htp	390/335	3510	10.5	6.8	15.2	$2843
1968	Fairlane Torino GT 2d htp	390/335	3780	11.3	7.2	15.1	$2772
1969	Fairlane Cobra 2d htp	428/335	3725	11.1	6.3	14.5	$3139
1970	Torino GT 2d htp	351/300	3830	12.8	8.1	15.6	$3105
1970	Torino Cobra 2d htp	429/370	3913	10.5	6.0	14.5	$3105

[1]Advertised; [2]Typical acceleration based on contemporary tests; [3]Advertised list price in contemporary dollars; n = Net advertised horsepower; cid = cubic inch displacement; bhp = brake horsepower; conv = convertible; cpe = coupe; fastbk = fastback; htp = hardtop; rdstr = roadster (2-seat); sdn = sedan; d = number of doors.

1966 Fairlane GT (left) and '67 GTA (above) offered 390 V8. Modifieds (below) ran well at the strips. Fastback Torino (lower left) bowed for '69, followed by Cobra (lower right).

slotted its 427 into the Fairlane. A few of these appeared on the NASCAR circuit, although Ford officially sat out the season.

For 1967, the 427 was listed as a regular option, with 410 or 425 bhp as in the big Fords. This move turned Fairlane into the official factory racer for Grand National events that year. Richard Petty and Plymouth went on a rampage and took 31 wins, while Ford scored the same number as the year before, 10, one of which was the Daytona 500.

Fairlane's 116-inch wheelbase and chassis design went untouched for 1968. Bodies (except for wagons, which had a 113-inch wheelbase) were new from stem to stern, however, and about four inches broader of beam. The big attraction was a new fastback body style. It was offered as a Fairlane 500, or in new Torino and Torino GT guise. All looked fast even when standing still. A single version of the 427, with four-barrel carb and 390 bhp, was listed. After a few months it got the hook in favor of the 428 Cobra Jet. A longer stroke and smaller bore made the 428 easier to get through Uncle Sam's new emission tests than the 427. Outfitted with one four-barrel, the 428 CJ delivered 335 bhp.

The fastback body had good aerodynamics, of course, as it had been designed to put Ford back at the front of the stock-car wars. That it did. Fords took 20 wins in '68, more than any other make in NASCAR, and driver David Pearson won the championship. Meanshile, A. J. Foyt took the USAC stock crown, and Benny Parsons did the same in the Auto Racing Club of America (ARCA), all in '68 Torinos. Despite these wins, Torino drivers still had one problem on the superspeedways, namely the Torino's sibling, the Mercury Cyclone. Its grille design made it faster than the Ford in the long-distance sprints, a fact Cale Yarborough and company rubbed in every chance they got.

But Ford showed it still had a few tricks up its sleeve on the '69 Torino and Fairlane. First, it fielded a low-buck muscle car, a concept popularized by Plymouth with the 1968 Road Runner. Called Cobra, a name borrowed from Carroll Shelby's incredible pavement chewers, it was offered in notchback and fastback (now called SportsRoof) hardtops with rather basic trim. The 428 CJ was standard, as was a four-speed tranny, heavy-duty suspension, and a cartoon decal of the famed snake. Optional power was supplied by the Ram-Air 428 CJ.

For the NASCAR gang, Ford also had the Torino Talladega and Boss 429. First came the Talladega, named for the new 2.66-mile Alabama track which opened in 1969. It featured an extended and sloped nose which met a simple, flush-mounted grille, and a front bumper lifted from the rear of the regular Torino, all for improved aerodynamics. It also had the SportsRoof body to take on the recently announced Dodge Charger 500 (Mercury got the same thing as the Cyclone Spoiler II). To make it all go, Ford tried to legalize a semi-hemi, or crescent-head, version of its new 429-cid big-block engine for the '69 season. But NASCAR and Ford officials didn't exactly agree that this Boss 429 was a production mill. Ford claimed it would be installed in Mustangs. NASCAR was doubtful, but after several races had gone by, allowed it.

Ford somehow enticed Richard Petty, who had driven Plymouths since 1959, into its corner. He responded by winning the first race he entered under the Ford flag, the 500-miler at Riverside. The Talladega's first superspeedway win came soon afterwards as Lee Roy Yarborough took the Daytona 500. (Later a Dodge Charger Daytona won the first race held at the Talladega track.) All in all, Ford had a good year in NASCAR. Pearson repeated as champion, and Fords connected for 26 wins, more than any other make. Late in the season, however, they got a run for it from the winged Daytonas. As it turned out, 1969 would be the high-water mark for the racing mid-size Fords. No Ford driver would ever win another Grand National championship, and the make would never get more than a half-dozen wins per season.

The decline started with the 1970 line, now officially called Torino. Wheelbase grew an inch to 117, width spread by about two inches, and length stretched out by about four. The SportsRoof fastback now looked sexier than ever. But although it was described by Ford as being "wind-shaped," superspeedway tests proved otherwise: the 1969 Talladega was a good five miles an hour faster. The 1970's reverse-curve rear window was said to be one of the problems. Ford couldn't give away that much speed to the winged Daytonas and their new friends, the Plymouth Road Runner Superbirds, so it (and Mercury) would run last year's cars in 1970 NASCAR big-track events. Ford won just six of them. Petty returned to Plymouth, and the future didn't look rosy for Ford fans. One reason was a cutback in the racing budget, as Ford was in the process of getting out.

Torinos were no slouches on the street, however. The 429 was available in four versions, from 360 bhp (standard in the Cobra) up to 375 bhp, including the Ram-Air setup. For 1971, the line was a carryover. The Cobra now had a standard four-barrel 351 small-block engine. The 429 was still listed both with and without Ram-Air, and both claimed 370 bhp. Performance promotion cooled, and the number of Fords in NASCAR dwindled without factory backing. The make won only three events, its worst performance since 1955.

The all-new 1972 Torino featured body-on-frame instead of unit construction, and coil springs were substituted for leafs in the rear suspension. Wheelbase on two-doors went to 114 inches, while four-doors went up to 118. Weight also went up. The Cobra slithered away, and only the Gran Torino Sport gave any hint of days gone by. A fastback style was continued, but it hardly made stock-car racers jump for joy. You could still get the 429, but the only resemblance between this engine and those of the past was the displacement. It put out 205 bhp net, and got along nicely on regular gas. The fastback lasted through 1973, and the Torino label made it through '76. A couple of Torinos raced in NASCAR during this period, but the win record wasn't impressive: four for '75 and just one the following year.

Ford Falcon

The compact Falcon made only a few brief entries in Ford's performance journal. Premiering in the fall of 1959, it started out as a thoroughly conventional economy model with a small-displacement, inline six-cylinder engine.

Falcon was out only a few weeks when results of some performance work on its little 144-cube six came

Torino Talladega (upper left) did well on the high-speed tracks. Richard Petty (above) switched to Ford for '69 season. Left: 1971 Torino GT. Upper right: 1972 Gran Torino Sport.

Falcon

Year & Model		Engine (cid/bhp)	Curb Wt.[1]	lbs/ bhp[1]	0-60[2] (sec)	¼-mi.[2] (sec)	Base Price[3]
1964	Falcon Sprint 2d conv	260/164	3008	18.3	10.9	19.0	$2671

[1]Advertised; [2]Typical acceleration based on contemporary tests; [3]Advertised list price in contemporary dollars; n = Net advertised horsepower; cid = cubic inch displacement; bhp = brake horsepower; conv = convertible; cpe = coupe; fastbk = fastback; htp = hardtop; rdstr = roadster (2-seat); sdn = sedan; d = number of doors.

to light. An option kit was announced consisting of three single-barrel Holley carbs, special exhaust manifold, and high-compression head. This pushed output from the stock 90 to 128 bhp. In one early compact-car competition, kit-equipped Falcons went up against the more powerful Valiant Hyper-Paks, and got creamed.

Its next encounter with performance came during the 1963 model year. First a neat convertible was added to the lineup, then a slantback two-door hardtop. Both these new styles were offered in standard form or as the new Sprint powered by Ford's 260 cubic-inch, 164-horse V8, a little dynamo that had seen service in the Fairlane for about a year. For the Sprint, it received a "power-toned" air cleaner and muffler, but no more power.

To create a more prominent performance image for the Falcon, Ford entered a brace of Sprints in the 1963 Monte Carlo Rally. They finished one and two in their class, but 35th overall, as a Swedish Saab won outright. A few highly modified Falcon sedans were also entered in sports-car events, but these bore almost no relation to the production offerings.

Falcon was treated to the 289-cid derivative of the 260 as a 1965 option, but only the easy-going 200-bhp version. The Sprint was offered through the end of the model year.

From 1966 through the end of its life as a compact, Falcon was based on a shortened version of the 1966 Fairlane platform. Only two- and four-door sedans and four-door wagons were offered, all on a 110.9-inch wheelbase. For 1967 a four-barrel 289 with 225 bhp was added. Falcon continued through the end of 1969. A mid-year 1970 model also used the Falcon name, but this was a stripped-down version of the Torino, and lasted only half a year. Ironically, this final Falcon was the most powerful of them all, as you could theoretically get a 429 V8 with 370 bhp. It's doubtful, however, that many, if any, of these cars were produced.

Ford Mustang

If it hadn't been for the Corvair Monza, there might not have been a Mustang. Introduced in the spring of 1960, Monza was mainly a Corvair coupe with bucket-type seats and tastefully reserved trim. But its sporty appeal made it a hot seller in Chevy's line of rear-engine compacts, which hadn't been moving too well up to then.

Statisticians had pointed out that the postwar "baby boom" generation would be reaching car-buying age in the mid-'60s. Auto men concluded that the reaction to the Monza was an early sign of things to come. Soon, there was a raft of sporty, bucket-seat compacts. One of these came from Ford, the 1961 Falcon Futura. Ford staffers had wanted to do a small sporty car ever since the demise of the two-place Thunderbird. The Monza's success gave impetus to the idea. So did Ford Division's new general manager, the dynamic Lee Iacocca, who took the post in November of 1960 at the age of 36. One of his dreams was a low-cost personal car that would be fun to drive and could be equipped in any number of ways to suit any taste. Accordingly, Iacocca personally spearheaded work on what would become Ford's biggest success of the decade.

The result splashed on the scene April 17, 1964. Called Mustang, it was based on Falcon components, but had a fresh, eager, and youthful appearance. It was offered in two-door hardtop and convertible styles, both with appealing proportions featuring a long hood and a short rear deck. Falcon mechanicals and high production volume allowed Ford to keep prices quite low. The advertised base at announcement time was $2368. As we know now, the Mustang proved to be one of the most astutely targeted products in automotive history.

The 1964–65 Mustang utilized unit construction, sat on a 108-inch wheelbase, and measured 181.6 inches long and 68.2 inches wide. A 170 cubic-inch six, right out of the Falcon, was standard. For more go there was a 164-horse 260 V8 and a 210-bhp 289. The fastest models had

Left: Falcon got Ford's potent 260 V8 as a mid-year 1963 option, along with pretty slantback hardtop. Putting the two together resulted in the Falcon Sprint (shown). Above: 1964 Futura coupe shows that year's new boxier contours.

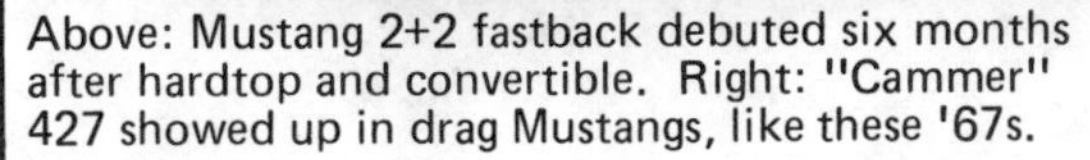
Above: Mustang 2+2 fastback debuted six months after hardtop and convertible. Right: "Cammer" 427 showed up in drag Mustangs, like these '67s.

the 271-bhp "Hi-Performance" 289.

Since Mustang debuted as an early '65 introduction, the main change for the "real" 1965 model year was addition of the 2+2 semi-fastback coupe.

Ford wasn't doing as well in drag racing as it would have liked, so it shoehorned its overhead-cam 427 into a few 2+2s. The company also sponsored teams to run them in the factory-experimental class. Les Ritchey topped A/FX competitors at the NHRA Nationals on Labor Day in one such car.

The competition was scrambling hard to get their own Mustang-type models on the market, so Ford made only minimal body and engine changes for 1966. A new racing series for compact sedans got under way that year, the SCCA Trans-American Sedan Championship, more commonly referred to as the Trans-Am. Run on road courses, it pitted both American and foreign models in a toe-to-toe slugging match. During the first season there were a half-dozen races, and four went to Mustangs. So did the championship, needless to say.

Mustang finally got some competition in the marketplace for the 1967 model year. Chevrolet launched its Camaro, Mercury its Cougar, and Pontiac had its Firebird at mid-year. The Plymouth Barracuda, which first appeared shortly after the Mustang premiered, got a new bodyshell and a wider model lineup. To meet the challenge, Ford gave the Mustang new sheetmetal below the beltline for a bit more bulk. Wheelbase stayed the same, but overall length went up two inches, width by 2.7, and most importantly, front tread was wider by 2.6 inches. This allowed for the installation of a big-block engine for the first time. The weight penalty for all this was about 130 pounds. In addition to three flavors of 289, buyers could now choose from a pair of 390s, one at 320 bhp, the other at 335. The 2+2 became a true fastback and all models got a somewhat rounder interpretation of the basic 1965–66 styling.

The new competition also turned up in the 1967 Trans-Am series. Roger Penske fielded some hot, but trouble-prone, Camaro Z-28s, and Mercury put in the Bud Moore-prepared Cougars. At the end, though, Jerry Titus had taken the Shelby-prepared Mustangs to four wins, and Ford repeated as the manufacturers' champion.

The biggest change on the mostly unchanged '68 Mustangs was a wider selection of powerplants. There was an additional extra-cost 390 V8 with 325 bhp, and the mighty 427 became a production option for the first time. It was now at 390 bhp, compared to 425 in previous years when it was sold in other Ford lines. At mid-year, the 427 was hastily retired and replaced by the new 428 Cobra Jet, deliberately rated at a very low 335 bhp. A quarter-mile zip of 13.56 seconds at a trap speed of 106.64 seconds caused *Hot Rod* magazine to sing the praises of the new big-inch Mustang. Also announced was a high-tech version of the little 302 small-block, with special heads and a pair of four-barrel carbs. Rated at a humorous 240 bhp, it was clearly developed around the Trans-Am formula. After it got an OK from SCCA, Ford had trouble getting it into production, and few were actually made. But it didn't make much difference. Mark Donohue won 10 events with his Camaro, and Chevy collected the manufacturers' trophy. Mustangs only won three events.

There was one 1968 development that would effect the shape of future Mustangs. This was the arrival of Semon E. "Bunkie" Knudsen as Ford Motor Company president.

Mustang grew again in '69. It was 3.8 inches longer, 0.4-inch wider, and about 140 pounds heavier than before. The bodyshell was com-

Ford Mustang Performance

Year & Model		Engine (cid/bhp)	Curb Wt.[1]	lbs/ bhp[1]	0-60[2] (sec)	¼-mi.[2] (sec)	Base Price[3]
1965	2+2 2d cpe	289/271	2840	10.5	7.6	15.9	$2640
1967	2+2 2d cpe	390/335	3255	9.7	7.4	15.6	$2650
1969	Grande 2d htp	351/290	3125	10.8	8.0	15.6	$2866
1969	Mach I 2d htp	428/335	3220	9.6	5.5	13.9	$3139
1969	Boss 302 2d htp	302/290	3260	11.2	6.9	14.9	$3588
1969	Boss 429 2d htp	429/375	3400	9.1	7.1	14.1	$4900
1971	Boss 351 2d htp	351/330	3452	10.5	5.8	13.8	$4101
1971	Mach I 2d htp	429/370	3805	10.3	6.5	14.6	$3474
1973	Mustang 2d htp	351/266n	3475	13.1	8.9	16.3	$2872

[1]Advertised; [2]Typical acceleration based on contemporary tests; [3]Advertised list price in contemporary dollars; n = Net advertised horsepower; cid = cubic inch displacement; bhp = brake horsepower; conv = convertible; cpe = coupe; fastbk = fastback; htp = hardtop; rdstr = roadster (2-seat); sdn = sedan; d = number of doors.

Above: 1969 Mustang Boss 302 in street trim. Below: Parnelli Jones in the Bud Moore '69 Trans-Am car. Upper right: 1969 Boss 429, a rare animal. Lower right: 1970 Boss 302.

pletely new, though the successful appearance themes of the past were retained. The fastback (now called SportsRoof) gained rear-quarter windows of the flip-out variety. There were two new models besides the usual three—the luxury-oriented Grande hardtop, and the Mach I fastback, a car clearly oriented to performance enthusiasts. New to the engine chart was the 351 small-block, a half-inch stroke job on the 302, offering 250 and 290 bhp. The 390 returned with 320 horses. So did the 428 Cobra Jet in regular and Ram-Air form, both producing an advertised 335 bhp. These were joined by two mid-year offerings, the Boss 302 and Boss 429. Each of these last two powered a limited-production model, and each was built mainly for one reason—racing.

After a false start for the racing 302 in 1968, SCCA was out to make sure Ford did it right for '69. The Boss 302, designed for Trans-Am use, had canted valves, a high-rise aluminum intake manifold, and single four-barrel Holley carb. Power was quoted at 290. Also cataloged was a dual four-barrel version, though output wasn't specified.

The Boss 429 was created for NASCAR service. Based on Ford's new big-block unit, it replaced the 427 wedge, which had been around since the 1963 season. It featured semi-hemispherical heads, which Ford called crescent-shaped. It was cleared for competition, provided it went into a production model. But rather than put it into a Torino, which was Ford's main NASCAR contender, Knudsen put it in a series of Mustangs. NASCAR looked the other way, and declared the unit legal. After a slow start, 852 Boss 429 Mustangs were bolted up for the model year.

Among lesser Mustangs, the new Mach I took the performance role, and had a 250-bhp 351 standard. A trio of Mach Is, considerably altered by Mickey Thompson, an old friend of Knudsen, was sent to the Bonneville Salt Flats in September of 1968 to alter the record books. They ended up breaking 295 speed marks. One of the drivers here was drag racer (and later Indy competitor) Danny Ongais. Despite its pretentions, the Boss 302 bowed to Penske, Donohue, and Chevrolet in the Trans-Am, and accounted for but a third of the dozen events on the card.

Model year 1970 didn't see much change in the Mustang's looks or performance. The Boss 429, still with 375 bhp, was withdrawn after 505 were constructed, the last in December 1970. Ram-Air was now available for the 351, with the four-barrel edition now at 300 bhp. The 390 engine became history; the 428 Cobra Jet, with and without Ram Air, was continued. Parnelli Jones took five Trans-Am events and teammate George Follmer took one more to give Ford its third manufacturers' title.

Just after the 1970 models were announced, Knudsen was relieved of his duties as Ford president by chairman Henry Ford II. But the first major evidence of his design philosophy didn't appear until he had departed. Thus, the biggest Mustang of all galloped in for 1971. Installing 429s in the 1969–70 models called for special work, and left the engine just about impossible to work on. In order to accommodate it, and future big-block monsters, the '71 had a wider body that was beefier and predictably heavier. Ironically, the big-blocks would be gone after only a year. The usual three body styles were retained, as were the Mach I and Grande models. The Boss 302 and 429 models were deleted, replaced by the Boss 351. This was a SportsRoof fastback powered by the H.O. (High Output) version of the 351, with "Dual Ram Induction," meaning a hood with twin scoops. In the big-block division, four 429s were offered; the CJ at 370 bhp, the CJ-R (Ram-Air) also at 370, and "Drag Pack" editions of both rated nominally 5 bhp higher. The Drag Pack included mechanical lifters, and high-lift cam.

Upper left: 1973 Mustang, last of the "heavies." Lower left: 1977 Mustang II with Cobra II option. Above: 1979 third-generation Mustang. Below: 1981 McLaren Mustang semi-race special.

In all, Ford offered six different engines requiring premium fuel for the 1971 Mustang. At the same time, all of GM's engines and some from Chrysler and American Motors were retuned to run on regular or no-lead gas that year. Emission standards were starting to choke big-inch engines, and the demand for them. Ford brought out its "performance" engine of the future, the 351 CJ late in the 1971 model year. Its compression ratio was 8.6:1, compared to 11:1 for the 351 H.O., and advertised horsepower dropped to 280.

There was more of the same for '72. All the big-blocks were gone, as was the Boss 351. Two normal versions of the 351 were offered, a two-barrel with 177 bhp net and a four-barrel with 266. Later, the 351 H.O., now running on regular, made a brief return, still with all the good stuff like solid lifters and a respectable 275 bhp net. It then disappeared.

Compared to their immediate predecessors, the 1971–73 models were two inches longer and three inches wider. Against the first-generation Mustangs, they were over nine inches longer, nearly six inches wider, and over 500 pounds heavier. Sales, on the other hand, went the other way—from nearly 700,000 for 1964–65 to a low of 119,920 for the 1972 model year. They picked up slightly to 123,402 for 1973, but clearly, interest in ponycars of old was declining.

Ford tried to recapture the spirit of the original Mustang with the downsized 1974 Mustang II. Overall length went from 190 to 175 inches, wheelbase from 109 to 96, and width from 74.1 to 70.2. Weight dipped from over 3000 pounds to around 2700. In its first year, the II offered only four and V6 power, but the 302 V8 returned the following year. As for true high-performance, it would never return.

Ford Thunderbird

Originally conceived as an American reply to foreign sports cars, Ford's two-seat Thunderbird emerged as something quite different—a "personal" car.

Unlike its obvious home-grown rival, Chevrolet's Corvette, the Thunderbird had a body made of steel, not fiberglass, and was offered from the start only with V8 engines instead of a six. It could also be ordered with manual transmission as well as automatic. Base engine for the inaugural 1955 model was a 193-horse 292, teamed with the standard three-speed stickshift. Overdrive or automatic purchasers got five more horses, thanks to a boost in compression ratio from 8.0 to 8.5:1.

Minor cosmetic changes and substantial engine alterations came along for 1956. A 202-bhp 292 went with the three-speed, while overdrive buyers got a 215-bhp version of a new 312 V8. Automatics got this too, but with 225 bhp. As before, four-barrel carburetion was standard. There was a mid-year performance option for non-automatic cars which boasted 260 bhp.

Small fins, resembling those on the standard Ford, plus new grille work marked the last of the two-place 'Birds. The standard 292 now packed 212 bhp, and with overdrive or automatic you got a 245-horse 312, again with a single four-barrel. A second four-throater was optional, and yielded 270 bhp. Part way into the model year, two more tweaks were added. One was a second twin four-barrel carb bumping output to 285 bhp. The other was a supercharger, with which the 312 cranked out an even 300 horses.

The early Birds weren't really considered sports cars or stock passenger models, so they weren't raced much. However, a '55 ran at Speed Weeks at Daytona Beach, and topped both the standing-start and flying mile for American sports cars. Admittedly, there wasn't a lot

Speedy two-seat T-Birds lasted only three years, 1955-57 (shown left from top). Top right: 1958 T-Bird. Above: The 1960 edition. Below: 1963 Sports Roadster featured rear seat tonneau cover.

of competition. Ferraris were the overall sports-car winners by a considerable margin. The next year Chuck Daigh set an acceleration mark in a topless T-Bird, but the Corvette of John Fitch took the flying mile. The following season, Danny Eames took his modified '57 to an acceleration mark of 97.933 mph, and made the flying-mile run at 160.356 mph. Even so, Corvettes took the stock wins.

Thunderbirds were also entered in selected sports-car races in the early years, including a few with Ford's backing. But Chevrolet was turning its Corvette into a formidable competitor, too much for the T-Bird to handle. Besides, Ford's personal car didn't really need that sort of press. Production was 16,155 for the 1955 models, 15,631 for the 1956s and 21,380 for the extended 1957 model run. This far outclassed Corvette, but was not what Ford had hoped for. Nevertheless, the two-place T-Birds were among the first postwar domestic cars to be discovered by collectors.

The reason for the two-seater's "instant classic" status was the appearance of a new four-passenger model for 1958. Designed to appeal to a much wider group of buyers, this new Bird offered a claimed 300 bhp from its big-block 352-cid engine.

There was one final attempt at racing, however, one not as widely publicized as the 1955–57 efforts. Some stock-car pilots wanted to enter the '58 T-Bird in NASCAR events because it was smaller and lighter than the standard Ford, sitting on a 5-inch shorter wheelbase. NASCAR said wait until next year. It just so happened that the 1959 models offered the 430-cid Lincoln engine, rated at 350 bhp, as an option. The standard Ford engine had a best of 300. A three-speed manual transmission was also made available at mid-year. Holman & Moody,

Ford Thunderbird Performance

Year	& Model	Engine (cid/bhp)	Curb Wt.[1]	lbs/ bhp[1]	0-60[2] (sec)	¼-mi.[2] (sec)	Base Price[3]
1955	2d rdstr	292/198	2890	14.6	10.8	17.9	$2944
1956	2d rdstr	312/225	3038	13.5	9.1	17.5	$3151
1958	2d htp	352/300	3870	12.9	10.1	17.6	$3631
1959	2d htp	430/350	3813	11.6	9.0	17.0	$3696
1962	Sports Roadster 2d conv	390/300	4690	15.6	12.4	18.7	$5439

[1]Advertised; [2]Typical acceleration based on contemporary tests; [3]Advertised list price in contemporary dollars; n = Net advertised horsepower; cid = cubic inch displacement; bhp = brake horsepower; conv = convertible; cpe = coupe; fastbk = fastback; htp = hardtop; rdstr = roadster (2-seat); sdn = sedan; d = number of doors.

Ford's race-car builder and parts distributor before the factory left racing in 1957, prepped a few '59 Thunderbirds for NASCAR's Grand National circuit, and they actually won six events. These cars were campaigned again in 1960, but by then Ford had more power and the sleek Starliner hardtop that proved faster.

The 430 returned to Thunderbird's option list for 1960. For the all-new '61 models, Ford's 390 was the only engine available, and continued as such for quite a while. A triple two-barrel 390, rated at 340 bhp, was offered for 1962–63. A unique model in this third generation was the 1963 Sports Roadster, with wire wheels and a fiberglass tonneau cover that fit over the rear compartment to create a two-place seating arrangement.

Thunderbird went on through a variety of body style and size changes. With the possible exception of the Sports Roadster, no T-Bird after 1957 has any real muscle-car connotations.

Lincoln

William Crapo Durant was looking around for a luxury make as the crown jewel for his budding General Motors empire in 1917. After a long series of negotiations, he bought Cadillac from its founder, Henry M. Leland. Leland had earned the title "Master of Precision" because of his pioneering efforts in the use of interchangeable parts. Although he was no longer young at the time he sold Cadillac, Leland decided to build a rival to it.

His new firm, the Lincoln Motor Car Company, made some beautiful and lavishly furnished automobiles. But despite their obvious breeding and quality, they were not successful in the marketplace. After being forced into receivership in 1921, Lincoln was purchased by the Ford Motor Company a year later. Like Durant, Henry Ford needed a prestige car to sit at the pinnacle of his firm's product line. Unfortunately, Ford left the Lincoln Model L, Leland's last design, to stagnate for a good eight years before replacing it with something more modern. The replacement arrived for 1931, the Model K. The next year, a huge 448 cubic-inch V12 powerplant was introduced.

From then until World War II, Lincoln continued with 12-cylinder engines exclusively. It also pioneered streamlined styling and unitized body construction with its smaller, cheaper Zephyr series of the late '30s.

Lincoln returned with V12s in the immediate postwar years, then adopted V8 power for 1949. This was a 336.7-cid L-head unit producing 152 horsepower. Also that year Lincoln split into two series. The base line shared its basic bodyshell with the lower-priced Mercury, and rode a 121-inch wheelbase. The more expensive Cosmopolitan used the same 125-inch wheelbase as in the past, and had its own separate body.

An all-new Lincoln greeted the 1952 model year. Wheelbase split the difference between the two previous lengths at 123 inches. Notable under the hood was Lincoln's first high-compression overhead-valve V8. Though displacement was down to 317.5 cubic inches, output (with two-throat carb) was up to 160 bhp, six more than the '51 flathead engine. The front suspension was redesigned with ball joints instead of kingpins, a first for a mass-production U.S. car.

Among cars at the top end of the market, Lincoln had the smallest engine and the shortest wheelbase for '52. To make matters worse, it looked somewhat like its lower-priced Ford and Mercury cousins, which were also new that year. This was especially noticeable in sedans. Although there was some sharing of inner panels, Lincoln rode Ford Motor Company's longest chassis. Lincoln's engine had only a two-barrel carburetor and modest output, so it didn't look too good against Oldsmobile, Buick, and Cadillac with their four-barrel engines, or against Chrysler's hemi-head V8. A few changes and a successful racing program would help turn things around.

For starters, the 1953 models got a Holley four-barrel carb. Compression ratio was boosted from 7.5 to 8.0:1, and valves were enlarged. These, plus a few other minor tweaks, boosted output to 205 bhp, still five less than Cadillac, but well ahead of Chrysler's 180.

While other makes gained publicity in stock-car racing, Lincoln chose the Carrera Panamericana or Mexican Road Race, first run in 1950. Contestants assembled near the Mexico-Guatemala border, and dashed northward to the U.S. border at Ciudad Juarez. Now the 1952 Lincoln may have been down on power, but its ball-joint suspension endowed it with fine handling. With its twisty, rough roads, the Mexican race was made to order for the Lincoln's capabilities.

While Lincoln would have to run against both sedans and sports cars piloted by drivers from several countries, the race was also a test of stamina, not just pure speed. Because of all the publicity generated by the event, Lincoln entered the '52 race. But its team drove 1953 models, shown well ahead of their public introduction. Bill Stroppe and ace mechanic Clay Smith prepared three cars, and Indy veterans Chuck Stevenson, Johnny Mantz and Walt Faulkner were hired to do the driving. With preparation that would have put some stock-car teams to shame, Lincoln finished one-two-three that year. To cap the triumph, stock-car driver Bob Korf, aboard an independent Lincoln entered by outboard motor industrialist Carl Kiekhaefer, finished fourth. Thus, Lincoln swept the stock-car class in its first outing.

Tom McCahill of *Mechanix Illustrated* magazine panned the 1952 Lincoln for lack of power, but glowed after testing the '53: "The Lincoln is far ahead of any immediate American competitor in roadability and cornering . . . I can honestly state the 1953 Lincoln is

Lincoln Performance

Year & Model		Engine (cid/bhp)	Curb Wt.[1]	lbs/ bhp[1]	0-60[2] (sec)	¼-mi.[2] (sec)	Base Price[3]
1952	Capri 4d sdn	317/160	4140	25.9	16.7	21.6	$3331
1953	Capri 4d sdn	317/205	4150	20.2	11.0	18.5	$3453
1954	Capri 4d sdn	317/205	4245	20.7	12.3	18.4	$3711
1955	Capri 4d sdn	341/225	4470	19.9	12.4	18.5	$3752

[1]Advertised; [2]Typical acceleration based on contemporary tests; [3]Advertised list price in contemporary dollars; n = Net advertised horsepower; cid = cubic inch displacement; bhp = brake horsepower; conv = convertible; cpe = coupe; fastbk = fastback; htp = hardtop; rdstr = roadster (2-seat); sdn = sedan; d = number of doors.

Lincoln adopted new overhead-valve V8 for its 1952 models (Capri convertible shown at left). 1955 models (like Capri hardtop above) were readied for Mexican Road Race but didn't get a chance to compete.

America's finest automobile." He backed it up by buying one.

For the 1953 Carrera, Lincoln entered the same cars. Again the result was the same, a one-through-four sweep, with Stevenson in the lead.

Nothing drastic happened to Lincoln for '54, and didn't need to. Cadillac was all-new that year, Chrysler's V8 picked up a four-barrel carb and top rating of 235 bhp, and even Packard's straight eight was boasting more horsepower. But Lincoln had Mexico to talk about. For that year's race, new 1954 cars were prepared, all two-door hardtops as before. There were now five classes in the event, two for sports cars and three for stocks. The sports cars were again faster, but Lincoln was again victorious in the stock class. However, this time it only finished one-two. Ray Crawford, supposedly an independent, came in first beating Faulkner by a little less than two minutes. Cadillacs nailed down the third and fourth positions.

Lincoln was about the only car in the industry not to adopt the faddish wraparound windshield for 1955. What it did get was extended rear fenders, a larger engine, and a new transmission. A bore increase yielded 341 cid, and a tighter 8.5:1 compression ratio helped horsepower up to 225. The General Motors Hydra-matic four-speed automatic used through 1954 was finally replaced by a three-speed Borg-Warner unit dubbed Turbo-Drive. Race watchers had their doubts about how well this new tranny would do in Mexico. There were further questions when Chrysler introduced its 300, with that much horsepower. Unfortunately, the 1955 Lincoln never got a chance to prove itself in battle. The Mexican government cancelled the Carrera Panamericana for safety reasons before the scheduled '55 race could be run.

For 1956, Lincoln took on larger-than-life proportions, and scored more sales than it had in '55. For obvious reasons, racing, speed runs, and the like were left to other Ford Motor Company cars. To date, none of the later Lincolns has had any sporting or performance overtones.

Mercury

Mercury was a car bred for performance. Debuting for 1939, it was sent out to get a slice of the lower medium-priced market that Ford Motor Company had been missing. The first Merc was very similar to the contemporary Ford (as it would be in most years thereafter) but had a longer wheelbase, about 250 pounds of additional weight, and most important, a bigger flathead V8. With 239 cubic inches it produced 95 horsepower compared to Ford's 221 cubes and 85 bhp.

All-new postwar styling bowed for 1949, as did a new chassis with coil springs up front and longitudinal leaf springs in the rear. Also new was an enlarged V8, still a flathead and again bigger than Ford's. Displacing 255.4 cubes, available power was now 110 bhp. Despite these increases Mercury was overshadowed by Oldsmobile, which bowed the first modern high-compression overhead-valve V8 in 1949, and had 135 bhp.

Mercury's '49 styling continued through the 1951 model year when horsepower hit 112. The bodyshell in these years was shared with the junior Lincoln, and became very popular with customizers who could turn it into a very mean-looking machine. Yet, Mercury engines could provide little more than average performance. Mercury did score two NASCAR wins in both 1950 and '51, but it was no match for Oldsmobile and later Hudson.

A new overhead-valve V8 was supposed to go into the all-new 1952 models, but material shortages and production cutbacks caused by the Korean conflict put that off until 1954. Instead, a compression boost on the flathead from 6.8 to 7.2:1 brought 125 bhp for 1952–53. When the new V8 did arrive, it proved nothing to be excited about. Displacement stayed about the same, 256 cubes, but power did go

Mercury Performance

Year & Model		Engine (cid/bhp)	Curb Wt.[1]	lbs/ bhp[1]	0-60[2] (sec)	¼-mi.[2] (sec)	Base Price[3]
1955	Montclair 2d htp	292/198	3480	17.6	11.7	19.5	$2631
1956	Montclair 2d htp	312/225	3620	16.0	10.4	18.0	$2765
1957	Montclair 4d htp	368/290	3925	13.5	9.8	17.2	$3317
1962	Monterey S-55 2d conv	406/405	4208	10.4	7.7	16.5	$3738
1966	S-55 2d htp	428/345	4260	12.3	8.9	16.9	$3292
1969	Marauder X-100 2d htp	429/360	4290	11.9	7.5	15.8	$4091

[1]Advertised; [2]Typical acceleration based on contemporary tests; [3]Advertised list price in contemporary dollars; n = Net advertised horsepower; cid = cubic inch displacement; bhp = brake horsepower; conv = convertible; cpe = coupe; fastbk = fastback; htp = hardtop; rdstr = roadster (2-seat); sdn = sedan; d = number of doors.

Mercury was introduced for 1939 (cabriolet shown above), had V8 power from the start.

All-new '49s (above) had enlarged flathead engine. 1949-51 Mercs became very popular with customizers in the '50s.

up to 161. The V8 shared engineering notice with the ball-joint front suspension new to Mercury that year.

The 1955 models gave some sign that Mercury was ready to recapture its early performance image. Engine displacement now stood at 292 cubes. Custom and Monterey models had 188 bhp from 7.6:1 compression, while the new top-line Montclair was given 10 extra horses by an 8.5:1 squeeze. All had four-barrel carburetors. Bodies wore a combination of old and new styling themes. Grilles carried on the '54 look, but rooflines were different, as was the new wraparound windshield.

Lincoln-Mercury Division had been a winner in the heavy-stock class in the Mexican Road Race (see Lincoln). However, Dodge V8s were cleaning up in the light-stock class. With a decent suspension and adequate power, Mercury wanted to do something about that. Builder Bill Stroppe was recruited to prepare a few '55 cars for the event. When the Mexican government cancelled the series, division boss Benson Ford said race the things somewhere, so Stroppe put together a team and entered American Automobile Association (AAA) stock-car events. AAA was chosen over NASCAR because the drivers, who had piloted the Lincolns in Mexico, had run already in the AAA-sanctioned Indy 500. Mercury managed one win in a 250-miler at Milwaukee, but Chrysler 300s took 10 out of the 13 races.

Displacement rose to 312 cubes for 1956. Initially 225 bhp was to be tops, but as you could get that in a lighter, smaller Ford, the "Big M" needed something more. This turned up as a mid-year option consisting of a pair of four-barrel carbs and a kick in compression which rendered 260 bhp. Appropriately named M-260, it was heralded by small chrome plates on the front fenders, and was available for all models, much like Dodge's D-500 setup, which was also advertised at 260 and was a full-line option. Bill Stroppe was again retained to prep Mercury stockers for '56, which were to compete in both NASCAR and United States Auto Club (USAC) circuits. (USAC replaced AAA in 1956.)

The fireworks started at the Daytona Beach Speed Weeks. Stroppe brought three Monterey two-door hardtops to do battle in the

Modern ohv V8 was slated for Mercury's rebodied '52 line (upper left) but was delayed until 1954 (lower left). Above right: Bill Stroppe's JT-450X factory experimental. Above: Wild-looking 1957 "Mermaid" racer ran at Daytona.

flying mile and the oval-track race. Stroppe arrived amidst the publicity surrounding DeSoto's 138-mph flying-mile run in the factory-experimental class. He set out to beat it. He went to a local dealer, bought a new Custom two-door hardtop, and outfitted it with a roll bar, Indy-type magnesium wheels, and special Firestone tires. For power he bored out a Lincoln engine to 391 cubes and added fuel injection. With a couple of internal tricks, he had his own factory experimental, the JT-450X. He even gave it large lettering just to be sure it attracted attention. Despite troubles on the second run, Stroppe's car averaged 147.26 mph, and topped the class. The JT-450X toured the show circuit the rest of the year, and made demonstration runs at tracks where the factory Mercurys raced. In the 160-miler, Billy Myers finished second to winner Tim Flock in a Chrysler 300B. But only five NASCAR wins went to Mercs that season.

"Dream-Car Design" was the theme for the all-new 1957 Mercury. It was longer, lower, and wider in the custom of the times. Wheelbase went from 120 to 122 inches, which threatened to hurt the new model's racing prospects. Offsetting the extra bulk, Lincoln's 290-bhp, 368-cube V8 became the top power option for all models. But the hot number was the late-intro M-335, again featuring dual four-barrel carbs. Advertised horses predictably numbered 335.

Stroppe put together a fairly potent team for '57. The "Mermaid" special won the Daytona 160-mile convertible race with Tim Flock behind the wheel. But NASCAR banned dual carburetion in April, and the manufacturers pulled out of backing teams with the AMA ban in June. These developments left little reason for independents to choose the big Mercurys when they could run lighter Fords and Chevrolets, so the make nearly dropped from sight in the racing world.

Mercury's big splash for 1958 was announcement of a 400-bhp version of the 430-cid Lincoln engine. This "Super Marauder" power unit was to have had three two-barrel carbs and be optional for all models. But though a few cars were put together for test and press purposes, the hardware never reached the production line.

With its 1961 models, Mercury again shared the Ford bodyshell, something it hadn't done since '56. The new low-priced Meteor 600 offered the first six-cylinder engine ever in a big Merc. But being tied to Ford wasn't all bad. In mid-1962, Ford introduced a hot new 406-cid engine, so Mercury got it, too. There was also a new S-55 hardtop and convertible with bucket seats that made a gesture toward sportiness.

There were two versions of the new 406: a single four-barrel unit with 385 bhp and a triple two-barrel variation with 405. Buyers opting for either one got a four-speed manual transmission and a special chassis (shortened slightly in wheelbase from 120 to 119 inches) beefed up with heavy-duty suspension pieces. There was no factory racing program for 1962, but once Ford officially declared it would ignore the AMA ban in June, plans were made for such an effort for '63.

Mercury's debut 1963 models continued the 406 options, but their new "Breezeway" roof styling with reverse-slant rear window was hardly suited for high-speed race work. So, Mercury joined Ford in introducing a new slantback two-door hardtop at mid-year. Carrying the Marauder name at Mercury, it was offered in both the Monterey Custom and S-55 series. The Marauder tag was also applied to several renditions of a new 427 V8. The regular one had a single four-barrel carb and 410 bhp, while the "Super Marauder" had twice the carburetion and a nominal rating of 425 bhp. Marauders didn't exactly maul 'em in NASCAR, winning only the last race of the season. The USAC record was better. Parnelli Jones drove a Bill Stroppe car up Pike's Peak faster than the other guys and won the annual hillclimb, so Mercury picked up the phrase "Pike's Peak Champion" for its ad copy.

The slightly changed '64 models retained the Marauder and Super Marauder 427s. Slantback four-door hardtops were added, also called Marauders, making a total of five different models with that handle. Mercury scored five NASCAR wins that season, but none were major. USAC was again more profitable, with Jones winning eight of the 15 scheduled events to take the championship. One of them was a repeat at Pike's Peak.

The 1964 Mercurys with special 119-inch wheelbase, rear leaf springs, and big engines had just qualified for stock-car racing, but there was no way the all-new '65s could be competitive. Wheelbase (except for wagons) hopped up to 123 inches, coils took over for leafs on the rear suspension, and overall size increased greatly. The slantback roof design was retained, but the cars were now too big to race, and Mercury cancelled its stock-car program. The herd of Marauder engine designations was dropped, but the 427 was still available.

A mild 428 replaced the 427 for 1966. All of Mercury's performance promotion now centered on the intermediate Comet.

Mercury made another attempt at a full-size performance car for 1969–70. The Marauder name was revived for a pair of tunnelback hardtops on a 121-inch wheelbase, three inches shorter than that of other models. The pricer of the pair, called Marauder X-100, came with special trim and a 360-bhp 429 as standard. Marauder production was 14,666 for '69, of which 5635 were X-100s. The figures dropped for 1970 to 6043 and 2646, respectively, thus ending the big Mercury's performance career.

Mercury Comet

The first incarnation for the Mercury Comet was 1960–65. In this period it was a line of compacts. Later, the name was attached to what became the intermediate Montego series, and in the '70s to a badge-engineered version of the compact Ford Maverick. Here we consider only the first-generation Comet. And only a few of these can be considered performance cars, even if we stretch the definition of that term slightly.

Speaking of stretching, the 1960 Comet just barely qualified as a compact. Its 114-inch wheelbase (wagons were 109.5) put it in intermediate territory, except there was no such thing at the time.

At the start of the 1963 model run, a convertible body style debuted. Comet's first V8 was the 260-cube, 164-horse unit which made the roster at mid-season. This was accompanied by a pretty little two-door hardtop style, the Sportster, which had a twin in the Falcon line.

Meanwhile, the mid-size Meteor went nowhere in 1962–63, so Mer-

First of the sporty Comet compacts was the S-22 of 1961. Shown above is the '63 edition. Convertible was a new style that year.

Hot Cyclone debuted at mid-year on rebodied 1964 line. Shown above is the '65 model. Note simulated chrome-reverse wheel covers.

cury decided to upgrade Comet to fill the gap. A reskinned line arrived for 1964, and the new top-of-the-line series bore the name Caliente. These were the first of the compact Comets to have any connection with performance.

To get the Comet name up in lights, Mercury staged a 100,000-mile durability test at Daytona International Speedway. The test cars averaged over 100 mph for the entire run without major problems. After that, Comet was proclaimed the "World's 100,000 Mile Durability Champion." Later that year Comet's first sporty car, the Cyclone, blew in. It had all the usual cosmetic touches, including bucket seats, console, and a set of wheel covers that simulated chromed exposed wheels, like the hot rodders use. More important, it had Ford's little dynamo, the 289-cube V8 with 210 bhp via a four-barrel carb. Later the potent 271-bhp "hi-performance" version of this engine became an option.

Mercury wanted to reach the drag race set, so it ordered up a number of Comets, similar to the Ford Thunderbolts, stuffed full of 427. Not enough of these were made to qualify for the Super/Stock class, so the cars ran as factory experimentals. At the NHRA Winternationals at Pomona, Bill Shrewsberry took A/FX, and Ronnie Sox was crowned Mr. Factory Stock Eliminator, both in Comet 427s.

The 1965 Comet was basically the same as the year before. The 271-horse 289 returned as the hottest street setup. "Dyno" Don Nicholson, who ran Comets on the strips in 1964, did so again this year, as did "Fast Eddie" Schartman. Mercury didn't take the '65s on another 100,000-mile jaunt, but it did send three on a 16,247-mile trip from Alaska to Argentina. All this was merely groundwork. It was now time for the performance baton to pass to the intermediates.

Mercury Cougar

Mercury aimed its sporty Cougar at the luxury end of the ponycar market, and paid the price when it came to performance. Ford's Mustang had been an instant hit, yet Cougar didn't appear until the 1967 model year, nearly 2½ years behind its cousin. The debut edition was based on the reworked structure of that year's Mustang hardtop, but had different exterior sheetmetal, a 3.2-inch longer wheelbase, and 6.7-inch greater overall length. With similar equipment, the Cougar was over 200 pounds heavier than a Mustang. Ford and Mercury used the same engines, of course, so the Cougar moved somwhat more slowly. However, that didn't stop Mercury from bringing out speedier versions.

Unlike Mustang, Cougar was offered with V8 engines only right from the first. A two-barrel 289 rated at 200 horsepower was standard. A 225-horse four-barrel version was optional, as was a 390 V8 with 320 bhp, which was part of the extra-cost GT package. Later the plush XR-7 was added, outfitted more for sporty luxury than performance.

Ford had been the winner of the first SCCA Trans-Am series, so it was decided to send the Cougar onto the road courses as well. An impressive team was assembled, with Parnelli Jones, Dan Gurney, Ed Leslie and Peter Revson piloting cars built and prepared by ace tuner Bud Moore. Coinciding with this development was the announcement of a "Group Two" package. This put a pair of four-barrel carbs atop a solid-lifter 289, and supposedly yielded 341 bhp. Mercury also tossed in a heavy-duty suspension and quick-ratio steering. Despite the power on paper, the 289 Cougars were down on inches compared to the 302 Camaros, and up on weight compared to the Mustangs. The team did not do well, and Mercury abandoned the Trans-Am after only one season. In the future, drag racing would be the Cougar's playground.

The 1968 engine lineup became more complicated than a soap opera plot. Starting from the top, there was a new GTE option that brought the street 427 with 390 bhp and standard automatic transmission. The 390 V8, rated at 335 bhp, came standard with the GT option.

Mercury Comet Performance

Year & Model		Engine (cid/bhp)	Curb Wt.[1]	lbs/ bhp[1]	0-60[2] (sec)	¼-mi.[2] (sec)	Base Price[3]
1963	S-22 2d htp	260/164	2985	18.2	14.5	19.3	$2400
1964	Cyclone 2d htp	289/210	3160	15.0	9.7	16.2	$2655
1964	AFX 2d htp	427/425	3085	7.3	4.2	12.0	NA
1965	Cyclone 2d htp	289/225	3060	13.6	8.8	17.1	$2683

[1]Advertised; [2]Typical acceleration based on contemporary tests; [3]Advertised list price in contemporary dollars; n = Net advertised horsepower; cid = cubic inch displacement; bhp = brake horsepower; conv = convertible; cpe = coupe; fastbk = fastback; htp = hardtop; rdstr = roadster (2-seat); sdn = sedan; d = number of doors.

Mercury Cougar Performance

Year & Model		Engine (cid/bhp)	Curb Wt.[1]	lbs/ bhp[1]	0-60[2] (sec)	¼-mi.[2] (sec)	Base Price[3]
1967	Cougar Group II 2d htp	289/341	3174	9.3	7.0	15.1	NA
1967	Cougar 2d htp	390/320	3562	11.1	8.1	16.0	$2851
1968	Cougar GTE 2d htp	427/390	3662	9.4	6.2	15.1	$3232
1970	Cougar Eliminator 2d htp	302/290	3610	12.4	7.6	15.8	$3404

[1]Advertised; [2]Typical acceleration based on contemporary tests; [3]Advertised list price in contemporary dollars; n = Net advertised horsepower; cid = cubic inch displacement; bhp = brake horsepower; conv = convertible; cpe = coupe; fastbk = fastback; htp = hardtop; rdstr = roadster (2-seat); sdn = sedan; d = number of doors.

Initially, the 210-bhp 302 replaced the 289 as standard power, but the 289 returned at mid-year. Of more interest to muscle fans were two 1968½ powerplants. One was the CJ 428, with the same conservative 335-bhp rating it had at Ford Division. The other was the 302 Trans-Am setup, with a pair of four-barrels. Interestingly, it was rated at just 240 bhp, 101 less than the similar Group Two 289 the year before. Ford and Mercury were clearly playing games. Availability of the Trans-Am unit was extremely limited, and it's doubtful it was truly a production option.

Still looking for Cougar's niche in the racing world, Mercury signed "Dyno" Don Nicholson and "Fast Eddie" Schartman to campaign Cougar "funny cars" at the drags. A funny car was ideal, as only a fiberglass body faintly resembling the stock issue had to be used. The fact that the real-life Cougar had a weight disadvantage made no difference here. Another area where Cougar excelled was in NASCAR's newly created Grand Touring series for sporty compacts, run mainly on oval tracks. Tiny Lund won the title in '68 piloting one of the ex-Trans-Am Bud Moore cars.

Convertibles in base and XR-7 trim joined hardtops as Cougar was somewhat restyled and enlarged for 1969. Again, the model and engine lineup at the end of the model year turned out to be different than at the start. A new 351 cubic-inch small-block V8 took over at the bottom. With a two-barrel carb it put out a claimed 250 bhp, and a quad carb meant 40 more. The 390 was still around, at 320 bhp. Topping the list was the 428 CJ in regular and Ram-Air versions, both curiously listed at 335, though the latter no doubt had more. After a false start in 1968, a performance 302 called the Boss officially bowed at mid-year. It was offered for a new model, the Eliminator hardtop, which featured front and rear spoilers, special tape striping, and a standard 290-horse 351. Two Boss 302s were optional for it. For the street you got a single four-barrel carb and rating of 290 bhp. The racing version doubled the carbs, but power was not advertised. Enthusiast magazines that tested the 302 Cougars noted the small engine was really working to move this over-3500-pound ponycar. Late in the model year, the huge 370-bhp NASCAR 429 semi-hemi may have been installed in a few Cougars, though it's unclear if it actually was.

The 1970 model year was the last for the Cougar's original body and chassis. The Eliminator reverted to option status, and the racing engine was removed from the books. The 390 also departed, but a street 429, rated at 375 bhp, became a full-fledged option. Interest in sporty compacts fell in 1970, and Cougar felt the decline as much as any. Production dropped below 100,000 units for the first time as only 72,343 were called for. That was less than half the '67 total of 150,893.

Top left: 1968 Cougar GTE packed 428-cid V8. Lower left: "Dyno" Don Nicholson's Cougar funny car dragster. Top right: 1969 Cougar Eliminator. Note trunk spoiler. Lower right: Cougar Eliminator for 1970.

Bigger was the key word for 1971. Wheelbase went up slightly to 112 inches, and width and length increased significantly, as did weight. The Eliminator was now completely eliminated, and only the 351 and 429 engines were available. Late in the model year, the top 285-bhp 351 option was replaced by a regular-gas version rated at 280. The 429 was now offered with or without Ram-Air. Both versions demanded high-test fuel, and were rated at 370 bhp. Production dropped to another low, 62,864.

Like its competitors, the 1972 Cougar lost its big-horse options. Only three versions of the 351 could be had, the strongest with 266 bhp net. Even that disappeared the following season, leaving only two- and four-barrel 351s. Production climbed for the first time in Cougar history, rising from the 1972 total of 53,702 units to 60,628.

For 1974, Ford brought out a smaller ponycar, the Mustang II, but Mercury would have nothing to do with it. Instead, it transferred the Cougar name to the mid-size Montego line, where it stayed through 1976. For 1977 the Cougar name was applied to the division's full intermediate line. A downsized XR-7 coupe appeared for 1980, joined by two- and four-door sedans based on the Ford Fairmont/Mercury Zephyr compacts for '81. There isn't a performance-oriented model in the bunch for any of these years.

Intermediate Performance

Year & Model		Engine (cid/bhp)	Curb Wt.[1]	lbs/ bhp[1]	0-60[2] (sec)	¼-mi.[2] (sec)	Base Price[3]
1966	Cyclone GT 2d htp	390/335	3580	10.7	6.6	15.2	$2891
1968	Cyclone 2d htp	428/335	3740	11.2	6.2	14.4	$2768
1969	Cyclone CJ 2d htp	428/435	3880	11.6	6.1	13.9	$3224
1971	Cyclone GT 2d htp	429/370	3800	10.3	6.4	14.5	$3226

[1]Advertised; [2]Typical acceleration based on contemporary tests; [3]Advertised list price in contemporary dollars; n = Net advertised horsepower; cid = cubic inch displacement; bhp = brake horsepower; conv = convertible; cpe = coupe; fastbk = fastback; htp = hardtop; rdstr = roadster (2-seat), sdn = sedan; d = number of doors.

Mercury Cyclone/ Montego

Mercury's first venture in the intermediate field, the 1962-63 Meteor, was not a success. Near the end it was offered with the 271-horsepower version of Ford's potent 289, but it never caused more than a ripple in the performance pond. The second try turned out better. For 1966, there was a new intermediate line branded Comet.

The Comet faced some big performance guns: Pontiac's GTO, Oldsmobile's 4-4-2, and the Dodge Coronet and Plymouth Belvedere now offered with the street hemi. Mercury's initial salvo was a weak one. The Cyclone was back as the performance entry in two-door hardtop and convertible form. The GT option brought a warmed-up 390 V8, advertised at 335 bhp. It also included chrome engine dress-up, fiberglass hood with fake scoops, and rocker panel striping. Trouble was, the Cyclone GT didn't have enough go for its class, especially at the drags. It ran in C/Stock, and was usually eaten alive. Later the 427 was installed on a few cars, which helped considerably.

Comet's cause was also helped by Eddie Schartman and Don Nicholson, who again raced Comet funny cars. But the biggest accomplishment came in NASCAR. Bud Moore, who had fielded factory-backed Mercurys in 1964 and then went independent in 1965, built a full-house Comet racer for the '66 campaign. Darel Dieringer won two events in it, including the prestigious Southern 500 at Darlington.

Not much happened to the mid-size Mercs for 1967. The Comet name was played down, and now applied only to the lowest-priced series. The 427, in both single four-barrel form at 410 bhp and dual four-barrel at 425, was now available for all two-doors except convertibles.

Following this off year, Mercury's intermediates rebounded as the new Montego. The Comet name survived on the cheapest model, a two-door hardtop, but the action was at the top of the line where the Cyclone continued to carry the performance colors. It was available as a notchback hardtop and as a stunning new fastback. The GT option was continued. The racy fastback was quite popular, and made itself at home on NASCAR's superspeedways.

Initially a mild version of the 427, rated at 390 bhp, was listed for Montego two-door hardtops, but that was dropped part way into the run, replaced by the CJ 428, pegged at 335 bhp. That wasn't really as puny as it seemed, because, like most carmakers in those days, Mercury was looking at drag racing rules with one eye and nervous insurance agents with the other. *Car Life* magazine uncorked a CJ 428 with automatic, and found it could reel off 0-60 mph times of 6.2 seconds. The quarter mile came up in 14.4, stopping the clocks at 99.44 mph, putting Cyclone near the head of the rubber-burning class.

Some of Ford's NASCAR partisans switched to Mercury for '67, mostly on the strength of the Cyclone fastback's aerodynamics. Among those joining the field were the Wood Brothers. Cyclones did very well on the long tracks, giving Merc its best year ever in the Grand National campaign. The make took seven wins, the first of which was the Daytona 500 with Cale Yarborough taking the checkered flag in the Wood Brothers Cyclone. Yarborough also won the Atlanta 500, the July 4th Firecracker 400 at Daytona, and the Southern 500 at Darlington.

For 1969, the Montego line received only minor trim changes. Comet was still at the bottom, and the notchback Cyclone hardtops were axed. To compete with Plymouth's Road Runner, Mercury had the Cyclone CJ, with standard CJ 428 V8 (still at 335 bhp), four-speed stickshift, and heavy-duty suspension. With its rather stark interior, the CJ matched the Runner in everything except a gimmicky horn. Price came to $3224, $141 over its beep-beep rival. In January, the Cyclone Spoiler joined the lineup. This featured a large wing (which wasn't approved for NASCAR) mounted on the trunk. The model served to honor two Mercury hotshoes, Yarborough and Dan Gurney.

There was yet another Spoiler variation that came along because of the "aerodynamics war" with Chrysler Corporation. Dodge had brought out its slippery Charger 500 after the start of the model year, so to keep its supertrack speed advan-

Upper left: Comet Cyclone was rebodied for 1966 as Mercury's counterpart to the Fairlane GT. Lower left: Hot Cyclone CJ 428 for 1969. Above: One of two special versions of Spoiler II for '69, the Cale Yarborough edition.

tage Mercury countered with the Spoiler II. This had a sloped nose and special flush-mounted grille and front bumper, and was similar overall to Ford's Torino Talladega.

Besides this, the "Big M" had a new engine for NASCAR, a 429 cubic-inch monster with crescent-head design. A street version pretended to have 370 bhp, and was listed for the Cyclone. Due to a delay in getting the 429 approved, the Mercury teams had to start the season in Ford Torinos. It took awhile to get things sorted out, Cale had an off-year, and Mercury won only four events.

As good as the 1968-69 Cyclones looked and ran, the powers at Ford had been changing body tin on its mid-size cars every two years, whether they needed to or not. Accordingly, the Montego/Cyclone was reskinned for 1970. Convertibles were dropped, as was the fastback styling, and wheelbase went to 117 inches. A notchback two-door hardtop tried to be smooth, but its aerodynamics fell short of that of the previous models. That was confirmed by track tests that found the '69s nearly five mph faster. Mercury (and Ford) was in the somewhat embarrassing position of asking its factory-backed NASCAR teams to race year-old "used cars." Three Cyclones were offered for '70, base, GT, and Spoiler, the latter still sporting its airfoil. The 429 could now be installed in four states of tune giving 360-375 claimed horsepower. All had a single four-barrel carb.

The new Cyclones appeared on some NASCAR circuits that season. Together the old and new models gave Mercury four wins. NASCAR rules for 1971 prohibited the Cyclone Spoiler II, Talladega, and winged Chrysler products. Ford pulled the plug on its factory teams. With entrants free to choose, those running Ford products chose 1969 Cyclones. Led by Bobby Allison in a Holman & Moody car, Mercury had its best season total, 11 wins.

Only one version of the 429, a Ram-Air job rated at 370 bhp, was listed for the mostly unchanged 1971 production models. This was standard on the Spoiler and optional on the other two Cyclones. It was the last year for the unit body, and the last year for true high-performance engines.

Montego was completely redesigned for 1972, adopting body-and-frame construction and coil-spring rear suspension. Wheelbase on two-doors was cut from 117 to 114 inches, while four-doors went up to 118. The last hurrah for performance was the GT hardtop, which returned to fastback configuration, and there was a Cyclone option package for it. A fairly mild 429 with 205 bhp net was also listed, but it was not considered very muscular.

For the '72 NASCAR season the '69s were now too old, so teams switched to the 1971 Montego. Without the fastbacks around for competition, it did quite well, taking nine wins that year, and a record-equalling 11 in 1973. All the '73 victories were scored by David Pearson in the Wood Brothers car.

Cyclone vanished as an option for 1973, and the fastback didn't make it to '75. The Montego name lasted through '76, when the Cougar name took over. The Wood Brothers kept a fairly steady flow of NASCAR wins going for Mercury with Montegos, and later, Cougars. But by then there was little relationship between the racing hardware and the street machinery in the showrooms. The mid-size Mercs have become known more for a smooth ride than performance in recent years.

Shelby

Carroll Shelby hung up his bib overalls racing outfit for the last time in 1960. Now, he needed something to do. The doctor had told him something he couldn't do—race cars. Heart trouble was the main reason. Possessing considerable engineering as well as driving ability, Shelby decided that if he couldn't drive 'em any more, he'd build 'em.

It seemed that AC Cars, Ltd. of Surrey, England had lost the supplier of engines for its Ace, a two-place roadster with pleasant, if not terribly original, lines that dated back to 1953. At roughly the same time, Ford Motor Company was in the early stages of its "Total Performance" campaign.

Shelby got hold of an Ace and a new small-block Ford V8, and put them together in his California shop. The 260-cube engine and Ford four-speed transmission fit without major alteration. So in early 1962, development work began on the AC Cobra, powered by Ford. Under the name Shelby American Inc., AC bodies and chassis were received at the Los Angeles site, along with the Ford engines. Some 75 Cobras were built before the 271-horsepower 289 V8 replaced the 260.

The Cobra's racing success was not immediate. Its public introduction coincided almost exactly with that of the Sting Ray, and a showdown seemed inevitable. The first one came on October 13, 1962 at Riverside. A Corvette won, but the Cobras were faster though more fragile. Corvette engineer Zora Arkus-Duntov admitted later that unless something were done, the lighter Cobras would be superior on the track—and that was before he saw the 289. Cobras would go on to dominate the SCCA's A-Production class for most of the rest of the decade.

In 1966, Cobra 289 production ended at Shelby (though some were later built in England). In its place came the Cobra 427, powered by that mighty Ford big-block stuffed into an altered AC body on a beefier chassis. This turned out to be one of the meanest cars of all time.

By 1967 it was apparent the Cobra couldn't last. The government's new safety and emissions regulations were on the horizon for 1968, and Ford was starting to lose interest. The Cobra had done its thing on the track and in people's minds. Production was abruptly halted before year's end. In all, 630 small-block roadsters and 510 big-blockers were made.

Cobra, of course, is only part of the Shelby story. Having worked closely with Ford management on that project, Shelby American was the logical choice when Dearborn wanted to enhance the performance image of its new Mustang.

Arrangements were made, and Ford's San Jose, California plant began shipping "raw" Mustangs to Shelby American's new facility at Los Angeles International Airport. What it received was a hoodless 2+2 fastback painted Wimbledon White, and also missing its back seat. The suspension used heavy-duty production pieces, augmented by Koni shocks, traction bars, and other goodies. The 289 V8 picked up tubular headers and other tweaks from Shelby, which brought the advertised horses to 306. The standard Mustang rear axle was swapped with one from a Galaxie, a Detroit Locker differential was fitted, and a Borg-Warner T-10 four-speed manual trans was installed. A

Shelby Performance

Year & Model		Engine (cid/bhp)	Curb Wt.[1]	lbs/ bhp[1]	0-60[2] (sec)	¼-mi.[2] (sec)	Base Price[3]
1963	Cobra 2d rdstr	289/271	2350	8.7	5.8	13.8	$5995
1966	Cobra 2d rdstr	427/425	2529	5.9	5.3	13.8	$7495
1965	GT-350 2d htp	289/306	2800	9.1	7.0	15.7	$4547
1967	GT-350 2d htp	289/306	3000	9.8	7.5	14.9	$3995
1967	GT-500 2d htp	428/360	3286	9.1	6.2	15.4	$4195
1968	Cobra 2d conv	428/360	3665	10.2	6.5	14.8	$4439
1968	GT-500KR 2d htp	428/335	3500	10.4	6.9	14.6	$4473

[1]Advertised; [2]Typical acceleration based on contemporary tests; [3]Advertised list price in contemporary dollars; n = Net advertised horsepower; cid = cubic inch displacement; bhp = brake horsepower; conv = convertible; cpe = coupe; fastbk = fastback; htp = hardtop; rdstr = roadster (2-seat); sdn = sedan; d = number of doors.

Top left: 1965 Shelby GT-350 poses at Los Angeles International Airport near Shelby factory.

Top right: 1968 GT-500 convertible. 428 and ragtop were both new that year. Above: 1967 GT-350.

The 1969 Shelby GT-500 convertible (left) and fastback (right). Both were rebodied along the lines of production Mustangs. Production halted by the end of the year.

fiberglass hood with a small scoop was added, as were big, broad blue racing stripes along the rocker panels and on top of the car from hood to rear deck. The result was dubbed GT-350. There was also a lightweight racing version, the GT-350R. The regular model cost $4547, the racer $5950. Much to the distress of Corvettes and Jaguars, the competition jobs ran very well right out of the box, and took the national B-Production title in 1965, '66, and '67.

For 1966, there were more colors besides white, the temperamental differential was made an option, and (gulp!) you could now get automatic transmission. On the plus side, a scoop that really took in air was added to the rear quarter panels to help cool the rear brakes, and the stock air vents behind the side windows were replaced with clear plexiglass panels to give better visibility. The rear seat was reinstated as an option.

Mustang got new tin for 1967, with larger dimensions and an optional big-block 390-cid V8. Naturally, these changes were incorporated into the Shelby variants as the factory's influence further compromised their sporting nature. The Koni shocks were deleted, as were the traction bars, the locker diff, and the tube headers. Visual dress-up was added, including a new front.

For visceral appeal the big-block 428 was now available as the GT-500, though it wasn't for the "civilian" Mustang this year. The big-inch Shelby proved more popular, and 2050 were built against 1175 GT-350s. Again, only the fastback coupe was offered. A few GT-500s were run off with the hairy 427 engine from the Cobra.

For 1968, a convertible with padded rollbar was added to the line, which now carried Cobra emblems. At mid-year came the GT-500KR ("King of the Road") featuring Ford's high-performance Cobra-Jet 428. It was rated at a ridiculously low 335 bhp, less than the 360-bhp 428 it replaced. The reason was to qualify for a particular drag racing class, and to please nervous insurance companies. The GT-350's 289 was replaced by a garden variety 302 good for 250 bhp advertised.

If you think Carroll Shelby was less than pleased by all the things Ford was doing to his car, you're right. Though his public statements at the time were positive, his interest in the project was all but gone. At the end of 1967, Shelby production was shifted from California to the A. O. Smith factory in Ionia, Michigan. A year later it was moved again, right into Ford's own Southfield, Michigan plant.

Mustang was restyled for 1969, so the Shelby versions were, too. To again set them apart, they got a unique fiberglass front end with NACA-style hood ducts. The 302 was replaced by the 351 small-block rated at 290 bhp. Inside, the old basic-black days of 1965 were long gone, and fancy trim prevailed. You could even get air conditioning. Now furnished more along the lines of what mainstream America expected, the later Shelbys sold in higher volume than the more "purist" early models. The 1968 model-year production total was an all-time high of 4450 units. The 1969 version had little that you couldn't get cheaper in a Mustang, so output dropped to 3150.

Not all the '69s had been sold by the end of the usual model year, so leftovers were retitled as 1970s and got minor cosmetic changes. There were just over 600 of these cars built. By now, the Mustang had long been a performance car in its own right, something that wasn't the case when the Shelby project started. The later Shelbys just weren't different enough to attract many buyers. The project was also expensive for Ford, which was easing its way out of the performance picture by 1970.

Today, all Shelby GTs are considered collector's cars. Though 10,825 were made altogether, some, like the early 1965–66 models, hold more value than others.

Engine Charts

Edsel

Type	Bore × Stroke (in.)	CID	BHP @ rpm*	Torque @ rpm*	Fuel# System	Avail. (years)
ohv V8	4.20 × 3.70	410	345@ 4600	472@ 2600	4 bbl.	1958
ohv V8	4.05 × 3.50	361	303@ 4600	390@ 2900	4 bbl.	1959

Ford

Type	Bore × Stroke (in.)	CID	BHP @ rpm*	Torque @ rpm*	Fuel# System	Avail. (years)
ohv V8	3.75 × 3.30	292	198@ 4400	286@ 2500	4 bbl.	1955

*SAE gross ratings except where noted; † hemispherical heads; # carburetion: no. carbs × bbls.; e = estimated; FI = fuel injection; n = net advertised figures; SC = supercharged; TC = turbocharged.

Type	Bore × Stroke (in.)	CID	BHP @ rpm*	Torque @ rpm*	Fuel# System	Avail. (years)
ohv V8	3.80 × 3.44	312	225@ 4600	324@ 2600	4 bbl.	1956
ohv V8	3.80 × 3.44	312	260@ 4600	335@ 2600	2 × 4 bbl.	1956
ohv V8	3.80 × 3.44	312	270@ 4800	336@ 3400e	2 × 4 bbl.	1957
ohv V8	3.80 × 3.44	312	300@ 4500	340@ 3200e	SC 4 bbl.	1957
ohv V8	4.00 × 3.50	352	300@ 4600	395@ 2800	4 bbl.	1958-60
ohv V8	4.30 × 3.70	430	350@ 4400	490@ 3100	4 bbl.	1959-60
ohv I6	3.50 × 2.50	144	128@ 4200	145@ 2400e	3 × 1 bbl.	1960
ohv V8	4.00 × 3.50	352	360@ 6000	380@ 3400	4 bbl.	1960
ohv V8	4.05 × 3.78	390	375@ 6000	430@ 3400	4 bbl.	1961-62
ohv V8	4.05 × 3.78	390	401@ 6000	430@ 3500	3 × 2 bbl.	1961-62
ohv V8	4.13 × 3.78	406	385@ 5800	444@ 3400	4 bbl.	1962-63
ohv V8	4.13 × 3.78	406	405@ 5800	448@ 3500	3 × 2 bbl.	1962-63
ohv V8	4.24 × 3.78	427	410@ 5600	476@ 3400	4 bbl.	1963-67
ohv V8	4.24 × 3.78	427	425@ 6000	480@ 3700	2 × 4 bbl.	1963-67
ohv V8	4.00 × 2.87	289	271@ 6000	312@ 3400	4 bbl.	1963-67
ohv V8	4.05 × 3.78	390	335@ 4800	427@ 3200	4 bbl.	1966-68
ohv V8	4.13 × 3.98	428	360@ 5400	459@ 3200	4 bbl.	1966-68
ohv V8	4.23 × 3.78	427	390@ 5600	460@ 3200	4 bbl.	1968
ohv V8	4.13 × 3.98	428	335@ 5400	440@ 3400	4 bbl.	1968-70
ohv V8	4.00 × 3.00	302	290@ 5800	290@ 4300	4 bbl.	1969-70
ohv V8	4.00 × 3.50	351	290@ 4800	385@ 3200	4 bbl.	1969
ohv V8†	4.36 × 3.59	429	375@ 5200	401@ 3400	4 bbl.	1969
ohv V8	4.00 × 3.50	351	300@ 5400	380@ 3400	4 bbl.	1970
ohv V8†	4.36 × 3.59	429	375@ 5600	450@ 4000	4 bbl.	1970-71
ohv V8	4.36 × 3.59	429	370@ 5400	450@ 3400	4 bbl.	1970-71
ohv V8	4.00 × 3.50	351	330@ 5400	370@ 4000	4 bbl.	1971
ohv V8	4.00 × 3.50	351	280@ 5800	345@ 3800	4 bbl.	1971
ohv V8	4.00 × 3.50	351	266@ 5400n	301@ 3600n	4 bbl.	1972
ohv V8	4.00 × 3.50	351	275@ 6000n	320@ 3600ne	4 bbl.	1972
ohv V8	4.00 × 3.50	351	246@ 5400n	312@ 3600n	4 bbl.	1973

Lincoln

Type	Bore × Stroke (in.)	CID	BHP @ rpm*	Torque @ rpm*	Fuel# System	Avail. (years)
ohv V8	3.80 × 3.50	317	160@ 3900	284@ 1800	2 bbl.	1952
ohv V8	3.80 × 3.50	317	205@ 4200	305@ 2300	4 bbl.	1953-54
ohv V8	3.94 × 3.50	341	225@ 4400	332@ 2500	4 bbl.	1955

Mercury

Type	Bore × Stroke (in.)	CID	BHP @ rpm*	Torque @ rpm*	Fuel# System	Avail. (years)
ohv V8	3.75 × 3.59	292	198@ 4400	282@ 2500	4 bbl.	1955
ohv V8	3.80 × 3.44	312	260@ 4600	335@ 2600	2 × 4 bbl.	1956
ohv V8	4.00 × 3.66	368	335@ 5000	420@ 3200e	2 × 4 bbl.	1957
ohv V8	4.13 × 3.78	406	385@ 5800	444@ 3400	4 bbl.	1962-63
ohv V8	4.13 × 3.78	406	405@ 5800	448@ 3500	3 × 2 bbl.	1962-63
ohv V8	4.24 × 3.78	427	410@ 5600	476@ 3400	4 bbl.	1963-65, 1967
ohv V8	4.24 × 3.78	427	425@ 6000	480@ 3700	2 × 4 bbl.	1963-65, 1967
ohv V8	4.00 × 2.87	289	271@ 6000	312@ 3400	4 bbl.	1963-65
ohv V8	4.05 × 3.78	390	335@ 4800	427@ 3200	4 bbl.	1966-68
ohv V8	4.00 × 2.87	289	341@ 5800	320@ 3400e	2 × 4 bbl.	1967
ohv V8	4.24 × 3.78	427	390@ 5600	460@ 3200	4 bbl.	1968
ohv V8	4.13 × 3.98	428	335@ 5400	440@ 3400	4 bbl.	1968-70
ohv V8	4.00 × 3.50	351	290@ 4800	385@ 3200	4 bbl.	1969
ohv V8†	4.36 × 3.59	429	375@ 5600	450@ 4000	4 bbl.	1969-70
ohv V8	4.00 × 3.50	351	300@ 5400	380@ 3400	4 bbl.	1970
ohv V8	4.00 × 3.00	302	290@ 5800	290@ 4300	4 bbl.	1969-70
ohv V8	4.36 × 3.59	429	370@ 5400	450@ 3400	4 bbl.	1970-71
ohv V8	4.00 × 3.50	351	280@ 5800	345@ 3800	4 bbl.	1971
ohv V8	4.00 × 3.50	351	266@ 5400n	301@ 3600n	4 bbl.	1972
ohv V8	4.00 × 3.50	351	264@ 5400n	314@ 3600n	4 bbl.	1973

Shelby

Type	Bore × Stroke (in.)	CID	BHP @ rpm*	Torque @ rpm*	Fuel# System	Avail. (years)
ohv V8	3.80 × 2.87	260	260@ 5800	269@ 4500	4 bbl.	1963-64
ohv V8	4.00 × 2.87	289	271@ 5800	312@ 3400	4 bbl.	1964
ohv V8	4.00 × 2.87	289	306@ 6000	329@ 4200	4 bbl.	1965
ohv V8	4.24 × 3.78	427	425@ 6000	480@ 3700	2 × 4 bbl.	1965-67
ohv V8	4.24 × 3.78	427	480@ 6500	410@ 3700	4 bbl.	1966-67
ohv V8	4.13 × 3.98	428	390@ 5200	475@ 3700	4 bbl.	1966
ohv V8	4.00 × 2.87	289	306@ 6000	329@ 4200	4 bbl.	1965-67
ohv V8	4.13 × 3.98	428	355@ 5400	420@ 3200	4 bbl.	1967
ohv V8	4.00 × 3.00	302	250@ 4800	310@ 2800	4 bbl.	1968
ohv V8	4.13 × 3.98	428	360@ 5400	420@ 3200	4 bbl.	1968
ohv V8	4.13 × 3.98	428	335@ 5400	440@ 3400	4 bbl.	1968-70
ohv V8	4.00 × 3.50	351	290@ 4800	385@ 3400	4 bbl.	1969-70

*SAE gross ratings except where noted; † hemispherical heads; # carburetion: no. carbs × bbls.; e = estimated; FI = fuel injection; n = net advertised figures; SC = supercharged; TC = turbocharged.

General Motors Corporation

The company that started the "horsepower race" in 1949 makes the last high-performance cars on the market for 1981. In between, "The General" unleashed a squadron of bold, brassy barn-burners despite its anti-performance attitude. Even Cadillac got in on the act.

Buick

Some of the most underrated—and under-raced—cars of the postwar period came from Buick. Over the years Buick built some very good, very fast cars, but one or another competitor always managed to offer something hotter. Yet few muscle-car fans remember that in its early days Buick was one of the most popular race cars in the country.

David Dunbar Buick, after ventures in the plumbing-fixture and gasoline-engine fields, went into building passenger cars in 1903, when he formed the Buick Manufacturing Company. There were problems right from the start, however, and it wasn't until William C. Durant took control in 1904 that Buick began to show signs of success. Later, Durant formed General Motors, with Buick as its centerpiece.

Starting with its 1931 models, Buick moved exclusively to an inline overhead-valve eight-cylinder engine, after a successful run with an overhead-valve six. The new powerplant turned in good performance, especially in the Century series, offered from 1935 through 1942. Centurys usually had the largest-displacement engine in a lighter, smaller package than the top-line Roadmaster and Limited. After World War II, straight-eight production was resumed, but the Century did not return for several years.

Buick's first V8 arrived in time for its 50th anniversary in 1953, making it the third GM division to get a modern overhead-valve design. Buick's engine debuted at 322 cubic inches, right between Cadillac's 331 and Oldsmobile's 303. Horsepower ranged between 164 and 188, depending on model, but availability was limited to the bigger Super and Roadmaster lines. The smaller, lower-priced Special still got along with the straight eight. One feature of the new Buick unit was "pent-roof" combustion chambers, with both intake and exhaust valves mounted topside. This made for a narrower engine and a longer exhaust passage through the head.

The division's first serious entry in the horsepower race was the revived Century series for the all-new 1954 line. New styling, complete with the "panoramic" windshield, drew attention to the outside, but the Century did its talking from the inside. Following the prewar formula to an extent, the Century utilized the Special's 122-inch wheelbase, but got the most potent versions of the 322, with four-barrel carburetion as on the Roadmaster. Standard-shift models came with an 8.0:1 compression ratio and a rating of 195 bhp. If you opted for Dynaflow automatic, the CR jumped to 8.5:1 for an even 200 bhp.

"Car buff" magazines tested the

Buick's first V8 premiered for 1953 (Roadmaster shown above). Century series returned for 1954, was hot model in lineup, especially in its 1955 form (right).

Century, and were quick to find it among the quickest cars of the day. In the flying-mile contests at Daytona Beach in 1954, the fastest Buick averaged 110.425 mph. But as would happen in later years, Chrysler and Cadillac were faster, and Buick settled for fifth place.

Compression ratio was squeezed to 9.0:1 for the 1955 Century with automatic transmission, and output was up to 236 bhp. It was a nice jump, but not in the year of the Chrysler 300. At Daytona, the Century's best effort in the standing-start and flying miles netted a pair of fourths. A Cadillac and a swift Chevrolet duo nosed out Buick in acceleration, but at least it edged the fastest 300. The flying mile saw 300s one-two, and Cadillac third. Century was popular as a stock-car racer in 1954 and even more so in '55, with several top drivers running them. It was during 1955 that Buick got its only two wins in NASCAR Grand National competition.

Horsepower for 1956 was higher than ever, 255, still coming from 322 cubes. Notable was a new exhaust system with header-like exhaust manifolds. Road testers confirmed the '56 Century was the fastest ever, with many publications getting 0-60 mph clockings of less than 10 seconds for the first time. *Motor Life* magazine seemed to be the best at it, quoting a time of 8.9 seconds.

The first growth in Buick's V8 occurred for 1957, when a ⅛-inch bore increase yielded 364 cid. Advertised horsepower rose to 300, but weight went up by an average of 200 pounds because of all-new bodies that year. It also was the time when it was fashionable to inflate advertised horsepower figures. Tests confirmed that the '57s were slower on the average than the '56s. Even though the Century remained in the line through 1958, its image as a performance car was now tarnished. Competitors were offering more power in lighter packages.

Buick did not promote performance for the rest of the '50s and well into the '60s. Its V8 continued to expand, however, eventually reaching 425 cubes for 1963. But its valves were just too small for the size to be used for maximum performance. Car size grew as well in most years, except for 1961. A new 430 big-block came out for 1967. It remained in production through 1976, reaching 455 cubes, but its main performance application was in Buick's intermediates.

Above: Two '55s on the front row at Darlington before the start of the Southern 500 (Buck Baker in the middle). Right: '57 Century was heavier and slower than the 1956.

Strangely, one of Buick's more impressive performance feats was kept secret. In January 1960, Buick rented Daytona International Speedway, and ran a 1960 model 10,000 miles at an average speed of 120.12 mph, using race drivers and high-speed refueling. Speeds often approached 130 mph, which was not far from those of fully-prepared stock cars of the day. After it was over, the powers-that-be decided the exploit was not in keeping with the 1957 Automobile Manufacturers Association anti-performance edict, and it was never mentioned, much less advertised. The factory never really got involved in the racing or high-performance games, but stuck to building comfortable cars capable of very good performance. The Daytona tests make you wonder what *would* have happened had Buick really tried—like it had some 50 years earlier.

Buick Gran Sport

Buick's prime entry in the muscle-car sweepstakes was the Skylark Gran Sport, first announced in December 1964. Oldsmobile had reacted to the Pontiac GTO in 1964 with its 4-4-2 option. It took Buick over a year to come up with its answer, perhaps because it was waiting for returns on GTO sales. Though it started out rather mild, the Gran Sport eventually became rather wild.

Gran Sport was an option for the two-door sedan, hardtop, and convertible models in the Skylark series of Buick's mid-size Special line. The Special name, formerly attached to the lower-price Buicks of 1935–58, resurfaced for 1961 on a line of com-

Buick Performance

Year & Model		Engine (cid/bhp)	Curb Wt.[1]	lbs/ bhp[1]	0-60[2] (sec)	¼-mi.[2] (sec)	Base Price[3]
1954	Century 4d sdn	322/200	3805	19.0	12.1	17.9	$2520
1955	Century 4d sdn	322/236	3825	16.2	9.8	17.5	$2548
1956	Century 4d sdn	322/255	4000	15.7	9.6	17.1	$3025
1957	Century 4d sdn	364/300	4163	13.9	10.1	17.6	$3354

[1]Advertised; [2]Typical acceleration based on contemporary tests; [3]Advertised list price in contemporary dollars; n = Net advertised horsepower; cid = cubic inch displacement; bhp = brake horsepower; conv = convertible; cpe = coupe; fastbk = fastback; htp = hardtop; rdstr = roadster (2-seat); sdn = sedan; d = number of doors.

Hot Skylarks through the years, clockwise for top left: 1965 Gran Sport, 1969 GS 400, 1970 GSX 455, 1967 GS 340. All were fast, though a little behind Pontiac's GTO.

pacts with a 112-inch wheelbase. That dimension grew to 115 for the all-new 1964s, moving Buick into the intermediate field. These featured body-and-frame construction, coil springs front and rear, and a cast-iron version of the aluminum V8 used from 1961–63. This displaced 300 cubic inches, and was no match for the GTO's 389-cid engine and 348 horsepower.

General Motors had a ban on engines over 400 cid for its intermediates at the time. Buick had a 401-cube job it was putting into its bigger cars. Though the press releases said the Gran Sport option came with a 400 cid engine and the sales brochures didn't mention size at all, the truth was that Buick got away with an extra cubic inch.

Advertised horsepower came out to 325 with a single four-barrel. All three GS models had stiffer convertible frames and heavy-duty suspension. Available transmissions were a manual three-speed, four-speed, and a two-speed automatic.

Buick's publicity said the Gran Sport was capable of a seven-second 0–60 mph sprint. With its automatic model, *Car Life* magazine obtained a 7.4-second figure, which no doubt could be cut with the four-speed. Top speed came to 121 mph. In all, this was good performance, though behind the GTO's 6.6-second time a year earlier.

Gran Sport left the option ranks and became a full-fledged series for 1966. Initially the 325-horse setup was all there was, followed by a mid-year boost to 340 bhp as an option.

All kinds of things happened to Buick's muscle car for 1967. Most important, it got a new engine. The old pentroof design, which dated back to 1953, was retired, and a new big-block replaced it. For intermediates it was sized at 400 cid, while the big cars got 430 cubes. The head design was a semi-wedge type, and the block had room for expansion. There was also room for decent-sized valves to help breathing. There were new nameplates for the hot versions as GS 400 replaced the Skylark Gran Sport logo, and again there were three body styles. Horsepower remained at the 1966 high of 340. Automatics were now of the three-speed variety. Although there was some pretty hot stuff around that year, the GS 400 finished first in the 0–60 mph listings at *Car Life*, doing it in six seconds flat. It nosed out a Ram-Air GTO timed at 6.1. While many will argue that there is no way a GS 400 will down a Ram-Air GTO, most will agree that Buicks were now at least competitive in performance with the rest of the field.

Added at mid-year was a junior edition, the GS 340, with 260 bhp from a 340-cid V8 (an enlargement of the 300). While its performance was just in the "ordinary" class, the 340 was typical of a new breed of muscle car that appeared in the late '60s in reaction to rising insurance rates. GS 340 was offered only as a two-door hardtop.

Wheelbase hopscotched on GM's 1968 intermediates. There were

Buick Special/Skylark/Century Performance

Year	Model	Engine (cid/bhp)	Curb Wt.[1]	lbs/ bhp[1]	0-60[2] (sec)	¼-mi.[2] (sec)	Base Price[3]
1965	Special Skylark 2d cpe	401/325	3400	10.5	7.8	16.6	$2608
1967	GS-400 2d htp	400/340	3500	10.3	7.8	15.9	$3019
1968	GS-400 2d conv	400/340	3547	10.4	7.5	16.3	$3271
1970	GS-455 2d htp	455/360	3750	10.4	5.5	13.4	$3283
1972	Skylark GS 2d htp	455/275n	3850	14.0	5.8	14.1	$3225
1973	Century GS 2d cpe	455/270n	3975	14.7	7.4	15.3	$3013
1974	Regal 2d cpe	455/230n	4390	19.1	8.5	16.7	$3984

[1]Advertised; [2]Typical acceleration based on contemporary tests; [3]Advertised list price in contemporary dollars; n = Net advertised horsepower; cid = cubic inch displacement; bhp = brake horsepower; conv = convertible; cpe = coupe; fastbk = fastback; htp = hardtop; rdstr = roadster (2-seat); sdn = sedan; d = number of doors.

121-inch-wheelbase wagons, two-doors were mounted on a 112-inch chassis, and four-doors rode a 116. Interestingly, the two-door wheelbase was again the same as that of the original 1961-63 models. The GS 400 now came only in two models, a hardtop and convertible. Power was still advertised at 340 bhp from 400 cubes. A 0.05-inch bore increase on the 340 engine brought 350 cubes, and appropriately the GS 340 became the GS 350 that year, now boasting 280 bhp.

Instead of offering more horsepower with mid-year production options, Buick took a route somewhat unusual for such a conservative outfit: it offered them through its dealers. This practice was common at Chevrolet, Pontiac, Ford, and Chrysler, but must have really rattled the parts-department folks at the local Electra 225 emporiums. Among the new goodies was the "Stage I" setup, which improved breathing and output for the 400-cid engine. GM intermediates weren't permitted below the 10-pounds-per-horsepower limit that year, but the Stage I cars came close. For the second straight year, a GS 400 was the fastest *Car Life* test vehicle, hitting 60 mph from rest in 6.1 seconds to edge the Mercury Cyclone.

Functional hood scoops were standard on the 1969 GS 350 and 400 models. The design was far from practical, however, as it proved more adept at gathering rain than fresh air. Models and horsepower ratings remained the same as in '68, but the Stage I was now a production option, and included a high-lift cam, reworked carb, and free-flow exhaust system. Other speed goodies were still available from Buick dealers.

On paper, the wildest Buicks of all were the 1970 GS 455 and GSX models. GM dropped its 400-cubic-inch limit for mid-sized cars. Buick responded and bored out the 430 that was going into its big cars and the Riviera, and came up with 455 cid. The new engine was deemed just the thing for the GS series, thus the GS 455. The GS 350 became just plain old GS this year. Stage I became a bit more believable in the ratings department, and was now tagged at 360 bhp. It was all kind of phony anyway, as most high-performance engines of the day were underrated to keep the insurance underwriters from going crazy.

Visitors to the 1970 Chicago Auto Show were among the first to view Buick's mid-year performance option, the GSX. For $888 over the price of the GS 455 you got front and rear spoilers, striping, a hood-mounted tach, and four-speed transmission. Engines were either the 455 or 455 Stage I, as on the regular GS. The main purpose of the GSX was to tell the muscle-car world that Buick was a participant, something insiders had known for a long time.

As was the case in the rest of the industry, Buick's performance fortunes took a turn for the worse in 1971. All GM engines had to get by on regular or no-lead gas, meaning compression ratios and tuning were changed and performance reduced. The model lineup was shuffled, with hardtop and convertible offered under the GS label. A 350 V8 was now standard. If you wanted a 455, it was optional in regular tune at 315 bhp or in Stage I form at 345. The GSX option was also still listed.

GS returned for 1972, but the GSX didn't. Horses were now figured on a net basis, so the regular 455 was rated at 250 bhp and the Stage I at 20 more.

Buick rebodied its 1973 middle models, and used the old performance handle Century. Wheelbase remained at 112 inches for two-doors. Hardtops and convertibles were gone, replaced by pillared sedans. The GS was now reduced to an option for the base Century coupe. Hood scoops were erased, but that didn't hurt much. With the GS you got the 455, still at 250 net horses. The 270-bhp Stage I setup was continued. Century GS was the only Buick on which you could get a four-speed manual transmission. A *Motor Trend* test bore out the bad news. The 0-60 mph leap now took 8.9 seconds for the Stage I model.

The Gran Sport's final appearance came for 1974. Despite the fuel crisis, the 455 was still available, as was Stage I. Rating for the latter was now down to 255 bhp net. It made little difference, as sales of performance cars were in the cellar, and the gas shortages and price increases that coincided with the new-model introductions kept many customers away.

The 1975 Century was devoid of GS and Stage I options, and the biggest engine available was a 350 V8. Buick was back to being average again.

Cadillac

What business does the "Standard of the World" have in a book on muscle cars? Quite a bit, actually. From 1949 through the mid-1950s, Cadillac was as well-known for its performance as for its luxury. In fact, it was one of the first postwar muscle cars. Cadillacs were raced in speed trials, on road courses, and around oval tracks, all with success. And there were even some special production models with more performance than the rest of the line. Cadillac engines also became popular with the hot-rod and race-car builders of the early '50s. One of the notable examples is the Cadillac-Allard sports car.

Cadillac was founded by Henry M. Leland, the "Master of Precision," in 1902. Leland sold out to William C. Durant near the end of the decade, and the firm became part of his new General Motors company. Following a series of one- and four-cylinder engines, Cadillac started offering V8 power beginning in 1915. In the '30s, massive V12s and V16s appeared, some of the most magnificent powerplants of all time. The early postwar Cadillacs used a 346 cubic-inch L-head V8 rated at 150

Cadillac Performance

Year	Model	Engine (cid/bhp)	Curb Wt.[1]	lbs/ bhp[1]	0-60[2] (sec)	¼-mi.[2] (sec)	Base Price[3]
1949	62 4d sdn	331/160	3956	24.7	12.1	18.0	$3050
1950	61 2d htp	331/160	3829	23.9	12.9	18.1	$2761
1952	62 4d sdn	331/190	4140	21.8	13.2	18.4	$3684
1954	62 4d sdn	331/230	4370	19.0	11.3	18.4	$3933
1955	62 4d sdn	331/250	4370	17.5	10.0	17.6	$3977
1956	62 4d htp	365/285	4550	16.0	11.4	17.8	$4753

[1]Advertised; [2]Typical acceleration based on contemporary tests; [3]Advertised list price in contemporary dollars; n = Net advertised horsepower; cid = cubic inch displacement; bhp = brake horsepower; conv = convertible; cpe = coupe; fastbk = fastback; htp = hardtop; rdstr = roadster (2-seat); sdn = sedan; d = number of doors.

Cadillac's new V8 arrived for its 1949 models (above), which also featured the industry's first tailfins. Make was surprisingly strong in racing (right). Eldorado was new for 1953 (lower left), had more horses than other models. The 1957 (lower right) boasted 325 bhp.

horsepower. All-new styling arrived for 1948, followed by the significant new overhead-valve V8 for 1949.

Along with the Oldsmobile V8 introduced that year, the 1949 Cadillac engine set an industry design standard that would be followed for the next three decades. Bore was larger than stroke, reversing a long-time industry practice, and making for shorter piston travel. Displacement came to 331.1 cubic inches and compression ratio tallied 7.5:1. There was provision for even higher compression, up to 12:1, to take advantage of the super-high-octane fuels promised after the war, which never materialized. More importantly, the Caddy V8 weighed nearly 200 pounds less than the L-head it replaced, and even came out a pound or two lighter than the Oldsmobile V8. With a Carter two-barrel carb, advertised horsepower came to 160 bhp to tie Packard for the lead.

Road test magazines were few and far between in 1949, but Tom McCahill was already reporting for *Mechanix Illustrated*: "With this engine, Cadillac, despite its large size, outperforms just about every car being made." He backed up that claim by posting a 0–60 mph romp of 12.1 seconds and a top speed of around 105 mph. No other car he tested that year had better figures.

For 1950, Cadillac got heavily revised styling which lacked the smoothness and grace of the 1948–49 models. Wheelbase on the Series 61 went down to 122 inches, compared with 126 for the Series 62 and 130 for the Series 60 Special. With nearly 200 pounds less weight than the 62, and standard manual shift, the 61 was among the speediest cars in the business. Its potential was amply demonstrated at LeMans, of all places, where a pair were entered in the 1950 edition of the 24-hour endurance classic by sportsman Briggs Cunningham. One car had a special body on the 61 chassis, the other was a stock-appearing two-door hardtop. Suspension was beefed up and carburetion improved to allow speeds up to 120 mph, but these cars still made a strange sight among all the other smaller contestants. Both cars placed quite high. Surprisingly, the stocker finished ahead of the trick job in 10th place.

The 61 series returned for 1951 minus its manual shift. The line was not very successful, less than 6000 61s were produced that year, and the series was dropped for 1952. However, after three years without change, Cadillac horsepower took an upward turn for '52. Cadillac, along with Buick and Oldsmobile, got its first four-barrel carburetor. The result was a dramatic rise in horsepower, up by 30, to give Cadillac a rating of 190 bhp and first place in the industry, topping Chrysler's 180. *Motor Trend* magazine found the 1952 Series 62 sedan had a top speed of 109.6 mph, the highest of any standard passenger car it had tested up to that point. The 0–60 mph sprint took 13.2 seconds.

Cadillac bumped compression from 7.5 to 8.25:1 for 1953, good for 210 bhp, and good enough to stay on top in the horsepower race. Cadillac had usually been a contender in the Speed Trials at Daytona Beach, but its first outright win didn't come until 1954. Joe Lit-

continued on page 81

Muscle Cars Color Gallery Two

1. 1964 Shelby Cobra 427
2. 1963 Chevrolet Corvette Grand Sport
3. 1964 Shelby Cobra 427
4. 1964 Shelby Cobra 427 cockpit

1. 1965 Dodge Coronet 500
2. 1968 Chevrolet Corvette Stingray
3. 1969 Chevrolet Camaro Z-28
4. 1969 Pontiac Firebird Trans Am
5. 1969 Pontiac Firebird Trans Am
6. 1968 Shelby GT-500
7. 1969 American Motors AMX

4
TRANS AM
591 VAJ

5

6

7
STAGED
WINNERS
VICTORY
MOTOR CITY
AMX
A M X
1969

1
1969

2
GTO
1969

3
1970
CYCLONE

1. 1969 American Motors SC/Rambler
2. 1969 Pontiac GTO
3. 1970 Mercury Cyclone Spoiler
4. 1970 Plymouth Road Runner Superbird
5. 1970 American Motors Rebel Machine
6. 1970 Ford Torino Cobra

1
GS

2
PLY-472

3
DNB-4-72
FLORIDA

4
PLY-472
GREAT LAKE STATE

5
13M-292

1. 1972 Buick GS 455
2. 1972 Plymouth 'Cuda 340
3. 1972 Dodge Challenger Rallye 340
4. 1972 Plymouth Road Runner
5. 1973 Pontiac Grand Am
6. 1976 Ford Mustang II Cobra II
7. 1977 Chevrolet Camaro Z-28
8. 1973 Plymouth Road Runner

1. 1979 Ford Mustang Cobra
2. 1980 Pontiac Firebird Turbo Trans Am
3. 1981 Chevrolet Corvette

continued from page 72

tlejohn drove a Series 62 hardtop to a 76.251-mph average to win the standing-start mile. It beat back the 235-bhp Chryslers, which led the industry for horsepower that year.

Cadillac got larger for 1954. Wheelbase went up three inches, and other dimensions increased proportionally. But horsepower also went up by 20 to 230 bhp. That still fell five short of Chrysler, which got its first four-barrel carb. *Motor Trend* gave its "performance car of the year" award to Cadillac, noting its Daytona victory.

Most speed fans remember 1955 as the year the Chrysler 300 devastated racing, especially with that record 127.580-mph run in the flying mile. But few remember that Cadillac was again the fastest in acceleration at the beach that year, setting a record mark of 80.428 mph at the hands of Littlejohn in a 1955 model. That speed was better than two mph faster than that of the second-place car, a Chevrolet. The flying-mile winner, Warren Koechling, could do no better than fifth in the standing-start mile, better than 3½ mph off Littlejohn's pace.

For 1955, compression was again tightened to 9.0:1, so the four-barrel V8 now boasted 250 bhp. Standard on the flashy Eldorado and optional for other models was a dual-quad setup, which brought 270 bhp. But the days of the heavy high-performance car were drawing to a close. Only the Chrysler 300 would pull it off after 1955, and it was nearly 300 pounds lighter than a Cadillac, and more powerful.

A bore increase enlarged the Caddy engine for the first time in 1956—365 cid. The dual-quad setup was still available, bringing horses up to 305, but the make's racing days were over. More people were interested in how high the fins were, or how soft the ride was. Most Cadillac drivers were now used to the fact they no longer had the fastest or most powerful car on the road. Most didn't really care. The twin four-barrel engine was offered through 1960. Cadillac wouldn't make engine news again until 1970, when it offered the biggest postwar engine ever, a 500 cubic-incher—hardly the stuff of high-performance legends.

Chevrolet

Through 1954, no one could ever accuse Chevrolet of building speedy cars. The only race Chevrolet was good at winning was the sales race, which it did quite regularly starting in 1927. The first Chevrolet was a product of race driver Louis Chevrolet, a Buick factory team member, who helped design the first model. The firm was acquired by William C. Durant, who put together General Motors in 1908, lost control, then used Chevrolet to regain it in 1915. Durant was out by 1920, but Chevrolet flourished, and eventually passed Ford to become the industry sales leader. Chevrolets of the 1930s, '40s, and early '50s were known for their unspectacular overhead-valve six, nicknamed the "stovebolt" because of its commonness and ease of repair.

By 1955, most cars had or were ready to get overhead-valve V8s. Chevrolet had to have one no matter how successful its six had been. It was unveiled in the all-new 1955 models, with the most drastic Chevy restyling of modern times and a newly designed 115-inch-wheelbase chassis. The new 265 cubic-inch V8 was built with an eye to low cost rather than high performance. Yet some of the features that saved nickels boosted power, like the stamped-steel rocker arms of ball-stud construction. It had a 3.75-inch bore and a short three-inch stroke. With an 8.0:1 compression ratio, its rating was 162 horsepower at 4400 rpm. A "power pack" was also offered with a four-barrel carb and dual exhausts, good for 180 bhp at 4600.

One of the engine's most notable features was its ability to rev up fast, a benefit of its light valvetrain. This was of immediate interest to racers.

The stock-car world was in a state of change. The domination of the six-cylinder Hudson Hornet was at an end. The awesome Chrysler 300 was now the most powerful production car on the market, but it was expensive and not at home in short-track events or acceleration tests like drag racing. Ford had offered a V8 for many years, but had done little with it, as it had no competition in the low-priced field. So, there was a need for a low-cost car for racing that could approach the most powerful cars in performance at a fraction of the cost. The '55 Chevy was it.

The first big test for this upstart Chevrolet came at Daytona Beach, in the February Speed Weeks competition on the beach. Here, power-pack-equipped Chevys were in force. Cadillac won the acceleration tests, but Chevrolets placed second and third overall, beating out such big-engine makes as Chrysler and Buick.

In NASCAR Grand National racing, Chevrolets were usually no match for the big 300s on the long tracks, but did well on the shorter ones. Chevrolet advertised its relatively minor victories, and soon the nation knew about "The Hot One."

You couldn't stand still with the "horsepower race" going on, and Chevrolet didn't. Displacement re-

Chevrolet Performance

Year & Model		Engine (cid/bhp)	Curb Wt.[1]	lbs/ bhp[1]	0-60[2] (sec)	¼-mi.[2] (sec)	Base Price[3]
1956	150 2d sdn	265/225	3155	14.0	8.9	17.0	$1925
1957	Bel Air 4d htp	283/283	3550	13.1	9.9	17.5	$2464
1958	Bel Air Impala 2d htp	348/280	3669	13.1	9.1	16.5	$2693
1960	Impala 4d htp	348/305	3950	13.0	8.5	16.8	$2769
1961	Impala SS 2d htp	409/360	3700	10.3	7.8	15.8	$2704
1962	Impala SS 2d htp	409/409	3750	9.2	6.3	14.9	$2774
1962	Bel Air Super/Sport 2d htp	409/409	3500	8.6	4.0	12.2	NA
1963	Impala SS 2d htp	409/340	3877	11.4	6.6	15.2	$2786
1965	Impala Caprice 4d htp	396/325	4380	13.2	8.4	16.5	$3092
1966	Caprice 2d htp	427/390	4220	10.8	7.9	15.5	$3000
1967	Impala SS 2d htp	427/385	4200	10.9	8.4	15.8	$3003

[1]Advertised; [2]Typical acceleration based on contemporary tests; [3]Advertised list price in contemporary dollars; n = Net advertised horsepower; cid = cubic inch displacement; bhp = brake horsepower; conv = convertible; cpe = coupe; fastbk = fastback; htp = hardtop; rdstr = roadster (2-seat); sdn = sedan; d = number of doors.

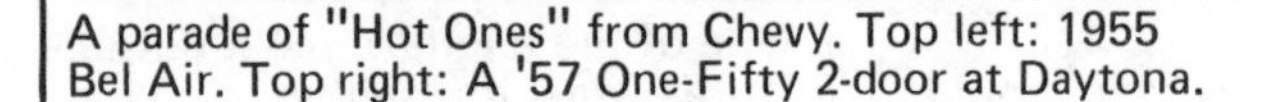

A parade of "Hot Ones" from Chevy. Top left: 1955 Bel Air. Top right: A '57 One-Fifty 2-door at Daytona. Bottom left: 1956 Bel Air Sport Sedan. Bottom right: 1957 Nomad.

mained the same on the facelifted '56 models, but power didn't. Upping the compression ratio and playing with the cam netted 205 bhp at the start of the model year for the hot setup. At mid-season, two four-barrel carbs and 225 bhp, again right out of the Corvette, upped the ante further. At the annual July 4th Pike's Peak hillclimb, a camouflaged '56 Chevy driven by engineer Zora Arkus-Duntov set a course record to win the stock-car division.

Indy legend Mauri Rose inked a contract to run Chevrolet's stock-car operation in NASCAR. Ford and Chrysler were also setting up factory-backed teams, touching off a scramble for drivers and mechanics. Chevy came up short, and got only three Grand National wins in 1956. It did win at Pike's Peak again, this time with Jerry Unser at the wheel. Like others, he drove the cheapest One-Fifty two-door sedan. Offering its hottest engine in its lightest models was to Chevy's advantage. Several makes took this route, while others, like Plymouth, didn't. There you could get the most powerful engine only in the top-line Fury.

There would be more checkered flags with the introduction of the 1957 models. A ⅛-inch bore increase brought displacement up to 283 cubic inches. A new mechanical fuel injection system plus a 10.5:1 compression ratio brought advertised horsepower up to 283 at a remarkable 6200 rpm. And Chevy *did* advertise it!

Ford pretty well walloped Chevy in NASCAR, taking 27 Grand National wins to Chevy's 18, though that figure was easily Chevy's best effort so far.

It has been said that perhaps the greatest thing ever to happen to the '57 Chevrolet was the 1958 model. To keep up with the competition, Chevrolet made it bigger, and introduced some new features which turned out to be unsuccessful. Wheelbase went up from 115 to 117.5 inches, length from 202.8 to 209.1, and width from 73.9 to 77.7. Average weight climbed nearly 100 pounds.

A 348 cubic-inch V8 was new at the top of the line, attached to the ill-fated Turboglide automatic transmission. This was a heavy powerplant originally designed for truck use, but with the low-priced competition going into the 350-cid area, its use in passenger cars was predictable. Two versions were on hand at the start of the model year.

It didn't take long for reports to come in from the dragstrips that the '57 Chevys were creaming the 348-cid '58s. There weren't many reports like that from the stock-car ovals, however, as few 1958s were raced. Most teams stuck with the lighter, better-handling '57s. Their success put Chevy on top in NASCAR for the first time, with 23 wins to 16 for runner-up Ford.

The '58 Chevrolet meanwhile turned out to be a one-year deal. Under GM's new corporate-wide body sharing program, Chevrolet got all-new styling again for '59.

There was plenty of power as well. The injected 283 was openly advertised with up to 290 bhp. The 348 also got some help. The 315-bhp police option was bettered at mid-year by a 320-horse four-barrel setup and a 335-bhp tri-carb option, both with 11.25:1 compression. To get the horses properly channeled, a Borg-Warner four-speed manual transmission, similar to the Corvette's, became an extra-cost item.

Fins were toned down for 1960, but there was little progress in the engine department. High-performance 283s were left to Corvette, and the 348 was now the lone power source.

Downsizing of a sort marked the 1961 Chevrolet. Wheelbase stayed the same, but size and weight shrunk, helping performance a bit. Frame design changed from X-brace to perimeter. Styling turned more conservative and smoother. Chevy was still in dire need of horsepower, though. Ford was up to 390 cubes, and Plymouth, Dodge, and Pontiac were all ready to go beyond 400. The 348 returned to start the model year. A four-barrel variation and one with tri-carbs delivered 340 and 350 bhp,

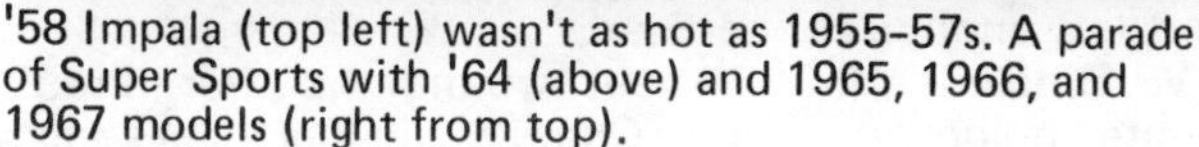

'58 Impala (top left) wasn't as hot as 1955-57s. A parade of Super Sports with '64 (above) and 1965, 1966, and 1967 models (right from top).

respectively, on paper. Chevy's ticket into the big-inch league came at mid-season with a bored-and-stroked 348, the soon-to-be-famous 409. At first it was equipped with a single four-barrel carb. Advertised power was conservatively pegged at 360. Also at roughly the same time a trim option for big-engine Impalas arrived, the Super Sport package. It was not tied to the 409.

Though the racers got their share of 409s, the public didn't. Manufacturing problems kept production very low. The bugs were squashed for 1962. Now two versions were available: a four-barrel at 380 bhp and a twin four-barrel unit with 409 bhp. Impala hardtops got more formal roof styling that resembled a convertible with the top up. This wasn't what the superspeedway racers wanted, but as luck would have it, the previous slantback smoothie was still around in the Bel Air series. Guess which one they used?

The Bel Airs took S/S and stock eliminator honors at the Nationals, and S/S laurels at the Winternationals, plus many drag trophies in between. On the '62 NASCAR circuit, Chevrolets won 14 events, most on the short tracks. Big-track events went to Pontiac, which took a total of 22 flags.

Chevy was ready for 1963, with a two-pronged attack that was supposed to help it in both NASCAR and drag competition. To start the model year, the 409's advertised output now topped out at 425 bhp.

The sleek Bel Air hardtop was gone, leaving only the squared-off Impala. That was used as the basis for RPO (Regular Production Option) Z-11, the drag racing package, about 100 of which were to be built for Super/Stock competition. It featured a hood, front fenders, front and rear bumpers and brackets, and other pieces made of aluminum. All extra insulation was left off, and weight came down 140 pounds. Other makes were doing similar things, but the Chevy ended up a bit heavier than the rest. Powering the Z-11 was a stroked version of the 409, coming right up to the new NHRA (and NASCAR) limit of 427 cid. With two four-barrels, it was rated at 430 bhp.

While the Z-11 was to be a production option, the new NASCAR engine was not. Of completely new design, this 427 powerhouse featured angled valves, thus earning the name "porcupine." There was a veil of secrecy surrounding this engine, and its non-production status raised all kinds of controversy. NASCAR legalized the setup because it thought a hot Chevy on the superspeedways would help bring in the fans.

All this might have worked out fine, except that GM's upper management told all divisions in early 1963 to cease all racing activity. Z-11 production stopped before enough had been made to make it legal in Super/Stock. Mystery-427 production also stopped, but not before the teams got enough to use for the 1963 season. Engineering development also stopped, of course, and the few teams using the 427 didn't have the know-how or the parts to do the job. While they ran, though, the 427 Chevys were the fastest cars on the track. Junior Johnson delighted the fans by winning two superspeedway races in a Chevrolet, a fourth of the eight wins Chevy scored that year.

After 1963, it was pretty well over for the big Chevrolet in stock-car and drag racing. It probably would have been in a year or two anyway, as intermediates were taking over. But the big Chevy was still good on the street. Through 1964 the 409 was the top engine, still with 425 advertised horses. The Super Sport became a distinct series in '64, still in hardtop and convertible form.

All-new styling marked the 1965 line. To start the year the 409 remained at the top of the list, but output was penciled in at 400 horses max. At mid-year it was replaced by a smaller version of the 1963 "mystery" engine, now at 396 cubes. Two ratings, 325 and 425 bhp, were shown.

A larger bore for '66 brought the 396 back to its original 427 size. Now rated at 390 and 425 bhp, it could be had in any full-size Chevy and the Corvette.

The big-block was sliced to a single 427 for 1968. This now pulled 385 bhp. The SS reverted to option status for the Impala.

Chevy's last stab at big-car muscle was 1969 with the SS-427 option for the Impala two-door hardtop and convertible. A 390-horse version of the 427 (RPO Z-24) was the heart of the package, and heavy-duty suspension and the usual external identification were included.

But the market for big supercars was long gone by now. Though Chevrolet would still have big-inch engines in the future (a 454 arrived for 1970), there was no further attempt to make the full-size Chevrolet a hot one.

Chevrolet Camaro

Chevrolet Camaro Performance

Year & Model		Engine (cid/bhp)	Curb Wt.[1]	lbs/ bhp[1]	0-60[2] (sec)	¼-mi.[2] (sec)	Base Price[3]
1967	SS-350 2d htp	350/295	3400	11.5	7.8	15.8	$2572
1967	SS 2d htp	396/325	3480	10.7	6.0	14.5	$2572
1967	Z-28 2d htp	302/290	3340	11.5	7.0	14.8	$2572
1969	SS 2d htp	396/375	3490	9.3	6.8	14.8	$2726
1970	Z-28 2d htp	350/360	3580	9.9	6.5	15.4	$2839
1974	Z-28 2d htp	350/245n	3640	14.9	8.1	15.4	$3159
1977	Z-28 2d htp	350/170n	3688	21.7	8.1	15.4	$5170
1979	Z-28 2d htp	350/170n	3560	20.9	8.5	16.4	$6115

[1]Advertised; [2]Typical acceleration based on contemporary tests; [3]Advertised list price in contemporary dollars; n = Net advertised horsepower; cid = cubic inch displacement; bhp = brake horsepower; conv = convertible; cpe = coupe; fastbk = fastback; htp = hardtop; rdstr = roadster (2-seat); sdn = sedan; d = number of doors.

Chevrolet was caught off guard by the success of the ponycar from Dearborn, so its sporty Camaro didn't arrive until the fall of 1966. Mustang was based heavily on existing components from the compact Falcon. The Camaro was a new design which would share pieces with a revamped Chevy II compact that would arrive a year later.

The '67 Camaro featured unitized construction with a bolt-on front sub-frame. Coil springs were mounted up front, and left enough width for a big-block V8. Single leaf springs, an unfortunate holdover from the Chevy II, suspended the live rear axle.

The engine lineup was extensive, with 230- and 250-cube sixes, two 327 V8s, and a new-size Chevy small-block, the 350, initially a Camaro exclusive. The 350 had a 0.23-inch longer stroke than the 327 from which it was derived. Rated at 295 advertised horsepower, you could only get it with the SS-350 package. SS cars had bumble-bee style stripes around the outside of the grille. Two body styles, a two-door hardtop and convertible, were offered, and a Rally Sport trim package was offered with all engines.

About two months after introduction, Chevy's big-block 396 joined the Camaro's option list, and was available only with the SS package. The SS-350 designation was dropped, and only SS was used after that. Further into the model year, the L-78 version of the 396 arrived. Because it was rated at 375 bhp, it violated GM's 10-pounds-per-horsepower rule, so technically it was listed as a dealer-installed option.

The most famous high-performance '67 Camaro was the

Top left: 1967 Camaro SS-350. Lower left: 1968 Z-28. Top right: Mark Donohue in the 1967 Penske Trans-Am car. Lower right: Big hood scoop and air dam marked '69 Z-28.

Lower left: Rally Sport was brought back for 1975.
Clockwise from top left: Z-28s for 1972, '77, and 1980.

least numerous. Only 602 hardtops with the Z-28 option were built. Production was deliberately limited because these were nearly race-ready flyers. Introduction came in late 1966.

The Z-28 was created to do battle in the Sports Car Club of America's Trans-American Championship. Rules called for a limit of 305 cubic inches for production engines. The 327 was the smallest Camaro V8, but it was obviously too large. Chevy still made the 283, but that was too small. The answer was to use the 283 crankshaft in the 327 block. This yielded 302 cubic inches, just about right. Chevy did the rest, coming up with a package that included heavy-duty suspension, cowl air intake, and even exhaust headers. A four-barrel carb was standard, but a kit with short ram-induction and two four-barrels was optional. Claimed output for the four-barrel 302 was 290 bhp, but that had no relationship to actual output.

Among early Z-28 "owners" were racers and race-car builders, including Pennsylvania Chevy dealer Roger Penske. He promptly set his up for the Trans-Am and other sports-car events. With development help from Chevrolet (which, of course, was officially not involved in racing), Penske and driver Mark Donohue got the bugs worked out of the Z-28, and won three Trans-Ams that season. Chevrolet finished third in points, behind winner Ford and runner-up Mercury.

Only minor alterations occurred for 1968 Camaros. Multi-leaf rear springs were now used on the more powerful models. The L-78 engine was back at the same 375 bhp, and was joined by the L-89 with aluminum cylinder heads. The Z-28 also returned with more racing-type options, but it no longer had the cowl air induction or headers. Chevy promoted the Z-28 a little, and production went up to 7199. Helping even more was its race record. Camaro won 10 of 13 Trans-Ams to take the manufacturers' title that year easily.

A variety of changes were made for 1969. There was noticeably altered sheetmetal and slightly increased length and width. Engines were shuffled. Two versions of the 350, at 250 and 300 bhp, plus a mid-year 307, wiped out the 327 V8. Four flavors of 396 could be had, with a new one at 350 bhp. Out for the last time was the 302-cube Z-28 engine. But all these stepped aside for the hottest production Camaro of all, the ZL-1. As Michael Lamm notes in his book *The Great Camaro*, 50 ZL-1s were made by the factory, mainly for drag racing. They came with an aluminum-block 427 with three two-barrels. Horsepower was mentioned as a ridiculous 425.

Production of the 1969 models continued through early calendar 1970, as the new second-generation design wasn't ready until then. Camaros controlled the Trans-Am again, taking the championship and eight of the dozen races. It was to be their last good season in the series.

The "real" 1970 models arrived in February of that year, and proved worth the wait. One body style was available, a semi-fastback coupe. Wheelbase was still 108 inches, length grew a couple of inches, and width was up a hair. Chassis design advanced. Styling looked advanced in 1970, and must have been, for it was retained with only modest alterations through 1981.

Engines were again shifted. SCCA changed its Trans-Am rules for the 1970 campaign to permit larger engines to be destroked to the limit. This allowed Chevy to use the 283 crank in the 350 block (which had the same bore as the 327), thus eliminating the need for the 302. The 350, rated at 360 bhp, was standard for Z-28, and was similar to the LT-1 Corvette engine. SS cars got a 300-horse version. Though advertised at 396 cubes, a bore increase now brought that engine to a true 402 cid. It was available in 350-bhp and L-78 375-bhp versions.

Model year 1971 marked the beginning of a downward slide for Camaro in the muscle-car world. All engines now had to run on low-test stuff, and some from 1970 didn't survive. A two-point drop in compression brought the Z-28 350 down to 330 bhp. Only one mild 402 was available, rated at 300 bhp, and there was no special stuff. Production hit an all-time low of 114,643, even less than the part-year 1970 run.

The worst year ever for Camaro was 1972. A strike halted production for almost one half of the model year, and production dipped to 68,656, the lowest annual total before or since. The industry's switch to net horsepower figures this year disguised some of the horsepower losses. The Z-28 went to 255, and the 402 was 15 below that.

With the sporty compact and performance markets both extremely soft, GM seriously considered dropping the Camaro and the companion Pontiac Firebird. But both cars had friends within GM, and production ultimately continued. Big-blocks became a thing of the past for 1973, and the SS option was gone, replaced by the more luxurious Type LT model. Power on the Z-28 was down to 245 bhp net. Hydraulic lifters replaced mechanicals on the 350, the aluminum high-rise intake manifold was gone, and the price of the whole Z-28 package dropped nearly $300 to just over $500. Camaro production went up slightly, but the 96,756 figure was not impressive. What *was* impressive was the rise in Z-28 production to 11,574 units, the highest since 1969.

New front and rear styling, featuring one-piece aluminum bumpers, marked the 1974 models. The Z-28 got bold graphics and wide stripes. Despite the problems for non-economy cars caused by the energy crisis, Camaro sales shot up, with production reaching 151,008, another high mark. Z-28 was up to 13,802. The Rally Sport was no longer available. Rather than dilute the Z-28 any further, management decided to drop it at the end of the model year.

Camaro returned for 1975, and only one other original ponycar, Pontiac Firebird, could make that statement. A wraparound rear window improved side vision. Powerplant offerings were the skimpiest yet, a six, and 145- or 155-horse 350 V8s. The Rally Sport option returned at mid-year with striking two-tone paint.

No major changes occurred for 1976, except that you could now get a 305-cid variation of the small-block V8. It was not a performance engine, with only 140 net horses. Demand increased as the market recovered from the effects of a recession and the fuel crisis. Production hit 182,981.

The 1977 models were also apparently little changed. The top engine, the 350-cube LM-1, now put out five more horses (170), but that was about it. A mid-year option, however, put Camaro back in the performance game. Though the Z-28 had been gone for two years, Pontiac never retired its Firebird Trans-Am, and had been selling a bundle despite what the market experts had forecast. Because of this, the Z-28 returned for 1977½. To back up its stripes, it pulled 185 net horses from the 350, yet met the strict emission standards. Dual exhausts helped, and without large mufflers they sounded neat. A four-speed Borg-Warner T-10 transmission was available. Most of the work on the Z-28 went into its suspension. It was actually engineered for good handling, and was not just a set of heavy-duty springs and shocks. Despite the late start, 14,349 Z-28s were made, second only to the long 1969 model run. Camaro production as a whole jumped to 218,854, also the best since 1969.

A rubberized nose and coated rear bumper distinguished the 1978 models, a look that would be continued through 1981, the last of this line. The engine lineup remained mostly the same, which was just fine with buyers. An all-time record 272,633 of the '78s were sold, despite the advanced age of the basic shape.

Tougher emission standards for '79 cost the 49-state Z-28 10 horses. Output was now down to 175 bhp net. Output from the production line was up again to 282,582, another record.

The Z-28 got stronger for 1980. While California customers had to be content with a 305 V8 and 165 bhp, buyers in other states got a healthier 350 with 190 bhp. Unfortunately, sales were not as healthy. Another fuel crisis had hit, and Camaro was wounded this time. Competition from more economical U.S. and import cars was too much, and production fell to 152,021, the worst since '75.

At this writing, '81 Camaro sales aren't doing well either, but this won't have any effect on the car's fate, for it's already sealed. For 1982, Camaro will be downsized with a new chassis and hatchback body. The rear leaf springs will be replaced by coils, and rear drive will continue. So will V8s, at least for a while.

Chevrolet Chevelle

In the first half of the 1960s, the domestic auto market scattered in several directions—compacts, sporty compacts, intermediates, personal-luxury cars. And in almost every direction, you could find a Chevrolet model. Chevrolet fielded the Chevelle for the intermediate segment.

At first, Chevelle followed the lead of early intermediates from Rambler and Ford by offering both six-cylinder engines and small-displacement V8s. There was a wide variety of body styles, including sedans, wagons, two-door hardtops, and convertibles for the inaugural 1964 line. Topping it were the Super Sport hardtop and ragtop.

Early in the model run, a 220-horsepower 283 V8 topped the power pole, but in December the larger 327-cid version of Chevrolet's small-block joined the slate as 250- and 300-bhp horse screamers. After that, a 365-horse screamer, right out of the Corvette, was offered to counteract Pontiac's popular GTO option.

Performance options for 1965

Chevrolet Chevelle Performance

Year	Model	Engine (cid/bhp)	Curb Wt.[1]	lbs/ bhp[1]	0-60[2] (sec)	¼-mi.[2] (sec)	Base Price[3]
1964	Malibu SS 2d htp	283/195	3260	16.7	9.7	17.4	$2590
1965	Malibu SS-396 2d htp	396/375	3650	9.7	6.5	14.9	$2590
1966	SS-396 2d htp	396/360	3800	10.6	7.9	15.5	$2776
1967	SS-396 2d htp	396/375	3850	10.3	6.5	14.9	$2825
1969	SS-396 2d htp	396/375	3900	10.4	7.6	15.4	$2673
1970	SS-396 2d htp	402/350	3990	11.4	8.1	15.5	$2809
1970	SS-454 2d htp	454/450	4000	8.9	6.0	13.8	$2809
1973	Laguna 2d sdn	454/245n	4225	17.2	8.0	15.7	$3147

[1]Advertised; [2]Typical acceleration based on contemporary tests; [3]Advertised list price in contemporary dollars; n = Net advertised horsepower; cid = cubic inch displacement; bhp = brake horsepower; conv = convertible; cpe = coupe; fastbk = fastback; htp = hardtop; rdstr = roadster (2-seat); sdn = sedan; d = number of doors.

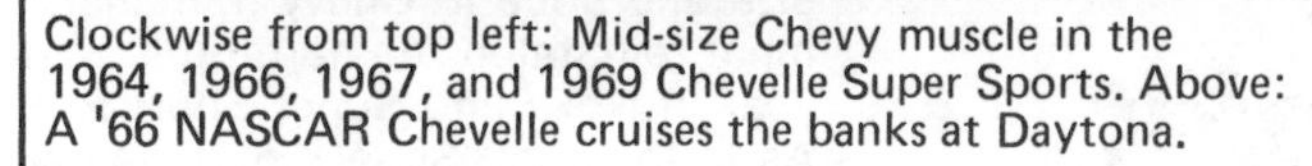

Clockwise from top left: Mid-size Chevy muscle in the 1964, 1966, 1967, and 1969 Chevelle Super Sports. Above: A '66 NASCAR Chevelle cruises the banks at Daytona.

again came in three waves. First was the 300-horse 327, then a 350-bhp 327 (a fact Chevrolet openly advertised this time). Finally, late in the year, came one of the hottest Chevelles of all time, the Z-16.

A special run of nearly 200 cars had this rip-roaring RPO. All were two-door hardtops with special trim, heavy-duty suspension, a 160-mile speedometer, and most important, a 375-bhp version of the new big-block 396. The combo added $1501.05 to the sticker price, and took seconds off the acceleration times. Allocation was supposed to be limited to Chevrolet officials (division general manager Bunkie Knudsen had a personalized one), but some were also sold to ordinary people.

There was no limited availability of the 396 the following year: SS-396 replaced the plain Super Sport series. Standard power was 325 bhp, and a 360-bhp setup was optional.

While competition from Ford, Chrysler, and even American Motors increased for 1967, several General Motors cars lost horses that year. The reason was a GM rule that no car, except Corvette, could have engines putting out more than one horsepower for every 10 pounds of automobile. The SS-396 was one of several victims of the edict.

Like other GM intermediates, the 1968 Chevelle came in two sizes. Two-doors had a 112-inch wheelbase, and four doors got a 116-inch spread. The Super Sport 396 still sat atop the model lineup, and 350 bhp was still tops. Now that some time had passed since the power-to-weight rule was issued, the 375s returned.

Little was changed for 1969, except that the SS-396 became an option rather than a separate model. The SS-396 was still an option for the top-line Malibu two-door hardtop and convertible, only you didn't get a true 396. A slight bore increase brought displacement up to an actual 402 cubes. Standard output was up to 350 bhp. This is not to be confused with the new 400 V8, which was simply the largest extension of

Above: Last blast for Chevelle Super Sport came in 1970 when Chevy offered a huge 450-bhp 454-cid V8. Performance tailed off rapidly after that. Right: Laguna Type S-3 (1975 shown) became popular as a NASCAR racer in the late 1970s.

the small-block. It put out 330 bhp and was not an SS engine. The big wallop came in the SS-454, based on the biggest big-block.

And that was only a warmup. Word leaked during the 1970 model year that all 1971 engines would have to run on regular or no-lead gas. That translated to lower compression ratios, detuning, and a drop in performance. As one last fling, Chevrolet offered the LS6, a no-holds barred 454 with 450 bhp.

After this last blast, the letdown was swift and deep. First off, the Super Sport option could be had with any V8 for '71, right down to the 307. Next, as threatened, compression ratios were cut. The rating on the 402 came down to 300 bhp, and the 454 was now pegged at 365. Though not promoted, the LS6 was still around, but down to 425 horses. Compression ratio was 9.0:1. A mid-year option was the "Heavy Chevy" package, which offered the performance look without a big-inch engine. Actually the SS was at that stage already.

Along with most other domestic cars, Chevelle's performance capabilities decreased with each ensuing model year. Net horsepower ratings for 1972 helped take the edge off the drop in output, though this temporarily confused some buyers.

The SS took its curtain call for 1973 on the Malibu two-door coupe. Styling was all-new, with only pillared coupes, sedans, and wagons available. Rating for the 454 was down to 245 bhp net. Both the 400 and 402 were gone.

By 1973, the muscular middleweights had died off. However, Chevrolet didn't let the ball drop entirely. Replacing SS was a new sports-oriented package, the Laguna Type S-3, which was a separate model, not just an option. At first this meant mainly a rubberized front end and fancier trim, but the 1975 edition got a sloped nose, too. It was an immediate hit in NASCAR, especially for superspeedway use, and continued through 1976. It was dropped in Chevelle's last year, 1977. Interestingly, the 454 was listed through 1975. Chevelle was downsized to a 108-inch wheelbase for '78 and retitled Malibu. No performance versions were offered.

Chevrolet Chevy II/ Nova

By late 1960, it was apparent that Chevrolet's Corvair couldn't handle the Ford Falcon in the sales race. So, a conventional economy compact was devised for 1962. Called Chevy II, it followed the Falcon by offering two- and four-door sedans and wagons, plus a hardtop and convertible. All were available with simple, economy-oriented four- and six-cylinder engines mounted in front.

Mid-way through the 1963 model run, parts were offered through Chevy dealers to convert the Chevy II to 283 or 327 V8 power. About the only real problem with this involved the single-leaf rear springs, which were prone to twist under the higher torque loading of the V8s.

For 1964 Chevy II gained its first production-line V8, a 195-horse 283, but lost its two-door hardtop and convertible models. Chevy had launched its Chevelle intermediate that season, and didn't want similar Chevy II styles to steal sales. With word that Ford would be bringing out the Mustang, a car very close in size and price to Chevy II, management reinstated the hardtop at mid-year in Nova and Super Sport trim. As in the past, Super Sport was an option package. Also added was a four-barrel version of the 283, producing 220 bhp, and this model's first four-speed manual trans.

Chevrolet's direct reply to the Mustang was still a couple of years away, and the Corvair was short on power and favor with the public. So, Chevy II would have to carry the performance ball in the sporty-compact

Chevy small-block was heart of Chevy II's muscle for (clockwise from lower left) 1966, 1965, and 1967. Big-block 396 could be had in 1969 Chevy Nova (lower right).

Chevy II/Nova Performance

Year & Model		Engine (cid/bhp)	Curb Wt.[1]	lbs/ bhp[1]	0-60[2] (sec)	¼-mi.[2] (sec)	Base Price[3]
1964	Nova SS 2d htp	283/195	3000	15.4	11.3	18.0	$2433
1966	Nova SS 2d htp	327/275	3040	11.0	8.6	16.4	$2535
1966	Nova SS 2d htp	327/350	3140	9.0	7.2	15.1	$2535
1968	Nova SS 2d sdn	327/325	3400	10.5	8.7	16.5	$2389
1971	Nova SS 2d sdn	350/270	3450	12.8	8.5	15.9	$2462

[1]Advertised; [2]Typical acceleration based on contemporary tests; [3]Advertised list price in contemporary dollars; n = Net advertised horsepower; cid = cubic inch displacement; bhp = brake horsepower; conv = convertible; cpe = coupe; fastbk = fastback; htp = hardtop; rdstr = roadster (2-seat); sdn = sedan; d = number of doors.

field. That was even more evident with the 1965 models, which were little changed in styling from the first '62. Topping the option list were two versions of Chevy's biggest small-block engine, the 327. Ratings were 250 and 300 bhp, the latter 29 horsepower higher than Mustang's hottest production mill.

New sheetmetal and more horsepower made the 1966 Chevy II look newer and go faster. You could now get the 350-bhp 327 found in Corvettes (a milder 275-bhp version was also available).

With that kind of power and a 3100-pound curb weight, the Chevy II made it to muscle city. *Car Life* magazine revealed a four-speed Super Sport could do the quarter mile in 15.1 seconds at 93 mph, do 0–60 mph in 7.2 seconds, and top out at 123 mph.

A demotion came for 1967. Camaro was the new star, so Chevy II lost its 350-horse option. It did keep the 275-bhp 327.

At first it looked like the all-new 1968 Chevy II would be the least sporty yet. Only two body styles were available, sedans with two and four doors. Wheelbase went up from 110 to 111 inches, length from 183 to 189.3, and width from 71.3 to 72.4. Weight was up by more than 200 pounds, and the Super Sport reverted to option status. But the new chassis design direct from the 1967 Camaro was encouraging. The front suspension and sub-frame were new, allowing room for Chevrolet's big-blocks for the first time. Initial engine options went up to the 275-horse 327 and 295-bhp 350.

Then, "budget" muscle cars were suddenly in style, due mainly to Plymouth's Road Runner. Again, Chevy II got the call to battle. A number of mid-year options appeared including the hot 327, downgraded to a rated 325 bhp to satisfy GM brass, and the first big-block, the 396, also suspiciously rated at 325. In testing a 1968 SS-396 Chevy II Nova, *Car Life* stated it was "quick in a straight line, but ill-suited to anything else."

Minor changes were all the 1969 models were due. Officially, the name was now Nova. From the sales catalogs you'd think the most powerful engine was the 300-bhp 350. Not so. Though Chevy didn't advertise the fact, you could still get the 396, including the L-78 option with 375 bhp.

For 1970 the SS package with 300 horses was as hot as Nova was supposed to get. But through Chevrolet's fleet-order program there were big-block Novas around.

The 1971 models were nearly identical to the 1968s, and the "double standard" ended as the 350 was shown as the largest engine, in and out of the sales catalogs.

Though out of the muscle-car class now, Nova continued to be a good compact performer through the '70s. In one form or another, the 350 was available through its last model year, 1979. The Super Sport (SS) option continued through 1976.

Chevrolet Corvair

With its air-cooled, rear-mounted six-cylinder engine, Chevrolet's first modern compact, the Corvair, cannot be considered a true muscle car in any of its guises. But there were some Corvairs capable of above-average performance, and worthy of note.

Corvair was one of the Big Three compacts introduced for 1960. Compared to the Ford Falcon and Chrysler Corporation's Valiant, its engineering was easily the most radical. Originally it had a 140-cid powerplant with 80 horsepower. Later in its first model year a power pack was offered good for 95 bhp.

Falcon easily outsold Corvair in the early months, as the public was not quite ready for such an unusual design from Detroit. Then at mid-year, the Monza 900 version of the Corvair coupe appeared. It had bucket seats, floor shift, and tastefully reserved trim. While the average buyer might not have been so game, the young buyers of the day were, and the Monza finally got Corvair sales in gear.

Early Corvairs, despite their sporty leanings, lacked power. Displacement grew to 145 cubes for 1961, and at the start of the 1962 series you could get up to 102 bhp—still not enough. Early in calendar '62 a convertible joined the Monza line, as did an option that would make it and the coupe much improved performers.

The most interesting part of this new Spyder package was its turbocharged engine. Horsepower went up to 150, making for more than one horsepower per cubic inch. Torque also shot up from 134 lbs-ft to 210. Other equipment included full instrumentation and special trim.

A longer stroke brought displacement up to 164 cubes for 1964, but Spyder output remained at 150 bhp. The Spyder was considered a separate model now instead of an option. Also notable for that year was a revised rear suspension on all Corvairs for more stable cornering.

Corvair got the only restyling of its career for 1965. Lines were more flowing, and pillars were eliminated to create a line of two- and four-door hardtops. Spyder was renamed Corsa, and convertibles were still of-

Chevrolet Corvair Performance

Year & Model		Engine (cid/bhp)	Curb Wt.[1]	lbs/ bhp[1]	0-60[2] (sec)	¼-mi.[2] (sec)	Base Price[3]
1962	Monza Spyder 2d conv	145/150	2570	17.1	12.1	18.5	$2779
1965	Corsa 2d htp	164/180	2540	14.1	10.9	18.1	$2465

[1]Advertised; [2]Typical acceleration based on contemporary tests; [3]Advertised list price in contemporary dollars; n = Net advertised horsepower; cid = cubic inch displacement; bhp = brake horsepower; conv = convertible; cpe = coupe; fastbk = fastback; htp = hardtop; rdstr = roadster (2-seat); sdn = sedan; d = number of doors.

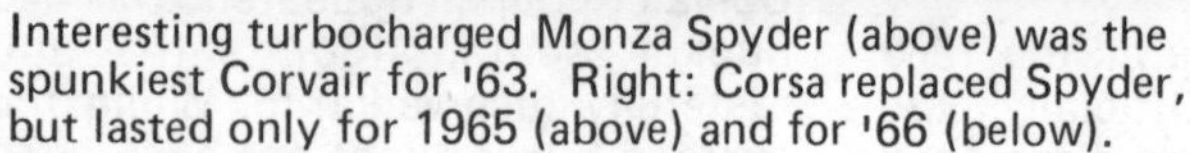

Interesting turbocharged Monza Spyder (above) was the spunkiest Corvair for '63. Right: Corsa replaced Spyder, but lasted only for 1965 (above) and for '66 (below).

fered. Standard for Corsa was a 140-horse version of the 164 with four one-barrel carbs. The turbocharged unit, now at 180 horsepower, was optional.

Corsa returned for 1966, but Corvair was in deep trouble. Mustangs were faster, and after 10,472 Corsas were made, the series was dropped. One reason for this was that Chevy didn't want any in-house competition for its new Camaro. At first, the 110-bhp engine was the peppiest available for 1967. Later, the 140 four-carb unit returned to the option list, and remained there to the end of the line, which came in May of 1969.

Chevrolet Corvette

Corvette is thought of primarily as a sports car, not a muscle car. However, it has followed muscle-car philosophy throughout its existence by offering large amounts of power at relatively low cost. Besides, no book on performance cars would be complete without it.

After successful public response to the Corvette show car, Chevrolet put the two-place design into production in late 1953. Just 300 were made. Chevrolet's 235.5 cubic-inch inline six was used, with three sidedraft carburetors and a rating of 150 bhp. The body was made of fiberglass. The frame, with a 102-inch wheelbase, was similar in concept to that of the regular passenger cars, with coil springs up front and leafs in the rear. All this didn't exactly excite the sports-car set, especially the fact that only the two-speed Powerglide automatic was available.

The 1954 models and first half of 1955 production continued with the six/automatic setup. Midway through the year, however, Corvette took a giant step forward with the availability of Chevrolet's new 195-bhp 265-cid V8. Also available, in limited numbers, was a three-speed manual transmission. The V8 weighed slightly less than the six, and was much more powerful.

A redesigned body and stronger horses marked the 1956 models, which were starting to show the imprint of the brilliant engineer, Zora Arkus-Duntov. Duntov would guide the Corvette's evolution from boulevard cruiser to one of the top sports/racing machines in the world.

Chevrolet Corvette Performance

Year & Model		Engine (cid/bhp)	Curb Wt.[1]	lbs/ bhp[1]	0-60[2] (sec)	¼-mi.[2] (sec)	Base Price[3]
1954	STD 2d rdstr	235/150	2800	18.7	11.5	18.0	$3513
1956	STD 2d conv	265/240	2910	12.1	6.3	15.0	$3144
1957	STD 2d conv	283/283	2950	10.4	6.4	14.4	$3465
1959	STD 2d conv	283/250	2940	11.8	7.6	15.6	$3875
1961	STD 2d conv	283/315	3040	9.7	5.5	14.2	$3934
1962	STD 2d conv	327/360	3080	8.6	5.9	14.9	$4038
1963	Sting Ray 2d cpe	327/360	3150	8.8	5.8	14.5	$4252
1964	Sting Ray 2d cpe	327/375	3100	8.3	6.3	14.6	$4252
1965	Sting Ray 2d conv	396/425	3260	7.7	6.0	14.1	$4022
1966	Sting Ray 2d conv	427/425	3360	7.7	5.7	14.0	$4084
1967	Sting Ray 2d conv	427/435	3340	7.7	5.5	13.8	$4141
1968	STD 2d conv	327/350	3445	9.8	7.1	15.0	$4241
1968	STD 2d conv	427/435	3500	8.0	6.3	14.1	$4241
1970	Stingray 2d cpe	350/370	3335	9.0	5.7	14.2	$5469
1972	Stingray 2d cpe	454/270n	3725	13.8	6.8	14.1	$5472
1972	Stingray 2d cpe	350/255n	3356	13.2	6.9	14.3	$5472
1973	Stingray 2d cpe	454/275n	3725	13.5	6.8	14.1	$5562
1973	Stingray 2d cpe	350/250n	3356	13.4	7.3	14.3	$5562
1975	Stingray 2d cpe	350/165n	3400	20.6	9.6	16.4	$6810
1977	Stingray 2d cpe	350/210n	3575	17.0	8.8	16.6	$8647
1979	STD 2d cpe	350/225n	3608	16.0	7.3	15.7	$10,515
1980	STD 2d cpe	350/190	3519	18.5	8.1	16.2	$13,140

[1]Advertised; [2]Typical acceleration based on contemporary tests; [3]Advertised list price in contemporary dollars; n = Net advertised horsepower; cid = cubic inch displacement; bhp = brake horsepower; conv = convertible; cpe = coupe; fastbk = fastback; htp = hardtop; rdstr = roadster (2-seat); sdn = sedan; d = number of doors.

There was a choice of a four-barrel 265 at 210 horses, or a twin four-barrel at 225.

A stroke increase enlarged the 265 to 283 cid for 1957, and brought with it Chevrolet's new Rochester mechanical fuel injection. The injection versions offered 250 and 283 bhp, or you could get four-barrel and dual four-barrel setups. Also notable was the first appearance of a four-speed manual transmission.

Top power output rose to 290 horses for 1958–59, then jumped to 315 for 1960–61, all from the 283. Basic styling remained the same through 1960. The rear end got a "ducktail" cutoff design for 1961.

The 1962 models meant more than the end of the line for the old Corvette design. It also was the first year for a larger version of the small-block V8, the 327, which had a larger bore and stroke than the venerable 283. Horsepower rose, with the injection engine topping the list at 360 bhp. A trio of four-barrel versions were rated at 250, 300, and 340 bhp.

The 327 was one of the few things to return for 1963 as Corvette underwent the most dramatic changes in its history. Two Sting Ray models, a convertible and fastback coupe, replaced the previous roadster. Wheelbase contracted to 98 inches. Independent rear suspension, with a cross-leaf rear spring, replaced the solid axle, and the frame design was altered. Bodies were still fiberglass. The radical new styling wowed the press and public alike. A newcomer to the race tracks, Carroll Shelby's Ford-powered Cobra threatened to spoil the Chevy show. To meet this hybrid sports-car challenger head on, a few rebels within Chevy engineering created a lightweight version of the Sting Ray, the Grand Sport, just for racing. General Motors, however, cracked down on such things in early 1963, so only five Grand Sports were actually completed. They raced with some distinction in private hands, but couldn't beat the Cobras.

Output from the 327 grew to a remarkable 375 bhp with injection for 1964. For 1965, Chevrolet's new Mark IV big-block appeared, sized at 396 cubes that year only and rated at 425 bhp.

More bore brought the 396 up to 427 cubes for 1966, but the advertised power output remained the same. The addition of 100 cubic inches over the original Sting Ray was some help on the race tracks, but not as much as the end of Cobra production in 1967. The advent of the 427 also spelled the end of the fuel-injection system on small-block Corvettes after '65.

For some reason, GM policy dictated that all its cars, except Corvette, had to lose their multi-carb setups for '67. Corvette hadn't had one for years, but the 427 now gained three two-barrels, boosting output to 435 bhp.

For 1968 there was an all-new body on the same basic chassis as before. Replacing the fastback was a notchback hardtop with "flying buttress" sail panels and a T-top

"Fuelie" 283 made '57 Corvette (top left) very rapid. Power rose for 1958 (middle left). '62 shows "ducktail" rear (lower left). Right: Sting Ray has become a near classic today ('65 top, '67 middle). Current 'Vette appeared for '68 (bottom).

Top left: 1970 Corvette. Bottom left: New nose was added for '73. Top right: 1977 Corvette. Bottom right: 1980 Corvette. Fastback came along for 1978.

roof. The convertible was retained. Not much happened under the hood.

Several versions of the 427 were available for 1969, including the 430-horse L-88 and the 435-horse L-89 with aluminum heads. But the biggest blaster was the ZL-1. This featured both aluminum block *and* heads, and cost an astounding $3000.

On paper at least, the most powerful Corvette ever came along in 1970 when the 427 grew into the rumbling 454. The most muscular version, the LS-7, was supposed to be available with 465 big ones, but after a few pilot models GM abandoned production. This left the 390-bhp LS-5 as the top dog.

All powerplants for 1971 had to run on regular or no-lead fuel, and Corvette wasn't exempt from this management edict. The most powerful offering was the LS-6 at 425 bhp, the toughest small-block the mechanical-lifter LT-1 at 330. Starting with the 1969 models, 350-cid engines had replaced the 327 as the Corvette small-block.

Net output figures replaced gross horsepower for 1972, magnifying the tumble of numbers that started the year before. The lone 454 was now rated at 270 bhp net.

The LT-1 was gone for 1973, and the top small-block now put out 250 net horses. After 1974, all the big-blocks vanished, so the 350 had to satisfy both customers and the government's increasingly tough emission standards.

Chevrolet went about as far as it could in putting hot engines into later Corvettes. It kept the L-82 350 above 200 bhp through 1980, when it was rated at 230. In that year, California customers had to make do with a 305 V8. For 1981, there was one engine for all, a milder version of the L-82, dubbed L-81. It has a stainless-steel exhaust manifold and a power rating of 190 bhp net. While the '81 will rank as one of the lesser Corvettes in performance, it's the fastest thing coming out of a U.S. factory in today's market.

Chevrolet Monte Carlo

Chevrolet's personal-luxury Monte Carlo was born at its performance peak. And although you might not think so, it got into the muscle-car act. Based on the new 1969 Pontiac Grand Prix, Monte Carlo appeared for 1970. Both models were based on a stretched intermediate platform. Wheelbase was 116 inches, and the Monte's overall length was 205.8. By comparison, Chevelle two-doors had a 112-inch wheelbase and a length of 197.2. Widths were very close. The Monte Carlo came out about 150 pounds heavier than a similarly equipped Chevelle.

The most potent 1970 model was the SS version. Its standard engine was a 360-horse 454, Chevrolet's biggest-displacement powerplant. All Monte Carlos had V8s. Only automatic trans was available, but four-speeds could be teamed with lesser engines. With a 0–60 mph capability of 7.7 seconds in loaded form, according to *Car Life* magazine figures, it ranked just behind the true muscle cars of the era.

The final SS equipment, which also included heavy-duty suspension, was seen in the 1971 model year. Despite a required drop in compression, advertised horsepower on the 454 went up slightly to 365. The SS group was withdrawn for 1972, but the 454 was still

Chevrolet Monte Carlo Performance

Year & Model	Engine (cid/bhp)	Curb Wt.[1]	lbs/ bhp[1]	0-60[2] (sec)	¼-mi.[2] (sec)	Base Price[3]
1970 STD 2d htp	454/360	4140	11.5	7.7	16.2	$3123

[1]Advertised; [2]Typical acceleration based on contemporary tests; [3]Advertised list price in contemporary dollars; n = Net advertised horsepower; cid = cubic inch displacement; bhp = brake horsepower; conv = convertible; cpe = coupe; fastbk = fastback; htp = hardtop; rdstr = roadster (2-seat); sdn = sedan; d = number of doors.

Monte Carlo (1970 model above) became favorite of drivers like Bobby Allison (right). Below: a trio of NASCAR MCs.

available, now at 270 bhp net horsepower. Chevrolet was concentrating on plush rather than push, and would from then on out.

Surprisingly, Monte Carlo became an extremely popular choice for stock-car racing. Short-track racers had discovered early that its engine sat further back in the chassis relative to overall length, making for more even front/rear weight distribution than in the shorter Chevelle.

Even though it left something to be desired in aerodynamics on the big tracks, Monte Carlo was nearly unbeatable on the shorter ones, and brought Chevrolet's victory total up from nowhere. After factory help ended in 1963, Chevy won eight Grand Nationals through 1970. From 1971 through '79, 98 wins went to Chevrolet, most of them scored by Monte Carlos.

Oldsmobile

If you had to credit one car with starting the postwar "horsepower race," it would have to be the 1949 Oldsmobile 88. A modern overhead-valve with 135 horsepower in a 3500-pound, lower-medium-priced car would set America's pulse racing faster than ever.

Over the years, fours, sixes, V8s, and straight eights have all been used in Oldsmobiles. Shortly before World War II, Oldsmobile and Cadillac had been working independently on new overhead-valve V8s. Cadillac's engine would go into all its models, while Oldsmobile's would go only into its top-line 98 series. Smaller models would still have the venerable flathead six.

The new Olds powerplant was unveiled in 1949. It was a short-stroke design, with a bore of 3.75 inches and a 3.4375-inch stroke for less piston travel per mile. Bore centers were widely spaced to assume plenty of room to grow. Compression ratio, at 7.25:1, took care of the needs of the day, and there was enough beef down under for the higher compression needed for higher-octane fuels in the future. With a 125-inch wheelbase and weight not far below two tons, the V8-powered 98s promised to be fairly good performing big cars.

Then a last-minute decision made the V8 proposition even more interesting. The "Rocket," as it was called, would also go into the lesser Olds models based on General Motors' A-body, shared with Pontiac and Chevrolet. The new series would be dubbed 88, with a 119.5-inch wheelbase and weight in the 3500–3600-pound range.

The importance of the Oldsmobile 88 cannot be overstated. Up until that time, only the more expensive cars had the biggest and most powerful engines, and usually the highest top speeds.

Hydra-matic transmission was standard for the 88, which hurt its performance potential somewhat. Helping it was a variety of body styles. The club coupe weighed 3550 pounds, and the fastback club sedan only 35 pounds more. Also, a nifty convertible and a couple of

Oldsmobile Performance

Year & Model		Engine (cid/bhp)	Curb Wt.[1]	lbs/ bhp[1]	0-60[2] (sec)	¼-mi.[2] (sec)	Base Price[3]
1949	88 4d sdn	303/135	3615	26.8	12.2	19.9	$2244
1952	Super 88 4d sdn	303/160	3649	22.8	14.0	19.0	$2462
1954	Super 88 4d sdn	324/170	3780	22.2	12.4	18.0	$2477
1955	Super 88 4d sdn	324/202	3762	18.6	10.6	17.6	$2503
1956	Super 88 4d htp	324/240	3869	16.1	10.8	17.8	$2881
1957	Super 88 4d htp	371/300	4117	13.7	9.1	17.3	$3257
1958	Super 88 4d htp	371/305	4073	13.4	8.7	17.3	$3339

[1]Advertised; [2]Typical acceleration based on contemporary tests; [3]Advertised list price in contemporary dollars; n = Net advertised horsepower; cid = cubic inch displacement; bhp = brake horsepower; conv = convertible; cpe = coupe; fastbk = fastback; htp = hardtop; rdstr = roadster (2-seat); sdn = sedan; d = number of doors.

four-door models were available, plus a wagon.

There weren't many auto enthusiast publications in 1949, but there *was* a new stock-car sanctioning body in Daytona Beach, the National Association for Stock Car Racing (NASCAR). Operated by a former race driver, Bill France, it sought to bring organization to the sport, and promote competition among new production cars. A race for the late-models was held on the oval track at Daytona, consisting of part paved road and part beach. Red Byron won the event in a '49 88. A total of eight races were held that year, all called Grand Nationals. Oldsmobile took five of them (two by Byron), leaving two to Lincoln and one to Plymouth. Byron scored the most points, and became the first Grand National champion. A 1949 Oldsmobile also paced the Indianapolis 500 that year, giving further exposure to the new star of the performance world.

For 1950, a two-door hardtop and sedan joined the 88 lineup. Three-speed manual transmissions were advertised, but hard to come by.

Grand National was growing in popularity, with 19 events being held in 1950. Olds took 10, and Bill Rexford took the driving crown, marking the second time in two years the champ was Rocket-powered.

As it turned out, 1950 would be the competition highpoint for the Rocket 88. Its two years of going almost unchallenged were over when the 1951 models appeared.

Olds didn't exactly help itself by dropping the club coupe, fastback, and two-door hardtop from the 88 line. The new 1951 Super 88 was mounted on a 120-inch wheelbase, and used the GM B-body shared with the smaller Buicks.

Olds started off the '51 season pretty good, despite Marshall Teague's Daytona win in a Hornet. But as the year wore on, it became apparent that Hudson's handling, plus help from the factory in the form of heavy-duty parts, was too much for Olds in stock-car racing. However, Olds had its best year ever in NASCAR, taking 20 wins in 41 starts.

"Oldsmobile Rockets to New Highs" proclaimed the literature for the 1952 lineup. On a couple of points, like horsepower and weight, it was right. With three years under its belt at the original 135-bhp rating, the Rocket now got a boost. A new four-barrel "Quadra-Jet" carburetor and valve improvements brought horsepower up to 160 for the Super 88 and 98. The base 88 was dubbed Deluxe 88, and came with the two-barrel 145-bhp version. Both 88 series now rode the 120-inch wheelbase and carried the B-body.

Despite having more power, Oldsmobile was no match for the fine handling of the Hudsons in NASCAR. The win total dropped from 20 to three, while the Hornets zoomed from 12 to 27 of the 34 events. Olds did nail down a big one, however, the Southern 500 at Darlington on Labor Day.

Compression ratios jumped to

Top left: 1949 "Futuramic" 88. Top right: 1950 Futuramic 88 Holiday; Center: Olds dominated early stock-car racing. Lower left: 1951 Super 88. Lower right: 1954 88.

8.0:1, the first increase since 1951, for the 1953 Oldsmobiles. That brought power on the Super 88 and 98 up to 165 and to 150 on the Deluxe 88.

Hudson was now heavily promoting its stock-car victories before a more performance-conscious buying public. Olds finally realized the value of what it once had, and took steps to regain its position in stock competition. Using the Hudson system, it announced six different heavy-duty parts packages, complete with parts numbers, all aimed at racing. Included were modifications to engine, differential, axle, radiator, suspension, and fuel tank.

The packages were all approved, and a half-dozen beefed-up 1953s invaded Daytona Beach in February to take home the marbles—which they did. Bob Pronger shattered the flying-mile record with a run of 113.38 mph in his two-door sedan. Acceleration (standing-start mile) competition was added this year, and Pronger took that too, averaging 74.41 mph. In the 160-mile Grand National race on the 4.1-mile beach-road course, Pronger rolled his mount, but fellow Olds driver Bill Blair kept everything under control and went on to win. Olds won the Southern 500 again, too, its second straight. Buck Baker did the honors this time. The packages helped Oldsmobile triple its winnings from 1952, taking nine. The bad news for Rocket fans was that out of the 37 GN events Hudson took 22.

Almost everything was changed on the 1954 Olds. Bodies were completely new, with the wraparound or "panoramic" windshield the most noticeable feature. All 88s now rode a longer 122-inch wheelbase. Thanks to an ⅛-inch bore enlargement, the Rocket got its first displacement increase, now 324.3 cubes, a couple more than Buick and not far from Cadillac. The plain old 88 came with a two-barrel carb and 170 bhp, while Super 88 and 98 models got the quad and a 185-bhp rating. All engines now had a higher 8.25:1 compression ratio.

Though it took a year, NASCAR reacted to all the trick stuff from the factories, and banned it for 1954, going back to stock (more or less) equipment. Olds drivers still managed 11 wins, their best year since 1951, but Hudson was still on top with 17.

You didn't stand still in the horsepower race, and the 1955 Oldsmobiles didn't, having another boost in advertised output. Compression jumped to 8.5:1, and (with a few other adjustments) raised the 88 tally to 185 bhp and to 202 bhp for other models. Styling was mainly a facelift of the '54.

Another facelift and another horsepower boost marked the 1956 Olds lineup, but the competition had clearly caught up with the Rocket. Compression was now at 9.25:1, and ratings read 230 bhp for 88, 240 for others. With average weights around 3700 pounds and only average horsepower, Oldsmobiles were more in the mainstream of medium-priced cars than in the forefront. For example, in that year you could get a Dodge with 295 bhp, a DeSoto with 320, a Mercury at 260, and even a lower-priced Pontiac at 285.

Only a single NASCAR GN win went to Olds in 1956, its worst year ever. In the rapidly rising sport of drag racing, only the older 88s did well in the lower stock classes.

For 1957, Oldsmobile was restyled and repowered. One engine was standard for all lines, including the low-priced 88. A larger bore and stroke netted a displacement of 370.7 cid, the biggest among GM passenger cars. With a four-barrel carb, the standard rating came to 277 bhp. There was also a second phase, the J/2 Rocket. Contrary to its name, the J/2 featured three two-barrel carbs, a compression ratio of 10:1, and 300 bhp. Some reports put it at 312 bhp, the rating used in 1958. Cost was just $85.

To showcase this newfound muscle, Olds signed Lee Petty to race 88s in NASCAR. But before the car could prove itself, NASCAR banned multi-carb setups, fuel injection, and superchargers, forcing all stockers to run with four-barrels. Then the manufacturers pulled out of racing. Petty bought leftover racing parts at a giveaway price, and decided to race the cars on his own. Five events went to Oldsmobiles in 1957 Grand National competition.

Strangely, one of the biggest Oldsmobile wins of all times came nearly two years after the make left racing. Lee Petty had pooled his remaining racing parts to concoct a 1959 Olds two-door hardtop. He entered it in the first Daytona 500 in 1959 on the new 2½-mile speedway. In a literal photo finish, he won. He and Richard raced Oldsmobiles part of that season, giving the make four wins, but then switched to Plymouth. Lee won the driving crown again, but Olds only got part of the credit.

All Olds engines had 10:1 compression for 1958. The J/2 was still offered, still at 312 bhp, but the glow was off the performance market. The facelifted body was overchromed, and a far cry from the clean look of the early 88s.

The division did go after the full-size "personal-car" market, however, beginning with the 1961 Starfire convertible. It was initially listed as part of the Super 88 line, and shared its 123-inch wheelbase. Later, Starfire became a separate series. It featured four bucket seats and a full-length console running straight down the middle of the interior. For 1962, a hardtop version was added. The idea was extended downmarket for 1964 with the arrival of the Jetstar I, also on a 123-inch wheelbase. Both models were offered with up to 345 bhp from Oldsmobile's 394-cid V8, a bored-out version of the original Rocket engine. While all offered good handling and reasonable go, they were not popular. The Jetstar was retired after only three models years, and the Starfire disappeared after 1966. By then, the performance action had shifted to the mid-size cars.

Oldsmobile Cutlass/4-4-2

After being the first performance king of the '50s, Oldsmobile abdicated the throne as the decade progressed. The renewed interest in performance cars seen in the 1960s was reflected in the 1962 F-85 lineup when the mid-year Jetfire was unveiled.

The unique Jetfire two-door hardtop featured a turbocharger to boost power, and fluid injection to prevent detonation. Advertised horsepower came to 215, the same as displacement. All this thrilled the technically inclined, and the exhaust-driven blower put the Jetfire into some fairly hot company. *Car Life* magazine drilled one to 60 mph in 8.5 seconds, six seconds quicker than the '61 F-85 it had tested. Top speed was noted to be 107 mph. Jetfire

Left from top: 4-4-2 was Oldsmobile's most potent mid-size model in 1965, 1966, and 1967. Right from top: 1968 4-4-2 convertible; 1969 4-4-2 hardtop; 1971 4-4-2 convertible (note aggressive scoops on hood).

production continued only through 1963, a year in which all F-85s were stretched a bit. But it was doomed to extinction. It was costly, didn't sell in high volume, and was trouble-prone.

A complete redesign resulted in intermediate status for the F-85 in 1964. Body-on-frame replaced unitized construction, wheelbase moved up to 115 inches, and all other dimensions were expanded. Weight rose by some 400 pounds. The aluminum V8 had never worked out that well, so bowing to the old racing phrase "there's no substitute for cubic inches," Olds devised a newly sized cast-iron V8. This 330-cube unit had a different block, but was built on a lot of the same tooling used to make the original Rocket V8, which was still around in Oldsmobile's big cars at 394 cid.

When equipped with a four-speed manual gearbox, the Cutlass was one fast automobile. *Mechanix Illustrated's* famed tester Tom McCahill got one such animal, and tallied a 0–60 mph stomper of 7.6 seconds. Top speed came to 118 mph. Normally this sort of acceleration would have garnered laurels for the F-85 Cutlass, but it was overshadowed by Pontiac's new GTO option for its Tempest. The big-horse 389 in what was basically the same car blew the Olds and the rest of the competition off the road.

Oldsmobile wasn't in the weeds for long. While it wasn't ready to put the 394 into the F-85, it did have an option that would at least send its intermediate in the direction of the

Oldsmobile F-85/Cutlass Performance

Year & Model		Engine (cid/bhp)	Curb Wt.[1]	lbs/ bhp[1]	0-60[2] (sec)	¼-mi.[2] (sec)	Base Price[3]
1962	F-85 Jetfire 2d htp	215/215	2739	12.7	8.5	16.5	$3049
1964	F-85 442 2d htp	330/310	3500	11.3	7.5	15.5	$2784
1965	F-85 442 2d htp	400/345	3510	10.2	7.8	15.5	$2784
1966	F-85 442 2d htp	400/360	3605	10.0	6.3	14.8	$2923
1967	F-85 442 2d htp	400/350	3568	10.2	7.1	15.5	$3015
1968	F-85 442 2d htp	400/350	3603	10.3	7.0	15.1	$3204
1968	Hurst/Olds 2d htp	455/390	3870	9.9	6.7	13.9	NA
1969	Hurst/Olds 2d htp	455/380	3885	10.2	5.9	14.0	NA
1970	F-85 442 2d htp	455/370	3775	10.2	5.7	14.4	$3376
1972	Hurst/Olds 2d htp	455/270n	3990	14.8	6.8	15.2	NA

[1]Advertised; [2]Typical acceleration based on contemporary tests; [3]Advertised list price in contemporary dollars; n = Net advertised horsepower; cid = cubic inch displacement; bhp = brake horsepower; conv = convertible; cpe = coupe; fastbk = fastback; htp = hardtop; rdstr = roadster (2-seat); sdn = sedan; d = number of doors.

GTO. This was the "Police Apprehender Pursuit Package," Option B-09. Olds was trying to get a bigger share of the police-car market, and the package was developed to make the F-85 into a high-performance car that could rival Plymouth and Dodge, who did well in that area with their intermediate-sized cars. However, Option B-09 hardly had the name to light the fire of the young performance buffs that were going out of their way to sign contracts for GTOs.

After a little creative thinking, the package was renamed 4-4-2. Available on all models except wagons, it extracted 20 additional horses from the 330 V8, bringing the total to 310. The numbers stood for (4) four-barrel carburetor, (4) four-on-the-floor manual transmission, and (2) dual exhausts. While those features helped, performance was assured by a higher-lift cam, heavy-duty rod and main bearings, a dual-snorkel air cleaner, and a heavy-duty suspension, including rear stabilizer bar.

Early advertising showed a 4-4-2-equipped four-door sedan in police duty, but the theme was quickly changed to something along the lines of what Pontiac was doing, with the emphasis on power and sportiness. But while the 4-4-2 seemed a lot faster, road tests showed it was not much swifter than McCahill's 290-horse job. There was still no substitute for cubic inches.

Using a method similar to the one it had used to come up with the 330, Olds replaced the 394 in its 1965 big cars with a 425-cid V8. Bore was 4.125 inches and stroke a rather long 3.975. Cutting the bore to four inches brought displacement down to an even 400 cubes, deemed just right for the 4-4-2 option. A four-barrel carb resulted in 345 bhp and, more important, a hefty increase of 85 ft-lbs of torque. So for 1965 the 4-4-2 meant (4) 400 cubic inches, (4) four-barrel carb and (2) dual exhausts. The option was now restricted to two-door models only, but still could be had with cheap to fancy trim.

Boosting compression ratio a quarter-point to 10.5:1 yielded five extra horses for the mildly changed 1966 4-4-2. Late in the model year one of the rarest goodies of all made the option list. This was a triple two-barrel carb that brought the rating up to 360 bhp. It was the first (and last) tri-carb setup at Olds since the 1957–58 J/2 option. One of the triple-two 4-4-2s scored a 0–60 mph clocking of 6.3 seconds for *Car Life*, which dubbed it the "Civilized Supercar." Olds dealers also started offering a fresh-air intake over the parts counter. Ducting for the air cleaner went behind the grillework.

GM clamped an unwritten ban on multi-carb setups and cars with less than 10 pounds per horsepower, so 4-4-2 lost the triple two-barrel setup for 1967. Thus the few 1966s that have it are a rare commodity. It didn't lose its 360 bhp, however. The air-induction system now became a factory option (W-30) and produced the same power as the tri-carbs, or so it was claimed.

Like its GM intermediate cousins, Oldsmobile's mid-sized cars went the dual-wheelbases route for 1968. Two-doors had a 112-inch stretch, down three from the previous four years. The 4-4-2 now became a separate line, with two-door coupe, hardtop, and convertible offerings. The 350-horse 400 was still no-charge. The W-30 option gave 10 more horses, and picked up the name "Force-Air" system in ad copy. Air intakes were now under the front bumper.

Like its competition, Olds started catering to those who liked supercar looks but didn't want maximum horsepower. A bore job brought the 330 up to 350 cubes, and another Force-Air option was added at mid-year, this time for the 350 (W-31), lifting its bhp reading from 310 to 325.

The 425 grew into the 455. With ratings up to 400 bhp, there was no

Top left: 1970 Rallye 350. Bottom left: 1969 Hurst/Olds 455. Top right: 1972 Hurst/Olds hardtop. Bottom right: 1973 Hurst/Olds (note blanked-off sail panels).

Upper left: Hurst/Olds served as Indy 500 pace car for 1974; shown is one of the replicas issued. Lower left: 1975 Hurst/Olds was more "show" than "go." Upper right: Hurst/Olds package was reprised for 1979. Lower right: Richard Petty's 1977 Number 43 Cutlass S stocker.

way Oldsmobile could put this in mid-size car—GM wouldn't allow it. But what if someone else put in bigger engines? That someone turned out to be Hurst Performance Products, which swapped Force-Air 455 for the 400s. The package got by the top brass, so a 380-bhp 4-4-2 was waiting at your Olds dealer this year.

For the most part, the bold Olds models for 1969 were similar to their '68 predecessors.

After having been roundly assaulted, the GM ban on big-engine intermediates was lifted for 1970. Olds immediately dropped the 455 into the 4-4-2, without Hurst's help, and advertised output at 365. You also could get the 455 in other Olds intermediates. Air-induction on W-30 and W-31 cars now came via a fiberglass hood with a built-in scoop (less agresive than on the '69 Hurst/Olds). The hood also had built-in tie-downs.

At mid-year, F-85 and Cutlass S models picked up a new option package of their own, the Rallye 350. Based on the W-31, it came in Sebring yellow, had urethane-covered bumpers, color-keyed wheels, an optional rear spoiler, and black-and-red accents.

No more making excuses for 4-4-2. *Car Life* tested a 1970 W-30 automatic, and zipped to 60 in 5.7 seconds. That tied the LT-1 Corvette four-speed as the fastest car tested in the magazine's final year. The Olds also whipped through the quarter mile in 14.36 seconds, clearing the traps at 100.22 mph. Again only the 'Vette was faster.

What goes up, must come down. With pressure from insurance companies, increasingly stringent emission controls, and federal safety regulations, the future for performance models wasn't rosy as the 1971s arrived. All GM engines now had to live on regular or low-lead fuel. The W-30's 10.5:1 compression ratio dropped to 8.5:1, and advertised horsepower fell to 350, still 10 up on the standard 4-4-2. The 4-4-2 coupe, W-31, and Rallye 350 were all cut.

For 1972 the 4-4-2 returned to option status for the first time since 1967, but wasn't tied to a specific engine. It was listed as an appearance-and-handling package, and was available on the Cutlass and Cutlass S two-doors and Cutlass Supreme convertible. If you wanted the big 455, you ordered the W-30 and got 300 net bhp.

A complete restyling and even fewer performance mods were dictated for 1973. Only pillared styles ("Colannade" to Olds) were offered. True hardtops and convertibles were gone, as were the W-30 option and the fiberglass hoods. The 4-4-2 package survived, but Olds literature got more of a kick out of pointing out its stripes than its mechanical attractions.

Unlike other competitors, Olds was not quick to drop its 4-4-2 symbol. Through 1980 you could still get a Cutlass with a handling-and-appearance package bearing this designation.

The Hurst/Olds continued for 1974–75 (it paced Indy again in '74). Also revived was the W-30 nameplate. For 1975, the H/O was attached to the Cutlass Supreme. Powering it was the W-30 455 or "W-25" 350. Hurst was in the hatch-roof business, and touted that feature more than the model's engine output.

After taking a couple of years off, the Hurst/Olds returned for a 1979 encore on the downsized Cutlass Supreme. Also dusted off was the W-30 nameplate, and for once it meant something. You weren't supposed to be able to get a 350 in Cutlass Supremes, but the Hurst/Olds W-30 had one, rated at 165 bhp net.

Missing from this account so far is NASCAR Grand National competition. The reason is that through 1977, few mid-size Oldses were entered, and none won. Starting with the 1978 season, Chevrolet engines were permitted to be run in any GM make. So the sloped-front 1976–77 Cutlass S proved popular on the long tracks because of its aerodynamics. Several teams used the Olds sheetmetal, and 11 Grand Nationals were credited to the make for 1978, enough to tie its second-best season, 1954. Five more wins were added for 1979, bringing the career total to 101. One of the 1979 victories was the Daytona 500 by

Richard Petty, exactly 20 years after his father won the first one in a 1959 Oldsmobile.

Pontiac

It's easy to trace the performance history of Pontiac prior to 1955: it didn't have one. Well, maybe it wasn't quite that bad, but Pontiac did have a reputation for many years as a dull car. That stands in rather sharp contrast to the major shift that lay just ahead.

Pontiac had first appeared for 1926. It was made by the Oakland Motor Company, a division of General Motors. It quickly outsold its parent, and replaced it after 1931. From 1935 through 1954 Pontiacs came with a choice of inline-six or eight-cylinder engines, both L-heads, of modest horsepower and acceleration. Along with Chevrolet, Pontiac didn't get its first overhead-valve V8 until 1955.

Pontiac's V8 had 3.75-inch bore and 3.25-inch stroke for a displacement of 287.2 cubic inches. Its rocker arms were of ball-stud construction, like Chevrolet's. This permitted higher revs, and cost less to produce than engines with rocker arm shafts in the heads. Horsepower was very state-of-the-art.

Pontiac Performance

Year & Model		Engine (cid/bhp)	Curb Wt.[1]	lbs/ bhp[1]	0-60[2] (sec)	¼-mi.[2] (sec)	Base Price[3]
1955	Star Chief 4d sdn	287/180	3556	19.8	13.8	19.7	$2362
1956	Star Chief 4d sdn	317/227	3647	16.1	11.4	18.1	$2735
1957	Super Chief 2d sdn	347/290	3640	12.6	8.5	16.8	$2793
1958	Bonneville 2d htp	370/300	3710	12.4	7.6	16.0	$3481
1959	Catalina 2d htp	389/280	4000	14.3	8.8	16.9	$2768
1960	Catalina 2d htp	389/333	4050	12.2	7.8	16.0	$2766
1961	Ventura 2d htp	389/348	3800	10.9	8.2	15.5	$2971
1961	Catalina S/S 2d htp	389/348	3680	10.6	4.6	13.7	NA
1962	Catalina 2d htp	421/405	3875	9.6	5.4	13.9	$2860
1962	Catalina Royal Bobcat 2d htp	389/370	3960	10.7	6.5	14.5	NA
1963	Grand Prix 2d htp	421/370	4190	11.3	6.6	15.1	$3489
1964	Catalina 2+2 2d htp	421/370	4000	10.8	7.2	16.1	$3057
1965	Catalina 2+2 2d htp	421/338	4130	12.2	7.4	15.8	$2868
1965	Catalina 2+2 2d htp	421/376	4100	10.9	7.2	15.5	$2868

[1]Advertised; [2]Typical acceleration based on contemporary tests; [3]Advertised list price in contemporary dollars; n = Net advertised horsepower; cid = cubic inch displacement; bhp = brake horsepower; conv = convertible; cpe = coupe; fastbk = fastback; htp = hardtop; rdstr = roadster (2-seat); sdn = sedan; d = number of doors.

To go along with this new engine, Pontiac introduced all-new styling for 1955 based on GM's A-body, which it shared with Chevrolet. Two wheelbases were offered, 122 for the 860 and 870 Chieftains, and 124 for the top-line Star Chief. A record 530,007 cars were sold for the model year, a mark that would stand until 1963.

Like most of its competitors, Pontiac couldn't afford to stand still in the mid-'50s. For 1957, the "Strato-Streak" V8's bore was enlarged, and the cube count hit 316.6. Compression ratios were raised as well.

A factory-backed racing effort saw a couple of cars set up by Indy veteran Louie Meyer for Speed Weeks at Daytona Beach in February. More noteworthy was Ab Jenkins' run on the Bonneville Salt Flats on June 26, as his '57 car went for 24 hours at an average speed of 118.337 mph, breaking several national and international records.

Top left: Pontiacs were facelifted for '56. Top right: Fuel-injected '57 Bonneville. Lower left: 1960 Bonneville and Ventura. Lower right: '61 Catalina drag special.

Perhaps the most significant event of 1957 was the appointment of Semon E. ("Bunkie") Knudsen as Pontiac general manager. The son of former GM president William S. Knudsen, Bunkie moved quickly to change the division's image. To do that, he moved quickly by hiring Elliott M. ("Pete") Estes from Oldsmobile to be chief engineer.

The facelifted 1957 models were mostly finalized when Knudsen took over. Before production started, however, he did manage to remove their "silver streak" exterior trim that had been a Pontiac trademark since 1935, one started by Bunkie's father. A longer stroke brought engine size to 347 cid. Horsepower ratings ranged from 227 to 270, the latter with a four-barrel carb and 10:1 compression. At mid-year Tri-Power (three two-barrel carbs) arrived. One version had a 290-bhp, and the stronger one was 27 bhp higher (some reports put it at 310).

Pontiac may have had the power, but it needed a showcase like DeSoto's Adventurer or Mercury's Turnpike Cruiser to show it off. Answering the call was the Bonneville convertible, one of three mid-year models. A four-door hardtop and wagon were aimed at the family trade, but Bonneville was the glittering performance number. Under all its chrome and aluminum trim was a 124-inch wheelbase and a fuel-injected 347 V8. This used GM's mechanical injection, similar to Chevrolet's. Horsepower was not advertised, but reports put it at 300–310, less than the hottest Tri-Power, which could be had in models lighter than the nearly 4300-pound Bonneville.

The '58s should have been slower. They were nearly four inches longer, two inches wider, and better than 100–200 pounds heavier. Basic bodies were shared with Chevrolet, with 122- and 124-inch wheelbases as before.

Once again displacement was up, this time to 370 cubes thanks to a bore rethink. Engines were now referred to as "Tempest 395," the number taken from the torque output on one of them.

The '58 Pontiac turned out to be a one-year design, a rarity in auto manufacturing. Bodies were all-new again for 1959 to bring the division into line with GM's new body-sharing scheme. Wheelbase remained the same, but weight and dimensions went up, except for height, which came down. With all GM cars now looking somewhat alike, Pontiac needed something to set itself apart. It came up with two features, although it took it a while to realize the value of one, the split grille. The other was "Wide-Track" design, wider front and rear treads than those of competitors.

For the fourth consecutive year, Pontiac enlarged engines, this time to 389 cubes, a size it would stay with for a while. A longer stroke accounted for the additional 19 cid. Advertised horsepower wasn't all that radical.

For 1960 the split grille went away. Instead of just increasing displacement as in the past, Pontiac worked in other areas. On its top three engines compression ratios went up to 10.75:1, and the hottest "regular" powerplant was the 318-bhp Tri-Power unit. A stock-car version with four-barrel put out 333 bhp, while the drag-oriented engine with Tri-Power boasted 348 bhp. A special heavy-duty racing chassis was developed, and a Borg-Warner four-speed manual transmission was offered, too.

The 1960 models put Pontiac back in the performance spotlight. At Daytona Beach Bob Pemberton won the standing-start mile for the second straight year. Pontiacs also came into their own in drag racing, despite some strong competition from Chrysler. Highlight of the year was ad executive Jim Wangers' Super/Stock and stock eliminator wins at the NHRA Nationals in Detroit on Labor Day.

After years of growing, Pontiacs shrank a bit for '61. The move did not prove popular with customers, but did wonders for the make's performance prowess. Wheelbase on the lower-priced Catalina and Ventura series dropped from 122 to 119 inches, the same as Chevrolet's. Pontiac's famed Wide-Track tread also was sliced from 64 to 62.5 inches, but retained its title. Even the frame was redone, going from X-brace to perimeter design. The split grille, which would become a permanent styling fixture, returned.

Less weight meant there was no need to enlarge the 389, which started the new year in roughly the same form as the year before. The hottest production option was the 348-horse Tri-Power job. Dealer kits could up that to 363 horses. Late in the year the factory may have installed some Super-Duty 421s rated at 373 bhp with two four-barrel carbs. The 421 used a larger bore and longer stroke than the 389. The Borg-Warner four-speed now became a normal production item, and three-speed automatics replaced the old four-speed units.

If all that wasn't enough, Pontiac came up with aluminum front bumpers, radiators, sheetmetal, and other parts to make its medium-priced car even lighter than the Fords and Chevrolets.

Pontiac's 2+2 option for the Catalina produced some of the most roadable big cars of the late '60s. Shown is the 1965 (above) and the '66 (right).

The result of all this was one fantastic racing year. Pontiac took 30 out of 52 NASCAR Grand National events, an all-time record up to then. Notable was Marvin Panch's victory in the 1961 Daytona 500. Six of eight superspeedway flags were taken by Pontiacs.

The 1962 big Pontiac lineup saw things tame down a tad. Wheelbase for all but wagons went up to 120 inches. Other dimensions also grew.

Knudsen left Pontiac not long after the 1962 models were announced to become general manager of Chevrolet. Estes took over as Pontiac boss, so the division's performance fortunes were in good hands.

NHRA changed the rules for factory-authorized parts eligible for drag racing. It said engines and body parts for the stock classes must be strict production options. This forced the hot 389 and 421 onto the official equipment sheet. It also had Chrysler building actual race cars. Pontiac also built a few race cars—with all the lightweight parts. And there were more trick parts for 1962, including aluminum fender liners, intake and exhaust (yes, exhaust) manifolds. Putting everything in place reportedly took 159 pounds off the front wheels.

Once again, Pontiac dominated the NASCAR circuits, taking 22 wins in 53 starts. Fireball Roberts won the Daytona 500, and Joe Weatherly became the first Pontiac driver to win the GN driving title.

The big cars were facelifted for 1963, with new sheetmetal from the beltline down. The 421 was available from the start of the model year. Three hotter versions, known as Super-Duty 421s, were available.

For drag racing, Pontiac wanted to get down near the 3200 pounds of the winning MoPars. This led to a special Catalina some 300 pounds lighter than the 1962 model. Included in the diet program were front and rear bumpers and brackets, bell housing, front-end sheetmetal, and axle centers, all made of aluminum. Frames were lightened, batteries were moved to the trunk, and all insulation, sound deadeners, and sealers were left off.

Construction of the Super/Stock light cars and the Super-Duty hardware for the 421 was halted abruptly when GM brass ordered all divisions (mainly Pontiac and Chevrolet) out of the racing and high-performance biz in early 1963.

Pontiac would continue to produce big cars with good street performance for the rest of the decade.

Pontiac Firebird

Usually Pontiac management has been more interested in starting market trends than reacting to them. After Ford scored a sales hit with its sporty four-passenger Mustang, Pontiac general manager John Z. DeLorean started campaigning for a fiberglass two-passenger sports-type car. But he was overruled on that one, and had to settle instead for a version of the soon-to-be-released Chevrolet Camaro, a direct Mustang competitor. The result was introduced for 1967½.

Firebird shared the Camaro's 108-inch wheelbase, unitized body/chassis, and hardtop and convertible body styles. Its grille was different, a big combination affair incorporating the front bumper. The hood was different, too, and slightly altered rear fender stampings and taillights of Pontiac design were used. The interior was pretty much like the Camaro's.

Where the two were least alike was in the engine compartment. Pontiac power was used exclusively. Choices included two 230 cubic-inch overhead-cam sixes, two 326-cube V8s, and two 400 V8s.

Option packages provided several model variations. The base Firebird came with a 165-bhp ohc six. The Sprint model packed the 215-bhp, four-barrel six-banger. The Firebird 326 had the two-barrel 326 V8 with 250 bhp. The H.O. used a four-barrel 326 of 285 bhp. At the top was the Firebird 400 with 325-bhp 400s, with or without Ram-Air.

Only minor changes were ordained for the '68 Firebird. A bigger-bore 326 engine changed the name of the 326 model to 350, and the H.O.'s output rose to 320 bhp. Horses on the base 400 went up five to 330. A 400 H.O. was added with 335 bhp, the same power as the Ram-Air. At mid-year the 400 Ram-Air II came along with 340 bhp, 26 less than in the GTO, due to a minor carb change and that weight rule. The cammer six grew from 230 to 250 cubes.

Most cars of the '60s had a tendency to grow as they aged, and Firebird was no exception. Sheetmetal contours and grille were modified for 1969, resulting in a car 2.3 inches longer, 1.3 inches wider, and somewhat heavier. Engines also changed a bit. The 400 H.O. was dropped, and the Ram-Air IV replaced the Ram-Air II. Better-breathing heads gave the GTO 370 bhp with Ram-Air IV, but the equivalent Firebird had to be content with 345. There also were some special Ram-Air V engines with tunnel-port head design. These were intended mainly for drag racing, and were only available through parts channels.

Speaking of racing, it seemed natural that someone would want to try the Firebird in the SCCA's Trans-Am series. Rules called for engines to have a maximum of 305 cubic inches displacement in stock form. Pontiac was nowhere near that figure, though Ford and Chevrolet had 302s. Canadian Terry Godsall entered a '68 Firebird in the Trans-Am. This car was derived from a Camaro Z-28, including its powerplant. When officials questioned the Chevy engine, Godsall said this was a *Canadian* Firebird. Since full-size Pontiacs built in Canada used Chevrolet engines, SCCA officials bought the story. With Jerry Titus at the wheel, Firebird went racing, but scored no major wins.

Meanwhile, Pontiac was working on a 303-cid V8, which had the 400's 4.12-inch bore and an extremely short 2.8-inch stroke. Heads were tunnel-port, similar to those of the Ram-Air V. Development problems kept the 303 from production, though several engines did see action in some late-season Trans-Am events in 1969 and in NASCAR's Grand American small sedan series.

Firebirds raced again in 1970, but in a tragic accident at Road America Titus hit a wall and was killed. Firebird's first outright Trans-Am win wouldn't come until 1972, when the series was far less competitive than in earlier years. With that kind of background, it may seem strange Pontiac would want to talk about the Trans-Am at all. As it turned out, the name did more for the Firebird than the Firebird did in the racing.

The first Trans Am model was actually an option package for the 1969 hardtop and convertible. Included in it were rear spoiler, special stripes, decals, simulated air outlets on the front fenders, the

Left from top: 1968 Firebird 400 H.O.; the first Trans Am, 1969; 1972 Formula 400. Right from top: 1975 Trans Am; 1979 10th Anniversary Trans Am; 1980 Turbo Trans Am Indy Pace Car.

Ram-Air 400 engine, and other assorted goodies. First shown at the Chicago Auto Show in March, it cost $725 extra, somewhat more with Ram-Air IV. The 303 was supposed to be available, but very few cars had it.

The all-new 1970 Firebird got off to a late start, but it caused a sensation. The semi-fastback coupe (convertibles were dropped) had super sleek lines and an aggressive, taut appearance. The chassis was broadly the same as on earlier models, though suspension was considerably altered in detail. External dimensions were within fractions of the 1967–69 generation. The overhead-cam six was replaced by a Chevrolet overhead-valve inline unit. Only one version of the 350 V8, a two-barrel with 255 bhp, remained. The 400 came in at least three versions, a two-barrel at 265 bhp, a four-barrel at 330, and the Ram-Air IV at 345. There may have been a 335-bhp Ram-Air setup also, but details are sketchy. There were now four models. From the bottom up the order read base, Esprit, Formula 400, and Trans Am. The last two were of most interest to muscle-car fans.

The Formula 400, naturally, had a 400 V8 standard, the 330-bhp unit. Ram-Air IV was an option, and made the neat scoops built into the leading edge of the hood functional. Trans Am featured a bold rear spoiler, functional rear-facing "shaker" hood scoop, front and rear fender flares, broad hood and deck striping, and a small Firebird decal on its Endura nose. Ram-Air-fed 400s were also part of the package, as were heavy-duty underpinnings.

Because of the short model year, Firebird production reached a lowly 48,739. This compares to 87,011 for the extended 1969 run, and 107,112 for the record-setting 1968 models.

Though unchanged outside, the 1971 model had several changes in front of the firewall. All GM engines were revised to run on regular fuel. The Formula lost its 400 suffix, because you could now get it with a 350. You could also have Pontiac's biggest, the 455, in both 325-horse

Pontiac Firebird Performance

Year & Model		Engine (cid/bhp)	Curb Wt.[1]	lbs/ bhp[1]	0-60[2] (sec)	¼-mi.[2] (sec)	Base Price[3]
1967	Sprint 2d htp	230/215	3470	16.1	10.0	17.5	$2666
1967	400 2d htp	400/325	3585	11.0	6.4	14.3	$2666
1968	400 2d htp	400/335	3600	10.7	7.6	15.4	$2917
1970	400 2d htp	400/330	3730	11.3	6.4	14.9	$3370
1972	Espirit 2d htp	400/175n	3741	21.4	9.9	17.6	$3194
1973	Trans Am 2d htp	455/310n	3775	12.2	7.3	15.0	$4102
1975	Trans Am 2d htp	400/185n	3860	20.9	9.8	16.8	$4740
1979	Formula 2d htp	400/220n	3837	17.4	9.1	16.1	$6018

[1]Advertised; [2]Typical acceleration based on contemporary tests; [3]Advertised list price in contemporary dollars; n = Net advertised horsepower; cid = cubic inch displacement; bhp = brake horsepower; conv = convertible; cpe = coupe; fastbk = fastback; htp = hardtop; rdstr = roadster (2-seat); sdn = sedan; d = number of doors.

and 335-bhp H.O. configuration. Functional hood scoops were optional. The Trans Am came with the 455 H.O. unit as standard and the hood scoop still worked, but the special engine and exhaust trim were omitted. Total production rose slightly to 53,124 units.

Engines changed little for the hotter 1972 models, but ratings did as the industry went to net horsepower and torque figures that year. The 455 H.O. now put out 300 bhp net, while the top 400 was down 50 from that. A strike at GM's Norwood, Ohio assembly plant in April cut deeply into production, and only 29,951 were built. Rumors of the demise of both Firebird and Camaro were rampant. But though management considered that, the cars got a reprieve thanks to a successful intramural "lobbying" campaign by GM execs.

Standard on the 1973 Trans Am (which now had the big hood decal dubbed by some scribes as the "screaming chicken") was a 250-bhp 455. Optional (available late in the year due to production problems) was the Super-Duty 455, which reversed the trend to lower horsepower as it was rated 10 bhp above the previous 455 H.O. It was also listed as an option for the Formula, which could still be had with a variety of engines. Trans Am's hood scoop was now blocked off—unblocking it was left to customers. Production lines flowed again, and 46,313 Firebirds were produced for the model year.

New Federal bumper standards took effect for '74, so Firebird got new front and rear ends that even looked better than those of earlier models. The SD-455 was still available, but at a reduced rating of 290 bhp net. Otherwise, there was little new, except for a 225-horse 400 that was made standard for Trans Am.

Despite the fuel shortages and price hikes which followed the 1973-74 Arab oil cutoff, Trans Am sales set an all-time record. Production hit 10,255 for model year 1974, well over the 4802 of 1973. Total Firebird production was 73,729, the highest in five years. This ran totally counter to the market, and assured the car would return for '75.

That year's models featured the most major structural body change that would occur during the second-generation's 12-year run, a wraparound rear window. The Trans Am returned, but its 455 didn't, at least not at the start of the year. Engines were switched to catalytic converters as emission standards tightened, but performance sank. Standard Trans Am power came from a 185-bhp 400, also optional for Formula. At mid-year Pontiac had second thoughts and brought back the 455 rated at 200 bhp net. It was renamed 455 H.O. Car sales were generally poor in 1975, reflecting the state of the nation's economy. However, Firebird again bucked the trend, with production hitting 84,063. Trans Am production shattered another record, hitting 27,274.

Little was changed for 1976, nor was it needed. A knockout all-black "Special Edition" Trans-Am with gold striping and hatch roof was offered to honor Pontiac's 50th anniversary. As if to celebrate, Firebird set another all-time production record of 110,775. Of these, a record 46,701 were Trans Ams.

General Motors started its downsizing program beginning with the 1977 full-size models. Firebird stayed the same size that year, but lost its 455 V8. All models got new nosework. A 180-horse 400 was standard for Trans Am except in California or high-altitude areas where you got a 185-bhp Olds 403.

The hottest Firebird engine was warmed up for 1978 by a higher compression ratio bringing the advertised rating to 220 bhp net, the first such boost since 1973. Production set yet another record, 187,284 units. Trans Am now accounted for nearly half at 93,341.

The 1979 models were facelifted, with an elongated nose and inset quad headlights. A 10th Anniversary Trans Am appeared with the last of the 400 engines. Production had ended in 1978, but a few of these powerplants were crated and saved for this limited-edition model. Firebird topped all other Pontiac lines—and all previous model years—in production at 211,454 units. Not bad for a car that almost was killed off in 1972, now in its 10th year with the same basic styling.

Firebird was selected to pace the 1980 Indianapolis 500, and predictably a Special Edition Pace Car was issued. While the 1980 styling was basically a carryover, engines were not. California folks were blessed with a 155-horse version of Chevy 305 for both Formula and Trans Am. Buyers in the other 49 got to try Pontiac's new small-block 301-cid unit, now turbocharged to help make up for the loss of the old 400. A four-barrel non-turbo engine with 155 bhp was standard on Federal Trans Ams. The 210-bhp blown unit was optional. While the turbo's paper figures may have been impressive, street numbers were not. It was offered only with automatic, and was no match for the old 400. Another energy crisis produced even more severe price increases than the previous one, and Firebird didn't escape its effects. Production sank to 107,340, the worst since 1975.

It was no secret that the 1981 Firebird would be the last of the second-generation series. Plans call for the 1982 models to be smaller and lighter, but still very sporty in character and performance. Indications are that 1981 production has slipped even further from 1980 levels. No doubt collectors will order one of the last of these true ponycars before the model year is over.

Pontiac Tempest/ GTO

For all the performance of Pontiac's big cars, relatively little rubbed off on the compact Tempest. The debut 1961 was better known for its radical engineering than for its 0-60 mph capabilities.

Some 1963 models (enlarged a bit over the 1961-62 Tempests) had the 326-cube version of Pontiac's V8, and were good performers. But the best was yet to come after a switch to intermediate size for 1964. Body-and-frame construction, coils all around, the 326, and a conventional driveline made the 1964 Tempest a very nice car. Only problem was, a number of folks at Pontiac weren't content with just building a nice car.

Ad man Jim Wangers, who also liked to race Pontiacs, reportedly got the idea of using a 389 in the '64 Tempest. It would be combined with heavy-duty suspension, four-speed GM-made "Muncie" transmission, and special tires. Its name: GTO, from the Italian *Gran Turismo Omologato*, which roughly translates as high-performance touring car certified for competition. Ferrari had used the designation for one of its fancy flyers. Instead of being a model, the Pontiac GTO was to be an option for the Tempest/LeMans series. Somehow this trick got it past the GM big shots, and the package debuted shortly after the rest of the '64 line bowed.

While the 389 was no longer the hottest setup for Pontiac's big cars, it was perfect for the smaller, lighter LeMans GTO. A 10.75:1 compression and four-barrel carb were standard. Rated output was tagged at 325 horsepower or 348 bhp with Tri-Power. Pontiac hoped to rekindle its performance image with this car, and sell about 5000 of them in the process. Nearly 32,000 copies later (still less than the demand) Pontiac and GM decided they had a winner.

Road tests put the GTO's 0–60 mph time at about 6.5 seconds, top speed at 130-plus, and quarter-miles at well under 15 seconds with a terminal velocity of nearly 100 mph.

Pontiac Tempest/LeMans Performance

Year & Model		Engine (cid/bhp)	Curb Wt.[1]	lbs/bhp[1]	0-60[2] (sec)	¼-mi.[2] (sec)	Base Price[3]
1964	GTO 2d conv	389/325	3560	10.9	7.7	15.8	$3092
1964	GTO 2d htp	389/348	3470	10.0	6.6	14.8	$2852
1965	GTO 2d conv	389/335	3563	10.6	7.2	16.1	$3026
1966	GTO 2d cpe	389/335	3445	10.3	6.8	15.4	$2783
1966	GTO 2d conv	389/360	3555	10.0	6.8	15.5	$3082
1966	Tempest Sprint 2d htp	230/207	3336	16.1	8.2	16.7	$2362
1968	GTO 2d htp	400/360	3755	10.4	6.6	14.5	$3101
1969	GTO Judge 2d htp	400/370	3735	10.1	6.2	14.5	$3156
1970	GTO 2d htp	400/366	3830	10.5	6.0	14.6	$3267
1970	GTO 2d htp	455/360	3855	10.7	6.6	14.8	$3267
1972	GTO 2d htp	455/300n	3885	13.0	7.1	15.4	$2968
1973	Grand Am 2d cpe	455/250n	4090	16.4	7.9	15.7	$4179
1977	Can Am 2d cpe	400/180n	3980	22.1	10.0	17.0	$4205

[1]Advertised; [2]Typical acceleration based on contemporary tests; [3]Advertised list price in contemporary dollars; n = Net advertised horsepower; cid = cubic inch displacement; bhp = brake horsepower; conv = convertible; cpe = coupe; fastbk = fastback; htp = hardtop; rdstr = roadster (2-seat); sdn = sedan; d = number of doors.

Raves from the press and the unexpectedly high sales created a new demand for hot intermediates, and brought forth copies from the competition.

For 1965, the GTO option came

Left from top: "the original," the '64 GTO; 1965 GTO; 1967 GTO; the rare '69 GTO Judge. Right from top: the '69 GTO with Ram Air IV; 1972 GTO; a shadow of its former self, the Ventura-based '74.

with higher horsepower ratings, 335 for the four-barrel engine and 360 with Tri-Power. Production boomed, topping 75,000 units

Blessed with the rare ability to improve, rather than detract from, the looks of their cars with each facelift, Pontiac stylists did their thing for the 1966 GTO. It was now a series, comprising two-door coupe, hardtop, and convertible styles as before. Engines and their ratings remained the same at the start of the model year. At mid-year, Pontiac dealers began offering an over-the-counter option to open up the simulated hood scoop, and tossed in a hotter cam for good measure. Called Ram-Air, the change did let cool air get to the carbs, but ram effect was minimal as the scoop design was not aggressive. A few cars also came with Ram-Air right from the factory. No horsepower ratings were announced.

At the other end of the Tempest's 1966 engine lineup was a new overhead-cam inline six based on the Chevrolet block. It was the first high-performance inline since the 1954 Hudson Hornet. The cam was operated by a reinforced fiberglass belt. The top-spec version had 207 bhp with 10.5:1 compression and a four-barrel carb, and was included as part of a new Sprint option.

General Motors had another edict for all its 1967 models. None of them except the Chevrolet Corvette could have multiple carburetors. As a result, Pontiac lost its three two-barrel setup on both GTO and the big cars, something it had been using since 1957. Corvette, on the other hand, got triple two-barrels, something Chevrolet hadn't had since 1961, and which had never been seen before on a production Corvette.

Major changes marked the 1968 Tempest and GTO. Two-doors now rode a 112-inch wheelbase and four-doors a 116, in common with other GM intermediates. Attracting much attention was the GTO's new front end featuring a front bumper covered by Endura, a rubber/plastic compound, and painted the same color as the body. The coupe didn't make the team now, but the hardtop and convertible did. In the engine room, power ratings were raised to 350 horses on the standard unit and to 265 on the two-barrel economy job. Late in the model year a second Ram-Air engine was offered, with a new head design and 366 bhp.

Outside changes were minimal on the 1969 GTO, but there were revisions among the hotter engines. Replacing the 400 H.O. was a 366-bhp Ram-Air 400. The most powerful was the new Ram-Air IV at 370 advertised horses. In December 1968 GTO buyers started saying "here come da Judge." The Judge was an option group that comprised a rear spoiler, stripes, special decals, and the Ram-Air 400 engine.

GM finally gave up trying to keep big inches out of its intermediates for the 1970 model year. That brought the furthest extension of Pontiac's V8, the 455, to the GTO.

For 1971 the GTO featured a better-looking hood with the air intake nearer the grille. That was about all that improved, however. All GM engines now had to live on regular fuel as the high-compression era had ended. And as the final insult, the GTO's engines were now available in lesser LeMans models. The standard powerplant was now a 300-bhp 400. Optional was the 325-bhp 455, and the 455 H.O. was top dog at 335 bhp. Ram-Air was gone, and The Judge was on the bench for the last time.

Following the corporate plan with the Olds 4-4-2 and Buick GS, the GTO became an option again for 1972 LeMans two-door coupes and hardtops. It was also played up less, sharing the limelight with other options like the GT, Sport, and even the "Endura front bumper" package. Engines again numbered three, but a conversion to net horsepower figures that year watered down what little was left of GTO's killer image.

The 1973 LeMans shared in the corporate-wide intermediate restyle, with "Colonnade" styling that did away with hardtops and convertibles. The new top-line Grand-Am series was the darling of the promotion men, while the GTO could be found in the fine print under options for the LeMans and LeMans Sport coupes. Included were GTO decals, heavy-duty suspension and a 230-bhp 400.

Pontiac should have left well enough alone, but unfortunately it didn't. There *was* a 1974 GTO, but it was no longer an intermediate. Instead, it was based on the compact Ventura, a clone of the Chevrolet Nova, and enthusiasts laughed. Just over 7000 were made before the GTO name was laid to rest.

Engine Charts

Buick

Type	Bore × Stroke (in.)	CID	BHP @ rpm*	Torque @ rpm*	Fuel# System	Avail. (years)
ohv V8	4.00 × 3.20	322	200@ 4100	309@ 2400	4 bbl.	1954
ohv V8	4.00 × 3.20	322	236@ 4600	330@ 3000	4 bbl.	1955
ohv V8	4.00 × 3.20	322	255@ 4400	341@ 3200	4 bbl.	1956
ohv V8	4.13 × 3.40	364	300@ 4600	400@ 3200	4 bbl.	1957-58
ohv V8	4.31 × 3.64	425	340@ 4400	465@ 2800	4 bbl.	1963-66
ohv V8	4.31 × 3.64	425	360@ 4400	465@ 2800	2 × 4 bbl.	1964-66
ohv V8	4.19 × 3.64	401	325@ 4400	445@ 3200	4 bbl.	1965-66
ohv V8	4.19 × 3.64	401	340@ 4600	445@ 3200	4 bbl.	1966
ohv V8	4.04 × 3.90	400	340@ 5000	440@ 3200	4 bbl.	1967-69
ohv V8	4.19 × 3.90	430	360@ 5000	475@ 3000	4 bbl.	1967-69
ohv V8	4.31 × 3.90	455	360@ 4600	410@ 2800	4 bbl.	1970
ohv V8	4.31 × 3.90	455	370@ 4600	410@ 2800	4 bbl.	1970
ohv V8	4.31 × 3.90	455	345@ 5000	460@ 3000	4 bbl.	1971
ohv V8	4.31 × 3.90	455	270@ 4400n	390@ 3000n	4 bbl.	1972-73
ohv V8	4.31 × 3.90	455	255@ 4400n	370@ 2800n	4 bbl.	1974

*SAE Gross ratings except where noted # Carburetion: No. Carbs × Bbls.; FI = fuel injection; † = Hemispherical Heads; e = Estimated; n = Net Advertised Figures; TC = Turbocharged

Cadillac

Type	Bore × Stroke (in.)	CID	BHP @ rpm*	Torque @ rpm*	Fuel# System	Avail. (years)
ohv V8	3.81 × 3.63	331	160@ 3800	312@ 1800	2 bbl.	1949-51
ohv V8	3.81 × 3.63	331	190@ 4000	322@ 2400	4 bbl.	1952
ohv V8	3.81 × 3.63	331	210@ 4150	330@ 2700	4 bbl.	1953
ohv V8	3.81 × 3.63	331	230@ 4400	330@ 2700	4 bbl.	1954
ohv V8	3.81 × 3.63	331	250@ 4600	345@ 2800	4 bbl.	1955
ohv V8	3.81 × 3.63	331	270@ 4800	345@ 3200	2 × 4 bbl.	1955

Chevrolet

Type	Bore × Stroke (in.)	CID	BHP @ rpm*	Torque @ rpm*	Fuel# System	Avail. (years)
ohv V8	3.75 × 3.00	265	195@ 5000	260@ 3000	4 bbl.	1955
ohv V8	3.75 × 3.00	265	225@ 5200	270@ 3600	2 × 4 bbl.	1956
ohv V8	3.88 × 3.00	283	245@ 5000	300@ 3800	2 × 4 bbl.	1957-61
ohv V8	3.88 × 3.00	283	270@ 6000	300@ 3800	2 × 4 bbl.	1957-61
ohv V8	3.88 × 3.00	283	283@ 6200	290@ 4400	FI	1957
ohv V8	3.88 × 3.00	283	290@ 6200	290@ 4000	FI	1958-59
ohv V8	4.13 × 3.25	348	315@ 5600	350@ 3600e	3 × 2 bbl.	1958
ohv V8	4.13 × 3.25	348	335@ 5800	362@ 3600	3 × 2 bbl.	1959-61
ohv V8	3.88 × 3.00	283	315@ 6200	295@ 4100	FI	1960-61
ohv V8	4.13 × 3.25	348	350@ 6000	365@ 3600	3 × 2 bbl.	1961
ohv V8	4.31 × 3.50	409	360@ 5800	409@ 3600	4 bbl.	1961
ohv V8	4.31 × 3.50	409	380@ 5800	420@ 3600	4 bbl.	1961-62
ohv V8	4.31 × 3.50	409	409@ 6000	420@ 4000	2 × 4 bbl.	1961-62
ohv V8	4.00 × 3.25	327	340@ 6000	344@ 4000	4 bbl.	1962-63
ohv V8	4.00 × 3.25	327	360@ 6000	352@ 4000	FI	1962-63
ohv flat-6	3.44 × 2.60	145	150@ 4400	210@ 3200	TC 1 bbl.	1962-63
ohv V8	4.31 × 3.50	409	425@ 6000	425@ 4200	2 × 4 bbl.	1963-64
ohv V8	4.40 × 3.50	427	430@ 6000	430@ 4000e	2 × 4 bbl.	1963
ohv V8	4.00 × 3.25	327	365@ 6200	360@ 4000	4 bbl.	1964-65
ohv V8	4.00 × 3.25	327	375@ 6200	350@ 4400	FI	1964-65
ohv flat-6	3.44 × 2.94	164	150@ 4000	232@ 3200	TC 1 bbl.	1964
ohv V8	4.09 × 3.76	396	375@ 5600	420@ 3600	4 bbl.	1965
ohv V8	4.09 × 3.76	396	425@ 6400	415@ 4000	4 bbl.	1965
ohv V8	4.31 × 3.50	409	400@ 5800	425@ 3600	4 bbl.	1965
ohv flat-6	3.44 × 2.94	164	180@ 4000	265@ 3200	TC 1 bbl.	1965-66
ohv V8	4.00 × 3.25	327	350@ 5800	360@ 3600	4 bbl.	1966-68
ohv V8	4.09 × 3.76	396	360@ 5200	420@ 3600	4 bbl.	1966
ohv V8	4.09 × 3.76	396	375@ 5600	415@ 3600	4 bbl.	1966-69
ohv V8	4.25 × 3.76	427	425@ 5600	460@ 4000	4 bbl.	1966
ohv V8	4.00 × 3.00	302	290@ 5800	290@ 4200	4 bbl.	1967-69
ohv V8	4.25 × 3.76	427	435@ 5800	460@ 4000	3 × 2 bbl.	1967-69
ohv V8	4.00 × 3.48	350	370@ 5800	370@ 4000	4 bbl.	1969-70
ohv V8	4.25 × 3.76	427	430@ 5200	460@ 4000	3 × 2 bbl.	1969
ohv V8	4.00 × 3.48	350	360@ 6000	380@ 4000	4 bbl.	1970
ohv V8	4.13 × 3.76	402	350@ 5200	415@ 3400	4 bbl.	1970
ohv V8	4.25 × 4.00	454	360@ 4800	500@ 3200	4 bbl.	1970
ohv V8	4.25 × 4.00	454	390@ 4800	500@ 3400	4 bbl.	1970
ohv V8	4.25 × 4.00	454	460@ 5200	490@ 3000	4 bbl.	1970
ohv V8	4.00 × 3.48	350	330@ 5600	360@ 4000	4 bbl.	1971
ohv V8	4.13 × 3.76	402	300@ 4800	400@ 3200	4 bbl.	1971
ohv V8	4.25 × 4.00	454	425@ 5600	475@ 4000	4 bbl.	1971
ohv V8	4.00 × 3.48	350	255@ 5600n	280@ 4000n	4 bbl.	1972
ohv V8	4.25 × 4.00	454	270@ 4000n	390@ 3200n	4 bbl.	1972
ohv V8	4.00 × 3.48	350	245@ 5200n	280@ 4000n	4 bbl.	1973-74
ohv V8	4.25 × 4.00	454	275@ 4400n	395@ 2800n	4 bbl.	1973
ohv V8	4.25 × 4.00	454	270@ 4400n	380@ 2800n	4 bbl.	1974
ohv V8	4.00 × 3.48	350	205@ 4800n	255@ 3600n	4 bbl.	1975
ohv V8	4.25 × 4.00	455	215@ 4000n	350@ 2400n	4 bbl.	1975
ohv V8	4.00 × 3.48	350	210@ 5200n	255@ 3600n	4 bbl.	1976
ohv V8	4.25 × 4.00	454	225@ 3800n	360@ 2400n	4 bbl.	1976
ohv V8	4.00 × 3.48	350	170@ 3800n	270@ 2400n	4 bbl.	1977
ohv V8	4.00 × 3.48	350	210@ 5200n	255@ 3600n	4 bbl.	1977
ohv V8	4.00 × 3.48	350	185@ 4000n	280@ 2400n	4 bbl.	1978
ohv V8	4.00 × 3.48	350	220@ 5200n	260@ 3600n	4 bbl.	1978
ohv V8	4.00 × 3.48	350	175@ 4000n	270@ 2400n	4 bbl.	1979
ohv V8	4.00 × 3.48	350	225@ 5200n	270@ 3600n	4 bbl.	1979
ohv V8	4.00 × 3.48	350	190@ 4200n	280@ 2400n	4 bbl.	1980
ohv V8	4.00 × 3.48	350	230@ 5200n	275@ 3600n	4 bbl.	1980
ohv V8	4.00 × 3.48	350	190@ 4200n	280@ 1600n	4 bbl.	1981

Oldsmobile

Type	Bore × Stroke (in.)	CID	BHP @ rpm*	Torque @ rpm*	Fuel# System	Avail. (years)
ohv V8	3.75 × 3.44	303	135@ 3600	263@ 1800	2 bbl.	1949-51
ohv V8	3.75 × 3.44	303	160@ 3600	283@ 1800	4 bbl.	1952

*SAE gross ratings except where noted; † hemispherical heads; # carburetion: no. carbs × bbls.; e = estimated; FI = fuel injection; n = net advertised figures; SC = supercharged; TC = turbocharged.

Type	Bore × Stroke (in.)	CID	BHP @ rpm*	Torque @ rpm*	Fuel# System	Avail. (years)
ohv V8	3.75 × 3.44	303	165@ 3600	284@ 1800	4 bbl.	1953
ohv V8	3.88 × 3.44	324	185@ 4000	300@ 2000	4 bbl.	1954
ohv V8	3.88 × 3.44	324	202@ 4000	332@ 2400	4 bbl.	1955
ohv V8	3.88 × 3.44	324	240@ 4400	350@ 2800	4 bbl.	1956
ohv V8	4.00 × 3.69	370	300@ 4600	410@ 2800e	3 × 2 bbl.	1957
ohv V8	4.00 × 3.69	370	312@ 4600	415@ 2800	3 × 2 bbl.	1958
ohv V8	3.50 × 2.80	215	215@ 4600	301@ 3200	TC 1 bbl.	1962-63
ohv V8	3.94 × 3.39	330	310@ 5200	355@ 3600	4 bbl.	1964
ohv V8	4.00 × 3.98	400	345@ 4800	440@ 3200	4 bbl.	1965
ohv V8	4.00 × 3.98	400	350@ 4800	440@ 3600	4 bbl.	1966-69
ohv V8	4.00 × 3.98	400	360@ 5200	440@ 3600	3 × 2 bbl.	1966
ohv V8	4.13 × 3.97	425	385@ 4800	475@ 3200	4 bbl.	1966-67
ohv V8	4.00 × 3.98	400	360@ 5400	440@ 3600	4 bbl.	1968-69
ohv V8	4.13 × 4.25	455	400@ 4800	500@ 3200	4 bbl.	1968-70
ohv V8	4.13 × 4.25	455	365@ 4600	510@ 3000	4 bbl.	1970
ohv V8	4.13 × 4.25	455	370@ 5400	300@ 3600	4 bbl.	1970
ohv V8	4.13 × 4.25	455	340@ 4600	460@ 3200	4 bbl.	1971
ohv V8	4.13 × 4.25	455	350@ 4700	460@ 2800	4 bbl.	1971
ohv V8	4.13 × 4.25	455	300@ 4700n	410@ 3200n	4 bbl.	1972
ohv V8	4.13 × 4.25	455	270@ 4200n	370@ 3200n	4 bbl.	1973
ohv V8	4.13 × 4.25	455	275@ 4200n	370@ 3200n	4 bbl.	1974

Pontiac

Type	Bore × Stroke (in.)	CID	BHP @ rpm*	Torque @ rpm*	Fuel# System	Avail. (years)
ohv V8	3.75 × 3.25	287	200@ 4600	278@ 2800	4 bbl.	1955
ohv V8	3.94 × 3.25	316	285@ 5100	330@ 3600	2 × 4 bbl.	1956
ohv V8	3.94 × 3.56	347	317@ 5200	359@ 3600	3 × 2 bbl.	1957
ohv V8	3.94 × 3.56	347	300@ 4800e	350@ 3400e	FI	1957
ohv V8	4.06 × 3.56	370	310@ 4800	400@ 3600	FI	1958
ohv V8	4.06 × 3.56	370	330@ 5200	400@ 3600	3 × 2 bbl.	1958
ohv V8	4.06 × 3.75	389	315@ 4600	425@ 3200	3 × 2 bbl.	1959
ohv V8	4.06 × 3.75	389	330@ 5200	430@ 3200e	3 × 2 bbl.	1959
ohv V8	4.06 × 3.75	389	318@ 4600	430@ 3200	3 × 2 bbl.	1960-62
ohv V8	4.06 × 3.75	389	330@ 4800	420@ 2800	4 bbl.	1960
ohv V8	4.06 × 3.75	389	348@ 4800	430@ 3200	3 × 2 bbl.	1960-62
ohv V8	4.06 × 3.75	389	333@ 4800	425@ 2800	4 bbl.	1961-62
ohv V8	4.09 × 4.00	421	405@ 4600	425@ 4400	2 × 4 bbl.	1961-63
ohv V8	4.09 × 4.00	421	370@ 5200	460@ 3800	3 × 2 bbl.	1963-64
ohv V8	4.06 × 3.75	389	325@ 4800	428@ 3200	4 bbl.	1964
ohv V8	4.06 × 3.75	389	348@ 4900	428@ 3600	3 × 2 bbl.	1964
ohv V8	4.06 × 3.75	389	335@ 5000	431@ 3200	4 bbl.	1965-66
ohv V8	4.06 × 3.75	389	360@ 5200	424@ 3600	3 × 2 bbl.	1965-66
ohv V8	4.09 × 4.00	421	376@ 5000	461@ 3600	3 × 2 bbl.	1965-66
ohc I6	3.88 × 3.25	230	207@ 5200	228@ 3800	4 bbl.	1966
ohc I6	3.88 × 3.25	230	215@ 5200	240@ 3800	4 bbl.	1967
ohv V8	4.12 × 3.75	400	325@ 5200	410@ 3600	4 bbl.	1967
ohv V8	4.12 × 3.75	400	335@ 5000	441@ 3400	4 bbl.	1967
ohv V8	4.12 × 3.75	400	360@ 5100	438@ 3600	4 bbl.	1967
ohv V8	4.12 × 4.00	428	376@ 5100	462@ 3400	4 bbl.	1967
ohc I6	3.88 × 3.53	250	215@ 5200	255@ 3800	4 bbl.	1968
ohv V8	4.12 × 3.75	400	340@ 5400	455@ 3800	4 bbl.	1968
ohv V8	4.12 × 3.75	400	360@ 5400	445@ 3800	4 bbl.	1968
ohv V8	4.12 × 3.75	400	366@ 5100	445@ 3600	4 bbl.	1968-70
ohc I6	3.88 × 3.53	250	230@ 5400	260@ 3600	4 bbl.	1969
ohv V8	4.12 × 3.75	400	345@ 5400	430@ 3700	4 bbl.	1969-70
ohv V8	4.12 × 3.75	400	370@ 5500	445@ 3900	4 bbl.	1969-70
ohv V8	4.12 × 4.00	428	390@ 5200	465@ 3400	4 bbl.	1969
ohv V8	4.15 × 4.21	455	360@ 4300	500@ 2700	4 bbl.	1970
ohv V8	4.12 × 3.75	400	300@ 4800	400@ 3600	4 bbl.	1971
ohv V8	4.15 × 4.21	455	335@ 4800	480@ 3600	4 bbl.	1971
ohv V8	4.12 × 3.75	400	250@ 4400n	325@ 3200n	4 bbl.	1972
ohv V8	4.15 × 4.21	455	300@ 4000n	415@ 3200n	4 bbl.	1972
ohv V8	4.12 × 3.75	400	230@ 4400n	325@ 3200n	4 bbl.	1973
ohv V8	4.15 × 4.21	455	310@ 4000n	390@ 3600n	4 bbl.	1973
ohv V8	4.12 × 3.75	400	225@ 4000n	330@ 2800n	4 bbl.	1974
ohv V8	4.15 × 4.21	455	290@ 4000n	395@ 3200n	4 bbl.	1974
ohv V8	4.15 × 4.21	455	200@ 3500n	330@ 2000n	4 bbl.	1975-76
ohv V8	4.12 × 3.75	400	200@ 4000n	325@ 2200n	4 bbl.	1977
ohv V8	4.12 × 3.75	400	220@ 4000n	320@ 2800n	4 bbl.	1978-79
ohv V8	4.00 × 3.00	301	210@ 4000n	345@ 2000n	TC 4 bbl.	1980
ohv V8	4.00 × 3.00	301	200@ 4000n	340@ 2000n	TC 4 bbl.	1981

*SAE gross ratings except where noted; † hemispherical heads; # carburetion: no. carbs × bbls.; e = estimated; FI = fuel injection; n = net advertised figures; SC = supercharged; TC = turbocharged.

Hudson Motor Car Co.

Hudson was at its performance peak when it ceased as an independent. The reason was a determined race driver who created a six-cylinder powerhouse that beat many V8s.

In the early years of the auto industry it was common for new makes of cars to enter some sort of competition. It was usually good for free publicity, and gave the maker a chance to demonstrate his product's durability and speed. It was equally common to withdraw from competitive events once a make had established itself in the market. Hudson Motor Car Company was an exception. It became more involved in racing and competition-oriented activities as time passed, and was at the peak of its involvement when it ceased to exist as an independent company.

The first Hudson appeared in 1909 under the name of Detroit department store magnate J. L. Hudson, who helped finance the company. Over the years, the make became successful and the better things got, the more it raced. Hudson-powered cars were found at Indianapolis, at hill climbs, in record runs, and in stock-car events at one time or other. In August 1939, John R. Cobb drove a Hudson to a class record of 93.9 mph at Bonneville Salt Flats. In all, Hudson boasted 149 American Automobile Association (AAA) records in the years before World War II. After the war the huge pent-up demand for cars made all manufacturers more worried about how fast their production lines were running than how fast their cars would run. And like the rest of the industry Hudson was readying its first all-new postwar models. These arrived for 1948, and became the basis for Hudson's greatest racing triumphs.

The rakish new '48 models with "step-down design" rested on a 124-inch wheelbase. They were wider than they were high, rising 60 inches from road to roof and stretching 77 inches from door handle to door handle. Construction was unitized, with the main structural members located below door level so the floor was lower than the door sills. This helped lower the center of gravity. The suspension system featured front and rear stabilizer bars and splayed rear leaf springs. All this made for very good handling when compared to the higher and narrower competition.

Oldsmobile had raised the performance standard in the medium-priced field with its 1949 overhead-valve V8. With 135 bhp from 303.7 cubes in the light 88 model, Olds had the fastest thing in the class. Hudson had put some of its bucks into its "Super Six," which was also new for '48, but couldn't afford to tool up for a V8 at the same time. As it turned out, it never would. By 1951, the six had evolved into the 308-cid Hornet engine, the biggest production six at that time. It was dubbed the H-145, and its displacement came via a bore and stroke increase on the 262 unit. With two-barrel carb, the H-145 was rated at 145 bhp. A 6.7:1 compression ratio was standard. A 7.2:1 head was optional, but no additional power was claimed for it. Hornet was the new top-line 1951 series on the Step-down's 124-inch wheelbase. Chrysler's FirePower V8 and the new Studebaker V8 appeared that year as well, so the Hornet wasn't exactly the center of attention.

However, it did attract the attention of Daytona Beach garage operator Marshall Teague. A master at tuning as well as driving race cars, Teague figured the Hornet could be made to be competitive in the 160-mile stock-car race to be held in his hometown in February. Teague bought a new Hornet, set it up, and won the race. The car was boldly painted with words that proclaimed it the "Fabulous Hudson Hornet."

Encouraged by the win, Teague went, unannounced, to the Hudson factory in Detroit to see if he could get some heavy-duty parts to make the Hornet go even faster and last longer. After talking his way in, he found a receptive audience in both the engineering and advertising departments. Though the Hornet was not designed with racing in mind, Hudson was not unfamiliar with the publicity value of speed events. And at that point, it needed something to drum up some interest in its products, which were looking more dated each year. A deal was struck. Teague would get cooperation from engineering on the parts he needed. he would do the PR work with the public, press, and dealers on Hudson's behalf. The relationship would set the stage for similar arrangements through the '50s and into the '60s, getting the factories directly involved in racing and the racers involved in promotion. Soon some "severe usage" items began showing up on Hudson parts lists.

Hudson Performance

Year & Model		Engine (cid/bhp)	Curb Wt.[1]	lbs/ bhp[1]	0-60[2] (sec)	¼-mi.[2] (sec)	Base Price[3]
1951	Hornet 4d sdn	308/145	3600	24.8	14.6	19.4	$2568
1952	Hornet 4d sdn	308/160	3600	22.5	15.1	19.4	$2769
1954	Hornet 4d sdn	308/170	3620	21.3	14.8	19.1	$2769

[1]Advertised; [2]Typical acceleration based on contemporary tests; [3]Advertised list price in contemporary dollars; n = Net advertised horsepower; cid = cubic inch displacement; bhp = brake horsepower; conv = convertible; cpe = coupe; fastbk = fastback; htp = hardtop; rdstr = roadster (2-seat); sdn = sedan; d = number of doors.

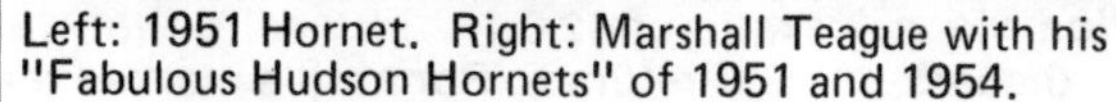

Left: 1951 Hornet. Right: Marshall Teague with his "Fabulous Hudson Hornets" of 1951 and 1954.

One of the more visible results of the Teague/Hudson agreement was Twin-H Power. An old hot-rodding trick for inline engines was to use two carburetors, equally spaced for better air/fuel mixture distribution. Teague knew it would improve output of the big Hornet six, and Hudson even had the hardware lying around. So in the summer of 1951, Twin-H was announced as an option for the Hornet.

As the 1951 season progressed, many drivers switched to Hudson as it became apparent this was the hot setup for big and small tracks alike. Oldsmobile, however, held sway in total wins, getting off to a better start. At year's end, Olds had 20 NASCAR Grand National victories to Hudson's 12.

More of the same was in store for 1952. Twin-H became a full production option, but had no horsepower rating. The flow of heavy-duty parts continued. With more drivers now in Hudsons from the start of the season, the year turned out to be the Hornet's best. Tim Flock won the NASCAR Grand National crown, and 27 of the 34 scheduled events fell to Hudsons. Oldsmobile's total was reduced to three. Teague concentrated on the American Automobile Association (AAA) circuit in the north, because he wanted to go Indy-car racing, which AAA sanctioned. Teague managed to take half of the 14 AAA stock wins; other Hudson drivers took five more, giving the Hornet a total of 39 wins in 48 major races that year.

The winning streak didn't mean Hudson could slack off, and the most famous of its engines, the 7-X, joined the parts list for dealer installation. This had a slightly overbored block capped by a high-compression head, and exhaust manifolding was split. Like the Twin-H, horsepower wasn't announced, but it was believed to be around 210 bhp.

Competition increased slightly in 1953 as Hudson took only 22 wins in 37 starts in NASCAR. Oldsmobile got nine and Dodge six. Thomas regained the championship. But the Hornets nabbed 13 of 16 AAA races.

NASCAR banned all factory-authorized parts for 1954, as the thinly disguised racing parts business was threatening to get out of hand. This actually helped Hudson. True, the competition had some mighty powerful engines, like Chrysler's 235-bhp FirePower V8. But without the "authorized" handling parts, they were no match for the agile Hornets.

Even without the special competition pieces, other makes were catching up to Hudson. It did take 17 of 36 NASCAR Grand Nationals, more than any other make for the third straight year. But Oldsmobile took 11 and Chrysler seven.

While Hudson was king of the racing world, the sales figures were anything but lofty. The old Step-down body style was still around in '54, and Hudson still couldn't afford to replace it. It also needed the V8 sought after by a power-hungry public in increasing numbers.

On May 1, 1954 came official word that Hudson and Nash-Kelvinator would merge to form American Motors. There was little question as to which would be the stronger partner. Hudson closed its Detroit factory, and switched production to the Nash facility in Wisconsin.

Engine Chart

Hudson

Type	Bore × Stroke (in.)	CID	BHP @ rpm*	Torque @ rpm*	Fuel# System	Avail. (years)
L-head 6	3.81 × 4.50	308	145 @ 3800	257 @ 1800	2 bbl.	1951-53
L-head 6	3.81 × 4.50	308	160 @ 4000e	260 @ 1800e	2 × 1 bbl.	1951-53
L-head 6	3.81 × 4.50	308	210 @ 4200e	280 @ 2800e	2 × 1 bbl.	1953-54

Type	Bore × Stroke (in.)	CID	BHP @ rpm*	Torque @ rpm*	Fuel# System	Avail. (years)
L-head 6	3.81 × 4.50	308	160 @ 3800	264 @ 1800	2 bbl.	1954
L-head 6	3.81 × 4.50	308	170 @ 4000	278 @ 2600	2 × 1 bbl.	1954

*SAE gross ratings except where noted; † hemispherical heads; # carburetion: no. carbs × bbls.; e = estimated; FI = fuel injection; n = net advertised figures; SC = supercharged; TC = turbocharged.

Studebaker Packard Corporation

South Bend's speedsters were unique among postwar high-performance cars in having supercharged engines. But the Hawks and the Avanti weren't enough to save the company.

Studebaker Avanti

The Avanti "is a car with a unique dual personality... that of an elegant prestige car and a car of high performance." That's how the sales literature read for Studebaker's dramatic new four-seat coupe announced for 1963. For once, the copy writers were right on the mark.

Sherwood H. Egbert, fresh from McCulloch Corporation, had assumed the president's chair at Studebaker-Packard Corporation in early 1961. He didn't spend much time in it as he set about to shape up the sagging company in whirlwind fashion.

Raymond H. Loewy, designer of Studebaker's beautiful 1953 Starliner coupes, was contracted to rush (everything around Egbert was "rush") through a design suitable for production. Loewy and associates delivered on schedule. The wedge-shaped Avanti (the name means "forward" in Italian) would utilize the 109-inch-wheelbase Lark Daytona convertible chassis. Despite a very limited budget, the car was a knockout. Though no wind

Standard for the 1963 Avanti was the R-1 "Jet-Thrust" version of the 289. With normal aspiration via a four-barrel carb, plus dual exhausts, it had an output of around 240 bhp. Studebaker never released horsepower and torque ratings for its R-series engines. One reason may have been that 240 bhp was nothing to get particularly excited about in 1963. Next step up was the R-2. It had the supercharger, a bit less compression, about 290 bhp.

Andy Granatelli, who came to Studebaker with Paxton, put an Avanti through its paces at Bonneville, and broke 29 records. But the car he used was far from stock. It had the R-3 engine, which was to have been an option for 1964, with 304.5 cid and around 335 bhp.

Production problems kept Avantis from reaching buyers just when demand was highest, between the announcement in the spring of 1962 and the fall of that year. By the time cars were available, many buyers had already turned to the all-new Chevrolet Corvette Sting Ray. As a result, only 3834 of the 1963 Avantis were built.

The R-3 engine from Granatelli's Bonneville car ostensibly became a production option on the little-changed 1964 edition, but only a handful were installed. Also announced, but not produced, was the R-4, which was to have two four-barrel carbs and a compression ratio of 12.0:1.

A return to Bonneville marked the pre-debut publicity for the '64 models. All kinds of Studebakers went out for an assault on the record books, including an R-5-equipped Avanti. Breaking his own record in the R-3 car, Granatelli stopped the clocks at 170.78 mph. Even Egbert took a crack at it, and hit 168. Records fell like rain.

Unfortunately, sales also fell, and in December of 1963, Studebaker called it quits at its South Bend, Indiana plant. Some Larks would be made in Canada for a while, but that was it. Total Avanti production for 1964 was just 809.

Avanti Performance

Year	& Model	Engine (cid/bhp)	Curb Wt.[1]	lbs/ bhp[1]	0-60[2] (sec)	¼-mi.[2] (sec)	Base Price[3]
1963	STD 2d cpe	289/240	3140	13.1	9.1	17.2	$4445
1963	STD 2d cpe	289/280	3140	11.2	8.0	15.8	$4445
1963	STD 2d cpe	304/335	3140	9.4	6.7	14.3	$4445

[1]Advertised; [2]Typical acceleration based on contemporary tests; [3]Advertised list price in contemporary dollars; n = Net advertised horsepower; cid = cubic inch displacement; bhp = brake horsepower; conv = convertible; cpe = coupe; fastbk = fastback; htp = hardtop; rdstr = roadster (2-seat); sdn = sedan; d = number of doors.

Studebaker Hawk

Like many carmakers entering the 1950s, Studebaker didn't hve much experience with performance. It had spent many years serving its customers in the territory between the low and medium-priced fields, venturing into one or the other or both at various times. But up until its sensational new '47s, Studebakers had been pretty dull for the most part. Studebaker's first postwar models with any performance potential came in 1951, along with a new overhead-valve V8 engine, which would serve Studebaker for the rest of its years as a carmaker. With a displacement of 232.6 cubic inches, it produced 120 horsepower and was offered in the Commander line.

The next ingredient in the performance recipe came in the beautiful form of the 1953 coupes. Styled by Raymond Loewy, they were absolutely right from a design point of view.

Studebaker's first true performance car arrived for mid-1955, the President Speedster. That year's coupes, like the rest of the line, had heavier grille work and more tinsel, which nearly ruined Loewy's original shape. The Speedster had even more chrome, plus wire wheel covers, triple-tone paint, and a well-designed dashboard with a 160-mph speedometer, tachometer, and full instrumentation. Power came from a new 259.2-cid V8, basically a bore job of the original 232 V8. A four-barrel Carter carb provided a rated 185 bhp. But the Speedster was not popular, so production was a meager 2215 units.

The 1953 design underwent a major facelift for '56. Sedans and wagons got more squared-off sheetmetal, but the coupes went in another direction. Still with the original bodyshell, they received a redesigned hood with an upright sports car-type grille and squared-off trunklid. The changes were successful, giving the cars character and dash. There were now four versions, all called Hawks.

The Flight Hawk (six) and Power Hawk (V8) were both fixed-pillar styles. The latter had the 259 V8. Sky Hawk was a hardtop equipped with a 210-bhp 289 V8, a stroked version of the 259. At the top of the nest perched the Golden Hawk hardtop. It was powered by an engine that made even the Studebaker mills look lightweight, the 352-cid Packard V8.

There were only two Hawks for 1957, Silver and Golden. The Silver Hawk was the pillared style, available with the six or the 289 V8, the latter with a choice of 210 or 225 bhp. Packard V8 production stopped in 1956, so Studebaker needed another path to high-performance for the hardtop Golden Hawk. Adding a supercharger to the 289 brought horsepower up to the same 275 bhp as the big Packard engine.

The Lark compact, actually a shortened version of the 1958 sedans, replaced all standard Studebakers for 1959. The Golden Hawk also departed that year along with its 289 power. The Silver Hawk remained, but could be had only with a six or two versions of the 259 V8. Production was off only slightly at 7788.

The Hawk returned for 1960. Just a single pillared coupe was listed. The model got back its 289 in 210- and 225-bhp forms, but not the supercharger. The six and 259 V8s were deleted. Production slipped to 3939. The 1961 model was mostly unchanged but somewhat sportier, getting bucket seats and an optional Borg-Warner four-speed transmission.

Studebaker's new president, Sherwood Egbert, hired stylist Brooks Stevens to redo the Hawk for 1962—only six months before it was scheduled to be introduced. Working on a minimal budget, Stevens got rid of the fiberglass fins, and redesigned the roof with Thunderbird-like lines. Interiors and dashboard were also changed, and trim was cleaned up. Stevens' transformation of the then nine-year-old body was amazing. The end product was called the Gran Turismo Hawk.

More horses were added for 1963. The 210-horse two-barrel 289 remained standard, as did the four-barrel 225-bhp option. But the GT

Studebaker & Hawk Performance

Year & Model		Engine (cid/bhp)	Curb Wt.[1]	lbs/ bhp[1]	0-60[2] (sec)	¼-mi.[2] (sec)	Base Price[3]
1951	Commander 4d sdn	232/120	3065	25.5	18.2	20.7	$2032
1955	Speedster 2d htp	259/175	3175	18.1	13.4	18.1	$2456
1956	Golden Hawk 2d htp	352/275	3360	12.2	9.2	17.3	$3061
1957	Golden Hawk 2d htp	289/275	3185	11.6	9.2	17.3	$3182
1960	Hawk 2d cpe	289/210	3207	15.3	12.3	18.4	$2650
1962	GT Hawk 2d htp	289/225	3230	14.4	11.4	18.2	$3095
1963	Super Hawk 2d htp	289/289	3280	11.3	8.5	16.8	$3095

[1]Advertised; [2]Typical acceleration based on contemporary tests; [3]Advertised list price in contemporary dollars; n = Net advertised horsepower; cid = cubic inch displacement; bhp = brake horsepower; conv = convertible; cpe = coupe; fastbk = fastback; htp = hardtop; rdstr = roadster (2-seat); sdn = sedan; d = number of doors.

Top left: 1963 Avanti. Lower left: 1957 Golden Hawk. Top right: 1962 GT Hawk. Bottom right: 1958 Packard Hawk.

Hawk could now be ordered with one of the Avanti R-series engines. Based on the 289, the R-1 "Jet Thrust" came with four-barrel carb, hot cam, and low-restriction dual exhausts. It was believed to produce 240 bhp (Studebaker never formally announced the ratings). Next up was the R-2, also a 289, but with a Paxton supercharger that put the unadvertised horses at 290–300. (Studebaker had earlier bought Paxton Products Company as part of its diversification program.) These powerplants were available as part of the mid-year "Super Hawk" option package that also featured heavy-duty suspension.

But even the fast ones were slow to move off the showroom floor. Only 4634 Hawks were built for '63.

For the slightly changed 1964 Gran Turismo Hawks two more engines were announced, both based on the 304.5-cid derivative of the 289. The R-3 with supercharger was rumored to give 335 bhp. The normally aspirated R-4 was in the region of 280 bhp thanks to a stiff 12:1 compression ratio and twin quads. It's doubtful if any R-3 or R-4 Hawks were made, for the model year was not a long one. Only 1767 of the 1964 Hawks were completed.

On December 9, 1963, management decided to close production at the South Bend plant, and shift to the firm's Canadian plant. The move spelled the end of the Hawk.

Packard

Before World War II, there was a direct correlation between a car's horsepower and its price. This tradition continued in the immediate postwar years. Accordingly, the prestigious Packard led the horsepower list for 1946–48, and tied for the lead in 1949–50.

Packard's first V8 didn't arrive until the 1955 model year. It came in two sizes, 320 and 352 cubic inches. The overhead-valve engine was of modern design, but was again quite heavy, like the cars it powered. The lower-priced Clipper models came with the 320-cid unit, rated at 225 horsepower with four-barrel carb. (American Motors bought these for installation in its top-line 1956 Nash and Hudson models.) Clipper Customs used the 352 in its 245-bhp form. In the senior Packards it was rated at 260 bhp, with 275 bhp reserved for the flashy Caribbean convertible and two-door hardtop.

A ⅛-inch stroke increase brought the largest Packard engine for 1956 to 374 cid, again the biggest in the industry. The Caribbean returned as the most powerful models, with two four-barrels and an unheard of 10:1 compression ratio.

Packard had into sales resistance with its '55 models, aggravated by body supply and quality control problems. At the end of the 1956 model year, the big V8 and all the senior cars (with a basic body that dated back to 1951) were cancelled, and with them, 57 years of tradition. Packard was temporarily saved by adopting the Studebaker body and drivetrains. The 1957 models weren't all that bad, if you considered them as high-price Studebakers, but they were hardly the Packards of old.

Sales of the '57 Packard sedan and wagon were very low, only 4809 were produced. Nevertheless, there were more Studebakers with the Packard badge for 1958. Tack-on fiberglass fins and quad headlights, plus a curious grille, make the standard models, including a new hardtop, rather ugly. The Clipper name was axed, and only the 225-bhp 289 was offered. There was also a high-performance model, the Packard Hawk, a twin to the Studebaker Golden Hawk. It, too, had rather odd styling, especially at the front. Inside was plush seating, and the vinyl door panel trim spilled over the window sills and on to the doors outside. The supercharged 275-bhp 289 was carried over from 1957, and made the Hawk one of the best performing Packards of all time. *Motor Life* magazine recorded 9.2 seconds in the 0–60 mph test.

But by now it was too late. Only 588 Packard Hawks were made for '58, along with 2034 sedans, wagons, and hardtops, the last cars to carry the Packard name.

Packard Performance

Year & Model		Engine (cid/bhp)	Curb Wt.[1]	lbs/ bhp[1]	0-60[2] (sec)	¼-mi.[2] (sec)	Base Price[3]
1955	400 2d htp	252/260	4250	16.3	11.4	18.6	$3930
1957	Clipper 4d sdn	289/275	3570	13.0	10.5	18.0	$3212
1958	Hawk 2d htp	289/275	3470	12.6	9.2	17.5	$3995

[1]Advertised; [2]Typical acceleration based on contemporary tests; [3]Advertised list price in contemporary dollars; n = Net advertised horsepower; cid = cubic inch displacement; bhp = brake horsepower; conv = convertible; cpe = coupe; fastbk = fastback; htp = hardtop; rdstr = roadster (2-seat); sdn = sedan; d = number of doors.

Engine Charts

Studebaker

Type	Bore × Stroke (in.)	CID	BHP @ rpm*	Torque @ rpm*	Fuel# System	Avail. (years)
ohv V8	3.38 × 3.25	232	120@ 4000	190@ 2000	2 bbl.	1951-53
ohv V8	3.56 × 3.25	259	185@ 4500	258@ 3000	4 bbl.	1955
ohv V8	4.00 × 3.50	352	275@ 4600	380@ 2800	4 bbl.	1956
ohv V8	3.56 × 3.63	289	275@ 4800	333@ 3200	SC 2 bbl.	1957-58
ohv V8	3.56 × 3.63	289	225@ 4500	305@ 2000	4 bbl.	1957-58, 1960-64
ohv V8	3.56 × 3.63	289	240@ 4000e	305@ 3200e	4 bbl.	1963-64
ohv V8	3.56 × 3.63	289	289@ 4800e	335@ 3200e	SC 4 bbl.	1963-64
ohv V8	3.66 × 3.63	304	335@ 5350e	340@ 3600e	SC 4 bbl.	1963-64
ohv V8	3.66 × 3.63	304	280@ 5000e	320@ 3200e	4 bbl.	1963-64

Packard

Type	Bore × Stroke (in.)	CID	BHP @ rpm*	Torque @ rpm*	Fuel# System	Avail. (years)
ohv V8	4.00 × 3.50	352	275@ 4800	380@ 2800	4 bbl.	1955
ohv V8	4.13 × 3.50	374	310@ 4600	405@ 2800	2 × 4 bbl.	1956
ohv V8	3.56 × 3.63	289	275@ 4800	333@ 3200	SC 2 bbl.	1957-58

*SAE gross ratings except where noted; † hemispherical heads; # carburetion: no. carbs × bbls.; e = estimated; FI = fuel injection; n = net advertised figures; SC = supercharged; TC = turbocharged.